KU-570-711

Ethnopolitics

Volume 13   Issue 4   September 2014

Articles

Debate

Ethnopolitics

Subscription Information:

Ethnopolitics (USPS permit number pending) is a peer-reviewed journal, published five times a year (in January, March, June, September and November) by Routledge Journals, an imprint of Taylor & Francis, an Informa Business, 4 Park Square, Milton Park, Abingdon, Oxfordshire OX14 4RN, UK.

Annual Subscription, Volume 13, 2014

Institution	$637	£384	€506
Individual	$192	£114	€150
Online	$558	£336	€443 (plus tax where applicable)

A subscription to the institution print edition, ISSN 1744-9057, includes free access for any number of concurrent users across a local area network to the online edition, ISSN 1744-9065.

Subscriptions purchased at the personal rate are strictly for personal, non-commercial use only. The reselling of personal subscriptions is prohibited. Personal subscriptions must be purchased with a personal cheque or credit card. Proof of personal status may be requested.

Dollar rates apply to all subscribers outside Europe. Taylor & Francis has introduced a euro rate for all titles, which applies to all subscribers in Europe, except the UK and the Republic of Ireland where the pound sterling price applies. For a list of countries in which the euro rate applies or if you are unsure which rate applies to you, please contact Customer Services in the UK. All subscriptions are payable in advance and all rates include postage. Journals are sent by air to the USA, Canada, Mexico, India, Japan and Australasia. Subscriptions are entered on an annual basis, i.e. January to December. Payment may be made by sterling cheque, dollar cheque, euro cheque, international money order, National Giro or credit cards (Amex, Visa and Mastercard). For more information, visit our website: http://www.tandf.co.uk/journals

For a complete and up-to-date guide to Taylor & Francis journals and books publishing programmes, and details of advertising in our journals, visit our website: http://www.tandfonline.com/journals

Ordering Information:

Please contact your local Customer Service Department to take out a subscription to the Journal: **India:** Universal Subscription Agency Pvt. Ltd, 101-102 Community Centre, Malviya Nagar Extn, Post Bag No. 8, Saket, New Delhi 110017. **Japan:** Kinokuniya Company Ltd, Journal Department, PO Box 55, Chitose, Tokyo 156. **USA, Canada and Mexico:** Taylor & Francis, 325 Chestnut Street, 8th Floor, Philadelphia, PA 19106, USA. Tel: +1 800 354 1420 or +1 215 625 8900; Fax +1 215 625 8914; Email: customerservice@taylorandfrancis.com. **UK and all other territories:** T&F Customer Services, Informa Plc., Sheepen Place, Colchester, Essex, CO3 3LP, UK. Tel: +44 (0)20 7017 5444; Fax: +44(0)20 7017 5198; Email: subscriptions@tandf.co.uk

Periodicals Postage Paid at Jamaica, NY and additional mailing offices. **US Postmaster:** Please send address changes to RENO. c/o Air Business Ltd, 155-11 146th St., Jamaica, New York, NY 11434.

Typeset by Techset Composition India (p) Ltd, Chennai, India, and printed and bound by Henry Ling Ltd, UK.

Copyright © 2014 All rights reserved. No part of this publication may be reproduced, stored, transmitted, or disseminated, in any form, or by any means, without prior written permission from Taylor & Francis, to whom all requests to reproduce copyright material should be directed, in writing.

Disclaimer: The Editors of *Ethnopolitics* and Taylor & Francis make every effort to ensure the accuracy of all the information (the 'Content') contained in its publications. However, the Editors of *Ethnopolitics* and Taylor & Francis and its agents and licensors make no representations or warranties whatsoever as to the accuracy, completeness or suitability for any purpose of the Content and disclaim all such representations and warranties whether express or implied to the maximum extent permitted by law. Any views expressed in this publication are the views of the authors and are not necessarily the views of the Editors of *Ethnopolitics* or Taylor & Francis.

Taylor & Francis grants authorization for individuals to photocopy copyright material for private research use, on the sole basis that requests for such use are referred directly to the requestor's local Reproduction Rights Organization (RRO). The copyright fee is £24/US$39/€29 exclusive of any charge or fee levied. In order to contact your local RRO, please contact International Federation of Reproduction Rights Organizations (IFRRO), rue du Prince Royal, 87, B-1050 Brussels, Belgium; email: IFRRO@skynet.be; Copyright Clearance Center Inc., 222 Rosewood Drive, Danvers, MA 01923, USA; email: info@copyright.com; Copyright Licensing Agency, 90 Tottenham Court Road, London W1P 0LP, UK; email: cla@cla.co.uk. This authorization does not extend to any other kind of copying, by any means, in any form, and for any purpose other than private research use.

Ethnopolitics, 2014
Vol. 13, No. 4, 309–327, http://dx.doi.org/10.1080/17449057.2013.864805

The Short and Brutish Life of Republika Srpska Krajina: Failure of a De Facto State

PÅL KOLSTØ* & DAVOR PAUKOVIC**

*University of Oslo, Norway, **University of Dubrovnik, Croatia

ABSTRACT   It is extremely difficult for a state to survive without international recognition; even so, some de facto states have been established and continue to exist. Others do not, and have been wiped off the face of the earth again. This article looks at one failed de facto state, the breakaway Serb Republic of Krajina (RSK) that existed for five years (1991–1995), before it was overrun by Croatian armed forces in Operation Storm. What did RSK do wrong that the surviving de facto states do right? Research has shown that in order to survive de facto states must have a patron that will protect them and supply them with financial and other resources; in addition, they must engage in state-building (the establishment of functioning state institutions) and in nation-building (fostering patriotism and a common national identity). RSK failed on all three scores. The Krajina leaders did initially enjoy the backing of the Milošević regime, but fell out with it and lost that support. Rather than build strong state institutions they pilfered the state and allowed the society to slide into anarchy. Finally, they never made any attempt to create a sense of separate RSK identity linked to the state. RSK was presented only as the westernmost outpost of Serbdom, and as a temporary structure pending the unification of all Serbs in one state. This is not the stuff successful de facto states are made of.

Introduction

In today's world, states that have achieved membership in the United Nations (UN) continue to exist even if they do not exhibit what Robert Jackson (1990) called 'empirical statehood', that is, even if they fail to perform the basic tasks expected of a state. International recognition serves as a protective shield that keeps them from collapse and from being absorbed by another state. States play hardball for influence and power, but they do not seek to eliminate each other. Saddam Hussein's botched attempt to incorporate Kuwait into Iraq forcefully only proves the point: it was nullified by the US-led invasion of Iraq in 1990. By contrast, no external actor interfered to save the self-proclaimed state Tamil Eelam in northern Sri Lanka when it was overrun by Sri Lankan government forces in 2009, even if serious war crimes seem to have been committed there. Unlike Kuwait, Tamil Eelam had no external legitimacy (Pegg, 1998).

Correspondence Address: Pål Kolstø, Department of Literature, Area Studies and European Languages, University of Oslo, Box 1003 Blindern, N-0315 Oslo, Norway. Email: pal.kolsto@ilos.uio.no

© 2013 The Editor of Ethnopolitics

Still, a few self-proclaimed states have continued to exist even in the absence of international recognition. This is the case with four secessionist states in the former Soviet Union—Abkhazia, the Nagorno-Karabakh Republic, South Ossetia and Transnistria (the Dniester Moldovan Republic)—as well as Somaliland and the Turkish Republic of Northern Cyprus. Other de facto states have failed and been wiped off the map again: Katanga (1960–1963); Biafra (1967–1970); Ichkeria (the Republic of Chechnya, 1991–2000); Tamil Eelan (1977–2009); and Republika Srpska Krajina (RSK, 1991–1995). In an earlier article one of the present authors discussed the sources of sustainability for de facto states (Kolstø, 2006). In this article, we approach the same issue from the opposite angle, by analysing one defunct de facto state, RSK. If the presence of certain qualities can sustain a state even in the absence of recognition, what circumstances may lead to its downfall?

State Recognition, State Performance and Sustainability

The diving line between fully fledged states and less-than-real states is not clear-cut. In addition to the member states of the UN (193 at present) there exist various more or less self-ruled territories around the globe. These run the gamut from warlord badlands in failed states and narcocartel-controlled regions in Latin America, to much more orderly quasi-states such as Northern Iraq (Iraqi Kurdistan) between the first and second Iraqi wars and the Palestinian National Authority (Kingston & Spears, 2004; Bahcheli *et al.*, 2004; Caspersen & Stansfield, 2011). What we are interested in here is the fate of would-be states that fulfil the following criteria: (1) they have control over (most of) the territory they lay claim to; (2) they have established at least the formal trappings of state institutions; (3) they have proclaimed independence from another state that continues to lay claim to their territory but (for the time being at least) is unable to recapture it; and (4) the declaration of independence has not been accepted by (the majority of) the member states of the UN. The statelets that fulfil these criteria are given various terms in the research literature, including 'pseudo-states' (Kolossov & O'Loughlin, 1999), 'quasi-states' (Kolstø, 2006), 'contested states' (Geldenhuys, 2009), 'unrecognized states' (King, 2001; Matsuzato, 2008; Protsyk, 2009; Caspersen & Stansfield, 2011; Caspersen, 2012), 'separatist states' (Lynch, 2002) and 'de facto states' (Pegg, 1998; Bahcheli *et al.*, 2004; Berg & Toomla, 2009; O'Loughlin *et al.*, 2011; Blakkisrud & Kolstø, 2011, 2012; Kolstø & Blakkisrud, 2012; von Steinsdorff & Fruhstorfer, 2012). In this article, we refer to them as *de facto states*, which increasingly seems to be the consensus term in the academic literature.[1]

The four conditions listed above whittle down the number of possible candidates for de facto statehood to about one dozen in post-Second World War history, of which roughly half are still with us today. However, even these seemingly clear-cut criteria leave some territories in a grey zone. Kosovo and Taiwan are recognized by 105 and 22 UN member states, respectively. The Sahrawi Arab Democratic Republic in Western Sahara is recognized by 82 states, but arguably should not be counted as a de facto state, as its government controls only about a third of the territory to which it lays claim, and is itself located outside it, in neighbouring Algeria.

Finally, we emphasize that our third criterion, proclamation of independence, is a formal one. While such proclamations normally signal a real aspiration for separate statehood, they may also be a tactical ploy to escape the control of one state in an attempt to join

another.[2] Conversely, when Iraqi Kurdistan did not issue any proclamation of independence between the first and the second Iraqi wars, even though it functioned as a self-
governed entity, this may well have been because the Kurdish leaders believed that
such a declaration would not serve the cause of consolidating its liberation from
Saddam Hussein's control (Caspersen & Stansfield, 2011).

The principles according to which states extend recognition to each other have changed
over time. In early modernity, dynasties recognized each other as legitimate rulers on the
basis of heredity. After the American and French revolutions, which proclaimed the
United States of America and the Republic of France 'in the name of the people', the legiti-
mist principle was gradually replaced by two other principles: popular sovereignty and de
facto statehood (Fabry, 2010). Already in the 1820s and 1830s, recognition of the new
states then being established in the former Spanish colonies of Latin America was
based on the fact that they wielded actual control over the territory to which they laid
claim. Roughly 100 years later, this empirical principle was codified in the Montevideo
Convention, adopted at the Seventh International Conference of American States in
Uruguay in 1933. Its Article 1 sets out four criteria for statehood: 'The state as a person
of international law should possess the following qualifications: (a) a permanent population; (b) a defined territory; (c) government; and (d) capacity to enter into relations
with the other states' (Montevideo Convention).

Some of today's de facto states have made reference to this convention in arguing
their right to acquire a legal status under international law.[3] After the Second World
War, however, the criterion of empirical statehood was set aside again, and we have
seen a return to a variant of the legitimacy principle of recognition: states that have
once been recognized continue to be so even when they lose control over their territory
and are unable to fulfil the basic functions of statehood. Thus, the Republic of Somalia,
for instance, continued to be internationally recognized even in periods when the body
that purported to act as its 'government' was physically located abroad (in Kenya) and
in practice wielded no authority at home. Under this type of legitimacy regime, so-
called failed states can continue to exist for indefinite periods of time, whereas, conversely, a de facto state will continue to be denied recognition. As Scott Pegg (2000,
p. 91) has remarked, 'the [internationally recognized] quasi-state is legitimate no
matter how ineffective it is. Conversely the de facto state is illegitimate no matter
how effective it is'.

Many de facto states are surprisingly robust, even well-functioning. In 2001, Charles
King (2001, p. 525) noted, 'The territorial separatists of the 1990s have become state
builders in the early 2000s, creating de facto countries whose ability to field armies,
control their own territory, educate their children, and maintain local economies is
about as well developed as that of the recognized states of which they are still notionally
a part'. Other researchers have reached similar conclusions (see Kimitaka, 2008; Kolstø
& Blakkisrud, 2008; Blakkisrud & Kolstø, 2011, Caspersen, 2012, chapter 4). Some de
facto states have impressive longevity. All the four extant post-Soviet such states—
Nagorno-Karabakh Republic, PMR, Republic of Abkhazia and South Ossetia—have
already celebrated their 30th anniversary of statehood, while the Turkish Republic of
Northern Cyprus, in existence since 1983, is even older.[4] However, the elimination of
the Tamil secessionist state in Sri Lanka—the Tamil Eelan—already established in
1977, warns us against assuming that if de facto states survive their infancy and adoles-
cence they will be able to hang on indefinitely. Other de facto states have suffered similar

fates, including the one under scrutiny here, RSK. So, why do some de facto state survive, and not others?

In an earlier article one of the present authors (Kolstø, 2006) focused on five factors that he deemed most important for the continuation of de facto states:

(1) *Military power.* Virtually all de facto states have achieved independence by military means, through a war of secession, and have been maintained by the same means.
(2) *External patron.* Most de facto states enjoy the explicit or tacit support of an external patron, a recognized state that supplies weapons, money, foodstuffs, perhaps also cadres.
(3) *Weakness of parent state.* If the parent state—the state from which the de facto state seceded—is weak, militarily and otherwise, the de facto state will need fewer resources to protect itself against attempts at reincorporation.
(4) *Role of the international community.* If the major international organizations and great powers see the secessionist conflict as peripheral and unimportant, they will not press hard, and the unresolved status of the secessionist region may be perpetuated.
(5) *Nation-building.* Through a process of nation-building, leaders of the de facto state often manage to achieve considerable internal legitimacy. They create a common national identity among the people through symbols, propaganda, history-writing, and the cultivation or 'invention' of traditions and national costumes. Such a sense of unity and shared fate is also fostered by cultivating an image of a common external enemy. Other facilitating circumstances include ethnic and cultural homogeneity of the population and deliberate strategies for creating a new national identity for the state-to-be. To the extent that such nation-building succeeds, the population will accept a greater degree of deprivation and hardship than they otherwise would.

But if the presence of these factors guarantees the continued existence of the de facto state, what of the converse: if any of these factors are absent, will the de facto state disintegrate? Of course, it is not possible to conduct controlled experiments, removing these factors from a de facto state, one by one, to see what happens. Here we have to fall back on historical evidence: examining the processes, internal and external, that led up to the collapse of a de facto state.

This article looks at one de facto state, the RSK in Croatia, which survived for five years before it was overrun by Croatian military forces in August 1995 in Operation Storm (*Oluja*).[5] This state had been proclaimed as a safe haven for the ethnic Serb minority in Croatia in protest against what its leaders claimed was rampant Croatian nationalism in Zagreb during the Tuđman regime. At the time of its establishment, the RSK enjoyed the explicit support of the Milošević regime in Belgrade, and also of the Yugoslav army (JNA). It seceded when the Croatian state was still in the process of being established and had not become consolidated—nevertheless, only half a decade later, the RSK was wiped off the face of the earth. What went wrong? Below, we give an account of the short but eventful history of this secessionist conflict, focusing on the circumstances around the establishment of the de facto state, the strategies its leaders employed for state-building and nation-building, and last but not least, the successes and failures of these strategies.

This article is based on primary RSK sources, partly original documents (copies) in the possession of the authors, partly on published collections of documents. Many official

RSK documents were captured by the Croatian army under *Oluja* and later published by the Archive of Croatian Information Centre and the Croatian Office for Cooperation with the International Criminal Tribunal for the former Yugoslavia (ICTY). The most important part of that documentation was published in book form in 2005 (Pauković, 2005), a collection that includes documents mainly from the official gazettes published in the territory of the RSK (*Glasnik Krajine, Službeni glasnik srpske oblasti Slavonija Baranja i Zapadni Srem, Službeni glasnik Republike Srpske Krajine*) as well as documents produced by RSK institutions. We have also drawn extensively on a book series with documentation from RSK archives published by the Croatian Memorial Documentation Centre of the Homeland War. There has been a much greater interest in research on the RSK in Croatia than in Serbia, where it is virtually non-existent, and this is reflected in the references used in this article. Most of the works published in Serbia are books by former RSK representatives; the most important of them have been consulted for this study.[6]

The Serbian Rebellion in Croatia and the Establishment of the RSK

State-building in 'Republika Srpska Krajina' on the territory of the Republic of Croatia commenced during the collapse of the Yugoslav state (SFRJ) and the Communist regime. The crisis of the 1980s and the awakening of nationalism showed that, despite what has often been asserted, the Croatian, Serbian and Slovenian questions had in fact *not* been resolved in Yugoslavia (Milosavljević, 2002, p. 87). Quite the contrary: the national question remained the most basic issue in Yugoslav politics, in the interwar as well as in the post-war period (Banac, 1992, p. 169).

The victory of the nationalist party Croatian Democratic Community (HDZ) in the first free elections in Croatia in spring 1990 did not help in achieving a political solution. The basic aim of the new power-holders in Zagreb was to establish sovereign Croatian statehood and regulate on that basis relations with the other Yugoslav republics—through a confederation, or by secession. Under these circumstances, preparations were made for a Serb uprising in Croatia. The ultimate goal of the Serbian politics and Serb nationalism (which peaked in 1989/90) was to keep the majority of Serbs in one state, whether a federal Yugoslavia or an enlarged Serbia.

The justification for the uprising and for the refusal to recognize decisions made by the newly elected HDZ government was that, in the Serb discourse, the Croatian government was anti-Serb and *Ustaša*-like—a continuation of the fascist regime in the 'Independent State of Croatia' (NDH) during the Second World War. (On the Serbian national discourse on the HDZ and Tuđman, see Pauković, 2008.) Admittedly, certain HDZ members did flirt with *Ustaša* symbolism, especially during the election campaign. Some anti-Serbian utterances could also be heard and Croatian nationalism was generally rising, but the atmosphere created in the Serbian media built on exaggerations.

The Serb uprising emanated from the Serbian Democratic Party (SDS), which was founded in Knin in February 1990 and was strongly influenced by Milošević's policies. In the months after the national elections in April/May 1990, the SDS established branches in all regions with substantial Serb populations. Gradually, it took over power from the reformed Croatian Communists (SKH-SDP), who had received the greatest number of votes in these regions. SDS had failed to organize significantly outside Knin and its surroundings and opinion polls showed that, before the elections, most Serbs in Croatia preferred SKH-SDP (46%); in fact, twice as many as preferred SDS (23%) (Šiber,

1991, pp. 98–100). But after the victory of HDZ a growing number of Serbs in the areas where they constituted a majority began to support SDS. Here it should be recalled that only around half of the total Serb population in Croatia lived in territories that constituted RSK at the beginning of 1992 (Barić, 2005, p. 566).

The first step in the creation of a Serbian autonomy in Croatia was the declaration, in the second half of June, that a 'Community of Municipalities of northern Dalmatia and Lika' had been established (Pauković, 2005, pp. 68–69).[7] The same day when amendments to the Croatian Constitution were adopted, 25 July 1990, confirming the sovereignty of the republic, the SDS organized a Serbian *sabor* ('assembly') for Serbs, which passed a 'Declaration on the sovereignty and autonomy of the Serbian people' (Pauković, 2005, pp. 70–71). This declaration emphasised the right of the Serbs in Croatia to decide for themselves under which regime they wished to live and how they would organize contacts with the other peoples of Yugoslavia. The key issue in the Serbian declaration was whether the right to secession was held by the republics or by the constituent peoples of Yugoslavia: here the Serbs insisted on the latter view.[8]

The events that followed marked the start of the rebellion against Croatian authorities in the 'log revolution' in August 1990.[9] By the end of 1990, a Serbian Autonomous Region or 'Oblast' was created in the territory controlled by the Serb insurgents. This was formally established on 21 December 1990 when the provisional presidency of the Community of Municipalities in Northern Dalmatia and Lika adopted the Statute of the Serbian Autonomous Oblast (SAO) of Krajina (Pauković, 2005, p. 73).

The tense situation in Croatia was aggravated in early 1991, making resolution by peaceful means seem increasingly unlikely. At a referendum held in May the same year (turnout was 83.56%), the vast majority (93.94%) of those voting defined Croatia as a sovereign and independent state that, together with other republics, could enter into an association of sovereign states (Sokol & Smerdel, 1995, p. 58). As the formal steps were taken to establish Croatia's sovereign statehood and to de-link the republic from Yugoslavia, the Serb insurgents continued to pass decisions formalizing the separation of the territory under their control from the Republic of Croatia in a parallel process. In the first half of 1991, rebel Serbs decided for separation from Croatia and merger with Serbia (Pauković, 2005, pp. 80–88).

The Serbian parliament in Belgrade, however, never accepted the accession of the rebellious Serb territories in Croatia. Belgrade clearly preferred the referendum question in Krajina to focus on the preservation of Yugoslavia, not on joining Serbia. The areas held by the Serb insurgents were protected by the JNA under Belgrade's control. The JNA had defended the Serb rebels since the beginning of the uprising in August 1990, and from the second half of 1991 it openly engaged in the fighting on the side of the Serb rebels (on the activity of the Yugoslav army, see Marijan, 2008). By the end of 1991 the rebels had succeeded in taking more territory, but not in toppling the Croatian authorities. It was becoming clear that neither side would be able to achieve major breakthroughs on the battlefield. This led to a cessation of hostilities and to acceptance of the UN peace plan known as the Vance Plan (Barić, 2005, p. 145), which was a de facto ceasefire, aimed at creating the preconditions for negotiations on a comprehensive solution to the Yugoslav crisis (Pauković, 2005, pp. 342–347).

Towards the end of 1991 some countries (notably Germany) declared that they extended international recognition to Slovenia and Croatia within the borders of their republics. For the Serb rebels only three possible arrangements were acceptable: attachment to Serbia;

unification with Bosnian Krajina and the creation of a common federal Krajina unit within Yugoslavia; or, finally, a Croatian Krajina as a separate federal unit within Yugoslavia. The adoption of the Croatian declaration of independence seems to have pushed the Knin leadership to go for the third option, and to proclaim a separate republic at the earliest possible opportunity. In December 1991 in Knin, a Constituent Assembly of the Krajina SAO was convened; it adopted a constitution and proclaimed the establishment of Republika Srpska Krajina (Barić, 2005, p. 146).

Symbolic Nation-building

An important element in any strategy aimed at giving a state an identity as a nation state is the creation and manipulation of symbols: coat of arms, flag, commemorations, *lieux de mémoire*, and so on. This was also done in the RSK, which issued both its own (rather unimpressive) stamps and bank notes (see Mønnesland, 2013, p. 225). Nation-building in RSK, however, was marked by certain peculiarities. First, even more important than the construction of new positive symbols associated with the putative state appears to have been the memorialization of negative symbols associated with Croatia. The post-Communist Croatian state was consistently identified with the wartime *Ustaša* regime, in particular through the red-and-white checkerboard coat of arms (the *šahovnica*), which was used by both. In symbolic terms, the Serb rebellion in 1991 was unleashed when police officers in Serb-dominated regions refused to wear the *šahovnica* on their uniforms (Pavlaković, forthcoming). In addition, the memory of the largest *Ustaša* concentration camp, Jasenovac, was constantly evoked in the speeches of RSK politicians, and the atrocities committed there were firmly linked to the Tuđman regime. More than 80,000 innocent people had been brutally killed in Jasenovac during the Second World War, but in Serb propaganda—in the RSK and elsewhere—this was inflated into a figure nearly 10 times higher (Kolstø, 2011), and the rebellion was explicitly justified as a step necessary to forestall a new genocide of Serbs (Pavlaković, forthcoming). Jasenovac is located on the Sava River in Western Slavonia, in a region that was controlled by the RSK. However, the museum that the Communists had erected in Jasenovac was not to the liking of the Serb nationalists. They demolished it and removed all the artefacts to Republika Srpska in Bosnia.

During the Second World War, Krajina Serbs had played a prominent role in Tito's Partisan army, but the RSK leadership increasingly distanced itself from this partisan legacy: Titoism was regarded as far too inclined towards multiculturalism and 'the brotherhood and unity of peoples'. Instead, they hailed as heroes the partisans' wartime adversaries, the *Četniks*, who could more directly be presented as defenders of the Serb national cause in a narrow sense. In fact, such *Četnik* imagery was not unique to the RSK: it became common symbolism for Serbs throughout the former Yugoslavia. Similarly, the official flag of the RSK was the standard red-blue-white Serb tricolour; its coat of arms featured a double-headed white eagle with a cross and four Cyrillic letters 's'—again, a pan-Serb symbol that in no way signalled any attempt to create a separate Krajina identity. This pan-Serb tendency could also be seen in the campaigns to erase Croatian and Communist names from streets and other place designations. Take the renaming of virtually all streets in the town of Svinjarevci in January 1992: the new names evoked the memory of Tsar Dušan, Saint Sava and Vuk Karadžić—none of whom had any connection to Krajina

(*Republika Hrvatska*, Book 4, p. 49). Similar name changes took place in virtually all towns under RSK control.

Turbulent Dependence on Belgrade

To a high degree, the RSK, as a Croatian by-product of the Serb national movement, shared the fate of this movement in Yugoslavia as a whole. From the very beginning, the Serb rebellion in Croatia, as well as the later creation of the RSK, depended on Belgrade as well as on the overall Yugoslav context. When the RSK was established, this was intended as a step towards the realization of the principle 'All Serbs in one state', although it was not quite clear how this goal was to be achieved: by creating a separate federal unit within Yugoslavia—alone or together with the Bosnian Serbs—or by joining Serbia at some convenient moment. Second, the territorial configuration of the republic, especially the fact that its constituent parts were geographically detached from each other, seriously hampered the functioning of the RSK. In addition, even though the peace plan had been accepted and UN peacekeeping forces deployed, the de facto state was in a permanent state of war, of varying intensity; also, this influenced how the RSK functioned or did not function. This was the context in which attempts at state-building had to be made. It greatly limited the state-builders' options and informed the discourse of the RSK ruling elites.

The dependence on Belgrade was strategic, military and economic. Serbian help was vitally important because all links to the other parts of the Republic of Croatia had been severed. The rebel leaders, no less than Milošević, realized that the RSK could not exist without outside help. Thus, for instance, most of the professional staff of the RSK military received their salaries directly from Serbia. In his testimony to the International Criminal Tribunal for the former Yugoslavia in 2002, former RSK leader Milan Babić confirmed that, economically, the RSK was totally dependent upon Serbia (Žunec, 2007, pp. 468–469).

The dominant influence of Belgrade was evident as regards whether the RSK should accept the Vance Plan. This was when the first serious conflict erupted between Belgrade and Knin—more specifically, between Milošević and Milan Babić as the first president of the RSK. Babić and his followers regarded the peace plan as unsatisfactory for the RSK, not only because it meant that the Yugoslav army would have to withdraw and the RSK armed forces be disarmed, but also because it would undermine Krajina statehood and reduce the Serbs to a national minority within Croatia. When Babić refused to accept the Vance Plan, this led to an open conflict with Belgrade. He was then removed from power and marginalized, while the peace plan was accepted (Barić, 2005, pp. 150–162; Žunec, 2007, pp. 276–278).

Repeatedly, the RSK leadership seems to have disregarded the basic fact that they were dependent on Belgrade's support. At many important crossroads they were willing to ignore the wishes of Milošević and bite the hand that fed them, with Babić's intransigent opposition to the Vance Plan as merely one example. Nina Caspersen, who has studied Serbia's relations with the secessionist regimes in Pale and Knin, notes that all RSK leaders either clashed with Milošević when they sought greater autonomy of action, or were abandoned by him if they failed to retain control in the statelet. She concludes:

> Milošević was not always able to control local developments ... Local leaders
> became increasingly rebellious and possessed means for limiting Belgrade's

influence. The analysis has shown that links between a kin-state and its ethnic brethren may be weakened despite the existence of extreme insecurity. (Caspersen, 2007, pp. 631, 640, original emphasis removed)

Despite the conflicts between Belgrade and the Serb rebel leadership in Croatia, the creation of a common Serbian state in the territory of Yugoslavia in order to let 'all Serbs live in one state' generally seems to have remained the final aim for all. Only later, at the end of 1993 and the beginning of 1994, did Milošević change his strategy, distancing himself from the aim of 'all Serbs in one state'. Under pressure of sanctions from the international community and with growing international recognition of Croatia, Belgrade realized that it was simply not realistic to expect to be able to attach any Serb-controlled Croatian territory to Serbia. Belgrade now began to adopt compromise positions, and tried to induce the RSK leadership to enter into negotiations with Croatia.

The negotiation framework foresaw three phases in a resolution of the conflict: a ceasefire; establishing economic relations between Zagreb and Knin; and, finally, a political settlement (Barić, 2005, pp. 259–271). With this strategy Belgrade was in no way disowning the RSK—simply continuing to adjust its policies to realities on the ground. Belgrade, and Milošević in particular, probably did not have a precise RSK strategy. To Belgrade, the fate of the Serbian-controlled part of Bosnia-Herzegovina seems to have been more important than the prospects of including the RSK in a future common Serbian state. For Croatia and the international community, a political solution would mean reintegration of the RSK into the Croatian fold, while the Serb insurgents tried to use the negotiations to strengthen their international standing and be recognized as an equal partner vis-à-vis Croatia. The sovereignty of the RSK was to them non-negotiable. Here it must be stressed that, until the very end, the Serb rebel leadership believed that they had the full support of Belgrade in their pursuit of statehood and in realization of the final aim, which was always a common Serb state. Therefore, when their state broke down, some RSK protagonists and apologists put the primary blame on Belgrade, accusing Milošević of first enticing them to rebel, and then abandoning them.[10] The ultimate disintegration of the RSK made clear its dependence on Serbia, and the lack of a proper policy and a real strategy among its leaders.

State Institutions and the Functioning of the Political and Legal System

From the very beginning, the leadership of the Serbian insurrection in Croatia sought to clothe their activities in a cloak of legitimacy and legality. After the proclamation of an independent RSK, the Serb insurgents rapidly set about establishing all institutions necessary for running a state. Indeed, one could say that the RSK possessed all basic state institutions, at least formally. The functioning and development of these institutions, however, did not meet the minimum standards of a democratic state. Normal constitutional and legal procedures were disregarded, the separation of powers rarely functioned, and the RSK political system was characterized by arbitrariness and abuse of power. The development of institutions was also hampered by the belief that these institutions were to function only temporarily, in a transitional period, until a common Serb state could be established. That this was the ultimate goal was not something they sought to hide from the public: on the contrary, it was written into the constitution of the RSK.[11]

The lack of material means and an enormous cadre deficit remained recurrent problems for the institutions of the RSK. It seems that Belgrade promised to supply reliable people to fill key positions, but the help provided was clearly insufficient (Žunec, 2007, p. 480). What Belgrade actually sent were primarily leading military personnel. The state of public security and the legal system clearly exemplified the poor functioning of the state and the social situation in the RSK. Like all other institutions, the legal structures suffered from a chronic dearth of professionals, in this case judges, whose positions were often filled by unqualified cadres. The police force largely engaged in the fighting effort, so there were not enough officers available for regular police duty. In this situation, and given the general political and social context, crime and violence flourished under the protection of state organs.

Valuable resources such as oil and wood were coveted items for smuggling, speculation and other criminal trade. There was a shortage of virtually all necessities, and the economy slumped further and further. Unemployment was rampant, and depreciation of the currency reached hyperinflation levels. The economy of the RSK could not function without substantial support from Serbia, as the de facto state was cut off from its natural catchment area—the other parts of Croatia. Moreover, its territory was disunited: the eastern part was adjacent to Serbia, while the western parts relied on a corridor through the Serb-controlled territory of Bosnia and Herzegovina. This territorial separation exacerbated the factional splits within the RSK leadership, as the eastern part was more under the sway of Belgrade than was Knin.

One might perhaps have expected the constant siege situation in the RSK to force its politicians to gloss over their ideological and personal disagreements and stand united in defence of the country. What emerged instead was an almost surrealistic degree of infighting and open quarrels. The first leader of the SDS party, Jovan Rašković (d.1992), had already been shunted to the sidelines before the war. With his moderation and willingness to accommodate the Croats, he soon became a hate-figure in the RSK, and could travel to Knin only at his own peril. The SDS soon split into several factions—or rather, several separate parties all using the SDS name. After falling out with Milošević over the Vance Plan, Babić was removed from the RSK presidency, but organized his own party, 'SDS of Krajina', in order to stage a comeback. For a while this party had to operate clandestinely, but was eventually allowed to participate in RSK elections.

As president of the RSK, Babić was replaced in February 1992 by Goran Hadžić, who throughout his term had difficulty asserting his authority. Hadžić organized his own 'SDS of the Serb Lands', which never became popular. One reason, apart from Hadžić's personal weakness, was that he hailed from Eastern Slavonia and had very little clout in Knin; in fact, he could travel to the putative capital only under heavy guard (Caspersen, 2010, p. 105). The strongman in Knin was the Minister of the Interior, Milan Martić, who initially enjoyed Milošević's support and also controlled his own paramilitary police forces. In the 1993/94 presidential elections, Martić bested Babić by a narrow margin—probably involving some electoral fraud. Babić nevertheless remained a strong player, not least because he had his own paramilitary structures, which, according to one source, engaged in 'selected assassinations' (Caspersen, 2010, p. 108).

In addition to the various parties using the SDS name, a plethora of other parties were active in RSK politics. Most important was the Radical Party, SRS, which was the local branch of the Radical Party led by Vojislav Šešelj in Belgrade; other players were two parties of Milošević loyalists, 'the Serbian party of Socialists' and 'the League of Communists—Movement for Yugoslavia'. Babić's party controlled the Krajina parliament in collaboration with die-hard nationalists in the Radical Party; together they ensured that relations with Belgrade remained frosty and that no concessions to Zagreb were accepted.

Apparently in an attempt to regain the initiative, President Martić in 1995 moved closer to the radicals' positions and distanced himself from Belgrade. When a new and remarkably generous peace proposal—the 'Z-4 plan'—was put on the table in early 1995, it was endorsed by Milošević, whereas Martić, along with Babić and the radicals, rejected it. However, this last-minute rapprochement could not detract from the fact that the RSK elites remained internally divided. As Caspersen explains, 'this [division] affected the positions taken by the leaders and the ultimate defeat of the radicals when Croatian forces retook Krajina in August 1995' (Caspersen, 2010, p. 100). Equally importantly, the RSK leaders forfeited the support of their own population by neglecting the task of nation-building and failing to provide basic security of life and property.

The Inner Life of the RSK: The Social Situation

Violence, crime and insecurity were central features of RSK society. According to the pro-Serbian author Marko Vrcelj (2002, p. 84), 'Krajina is characterised by violence and terror against its own people'. Numerous, often grotesque, examples provided by prominent participants in the insurrection testify to this (see, e.g. Jović, 1996, p. 437; Vrcelj, 2002, p. 30). Criminality, in which both the elite and the masses participated, paralysed the institutional system, and the fact that the RSK was always on a war footing exacerbated the situation. The highest political representatives of the state participated in crime and smuggling, actively impeding any improvements. Those who did try to rectify the situation were obstructed, removed and, in some cases, also liquidated (Žunec, 2007, pp. 482–494).

After Operation Storm, the Croatian authorities captured large parts of the RSK state archives, which contained a wealth of important information about the inner life of the breakaway republic. Much of this material has been published by the Memorial Centre for the Documentation of the Homeland War in Zagreb and made accessible to the public. The reports from military commanders are surprisingly frank in assessing the shortcomings and problems facing the Serb insurgents in their (faltering) attempts to establish a functioning state. Most of the documents cited below are various military reports.

In 1992, the first year after the ceasefire had been signed, some internal reports still retained a note of guarded optimism. War damage had destroyed much of the infrastructure in the Serb-controlled areas, but the chances for reconstruction and normalization were still deemed reasonably good. From Vukovar, one of the most devastated cities, Milorad Višić, head of the city council, claimed in August 1992: 'since the war ended nine months ago enormous efforts have been made to establish minimal life conditions in Vukovar'—specifically, the electricity grid, the water supply and the sewage system were functioning. However, Višić added that the tax inspectorate in the region was not working properly, and this created conditions favourable to economic crime. Moreover, the independent paramilitary organizations that had played a decisive role when the city had been captured from the Croats ought to leave: they brought unrest among the local population and obstructed the work of civilian institutions. The ineffectiveness of the legal system created an atmosphere of 'general anarchy', Višić claimed (*Republika Hrvatska*, Book 6, p. 115).

In September the same year a Ministry of Internal Affairs report noted that 'in general terms the situation has stabilized since the UNPROFOR [United Nations Protection Force] took over the protection of the territory of RSK. Satisfactory living and working conditions for the population, and for the authorities, including the police, have been created' (*Republika Hrvatska*, Book 5, p. 246). However, the report also noted that various irregular incidents had been observed, such as armed clashes among peoples settling accounts among themselves, leading to heavy violence and even murder. State property was stolen, and houses and churches set on fire. People were unlawfully arrested and incarcerated.

Reports from local field commanders were increasingly alarming. A mobilization assessment from Northern Dalmatia noted: 'in the territory of the RSK the political and security situation is extremely complicated.' The organs of power were not functioning, and the people's dissatisfaction with the ongoing clashes within the political leadership threatened to unleash social unrest. In a situation when everyone seemed to be armed, this could have tragic consequences, the reporting officer warned. Outmigration from the territory was on the increase, particularly among the young, and the slowness with which socio-economic problems were solved could lead to its further acceleration. The number of weapons stolen had increased enormously; some of these thefts were clearly the result of organized crime. 'The increased criminality has reached such a level that it threatens the economic foundations [of the state] and is targeting also military hardware. The citizens are in possession of a vast amount of weapons and munitions, mines, and explosives which for the most part have been acquired illegally' (*Republika Hrvatska*, Book 5, p. 244). Another report pointed out that 'well-known figures from public life' were involved in organized crime: they were in a sense above the law. 'When the judicial organs try to prosecute such individuals, their work has in several cases been obstructed' (*Republika Hrvatska*, Book 6, p. 124).

Military officers linked the social problems in the RSK directly to lack of political leadership and to infighting within the civilian elites. 'The clashes among various factions in the leadership, their power struggles, the problems of political-territorial organisation, the unfinished state of the poorly functioning legal system, the one-sidedness and lack of objectivity in the mass media—all this may lead to chaos and anarchy' (*Republika Hrvatska*, Book 5, p. 232). In a talk to the 92th police brigade in Benkovac in September 1992, Chief Inspector Momčilo Bogunović did not beat around the bush:

> Unfortunately, a power struggle has broken out for the wrong reasons and at a bad time. All forces and all capabilities of Krajina ought to be united in order to move the economy forward and prepare for the defence of the country. Instead, what is going on among us is precisely what the enemy would want to happen. Rather than strengthening our economy, we are weakening it and our defence capabilities. (*Republika Hrvatska*, Book 5, p. 258)

In February 1993 it was revealed that local RSK officials in Western Slavonia had struck a secret deal with local Croatian leaders about the resolution of certain practical problems such as the return of refugees. In both Zagreb and Knin, this 'Daruvar Agreement' was interpreted as a step towards a separate peace, and was disowned. The Serb leaders involved in the deal were taken to Knin and arrested—but, according to some RSK intelligence reports, the Agreement was supported by 'an increasing number of the Serb population' who wanted to return to the farms they had been forced to leave on the other side of the border. 'Those who are in favour of the "[Daruvar] peace plan" claim that Krajina is at war because some idiots have pushed the people into it. These people, [they say], are building their careers on the graves of Serbian boys even as they know that co-existence with the Croats is inevitable and the only possible solution' (*Republika Hrvatska*, Book 7, p. 248).

From 1993 onwards, the glimmers of hope and optimism that could be detected in some internal RSK documents one year earlier gave way to increasingly sombre reports. In February 1993 Colonel Milan Čeleketić of the Zone Staff of Western Slavonia noted with despair that the legislative, judiciary and executive branches were failing to provide people with even the most basic security. 'It is easier to kill a man than a hen' (*Republika Hrvatska*, Book 7, pp. 221–122). This brings to mind Hobbes' description of the natural condition of man in a stateless society: life as 'solitary, poor, nasty, brutish, and short'.

From Eastern Lika it was reported that the municipality of Donji Lapac had been 'privatized' by the mayor and some of his cronies. The market and finance inspectors in the city took their orders only from him and served their private interests (*Republika Hrvatska*, Book 7, p. 515). In Srijem, the town of Ilok had been taken over by members of the Serbian Radical Party. These 'radicals' had their own militia—the red berets—who did not heed any legal norms and satisfied their needs 'the *hajduk* way' (*Republika Hrvatska*, Book 7, p. 37). From Eastern Slavonia it was reported that members of paramilitary units had liquidated 150 non-Serbs in order to seize their property (*Republika Hrvatska*, Book 7, p. 23).

Reports of assaults on non-Serbs, ethnic Croats in particular, became a standard ingredient in nearly all situation reports from local commanders. These reports left the impression that Croats were fair game: anyone could do as they pleased with them. Such attacks were becoming 'increasingly common' (*Republika Hrvatska*, Book 7, p. 146). Atrocities against Croats became so commonplace that situation reports sometimes mentioned when they did *not* occur (*Republika Hrvatska*, Book 7, p. 494).

Violence against civilians, however, was not directed solely at Croats and other minorities. Paramilitaries from the Radical Party and Arkan's Tigers terrorized members of the local population indiscriminately, including Serbs. In Benkovac, a group of paramilitaries who had been billeted in a local school suddenly started shooting at a nearby house. After a while they forced their way into it and molested the women and the children who were living there. The attackers were later taken to the local militia station, but were released shortly thereafter and resumed their rowdy behaviour. The anger of the local population at this incident was directed not just against the paramilitaries but even more at the police who were unable to protect the populace against such attacks. According to a report, the local people declared that 'unless the police restore order, they will take matters into their own hands' (*Republika Hrvatska*, Book 7, p. 313, also p. 212). The bitterness of the assaulted women stemmed not least from the fact that they were exposed to such acts of violence while their husbands were away at the front, defending the RSK homeland. The uncontrolled behaviour of the paramilitaries directly undermined the morale of the RSK fighters, who would have preferred to return home and protect their families.

The Inner Life of the RSK: The Military Dimension

The situation in the army was characterized by desertions, plundering, internal clashes and smuggling. Even so, in early 1992 some situation reports from the military units were still quite upbeat: An assessment of combat preparedness in the 145th brigade from July that year claimed that the soldiers were firmly determined to fight for their people, for the RSK, and for Serbianness and Serbian honour. The news that a corridor had been established through Republika Srpska in Bosnia, connecting the RSK with 'our future homeland' (meaning Serbia), had been received 'with great enthusiasm' (*Republika Hrvatska*, Book 5, pp. 73–74).

The Croatian surprise attack during the Maslenica operation in January 1993 seems to have caused a burst of fighting spirit among the RSK insurgents (*Republika Hrvatska*, Book 7, pp. 52, 61ff). Also, the volunteers from Serbia played central roles in stemming this offensive, which petered out after a few weeks. This achievement, however, did not lead to a lasting improvement of discipline, morale or social unity. It was reported that during the Maslenica operation fresh atrocities were committed against Croatian civilians, and one brigade had to be withdrawn from the front to be cleansed of defeatist elements (*Republika Hrvatska*, Book 7, pp. 64, 69). One front soldier noted in his diary, 'We have a lot of drunks here who are unable to defend the state. The wine is brought in by the barrel, there is no control. We are unable to carry out any surprise attack. With this kind of spirit and responsibility we will lose the war' (*Republika Hrvatska*, Book 7, p. 109). In addition to wine and hard liquor, also large quantities of drugs, cocaine and marihuana in particular, were consumed at the front (*Republika Hrvatska*, Book 7, p. 277).

A May 1993 report from Chief of Staff Milan Mandić of the 75th motorized brigade painted an appalling picture of the situation at the front: disease, desertion, low morale and lack of discipline. On behalf of his unit, Mandić demanded 'the government must define the political goals of our struggle and announce them publicly through the mass media, so that each soldier can know what he is fighting for' (*Republika Hrvatska*, Book 7, p. 600).

The officers directly blamed the leaders of the political parties for the sorry state of affairs. Not only did the politicians fail to provide leadership in Knin, but they also interfered with the work of the military at the front. 'The activities of the party leaders make it virtually impossible to carry out leadership and command' (*Republika Hrvatska*, Book 7, p. 522). One report from May 1993 characterized the general situation in the 39th corps as 'almost chaotic with regard to order, discipline, and responsibility, in the military as well as in the civilian sector' (*Republika Hrvatska*, Book 7, p. 522).

Conclusions

There was no love lost between the military and civilian leaders in RSK. Having been trained in the Yugoslav army under Tito, the top brass were accused of being Communists, and not genuine Serb nationalists (*Republika Hrvatska*, Book 7, pp. 360, 388). They reciprocated by heaping scorn on the politicians for their incompetence, negligence and personal greed; political disunity weakened the people's motivation to defend their country, they lamented (*Republika Hrvatska*, Book 7, p. 499). Given this quarrelsome atmosphere, we should perhaps take some of the military's accusations against the civilian leadership of the RSK with a pinch of salt, but the fact that the officers and the politicians in the statelet did not see eye to eye was in itself a severe impediment to the construction of a functioning state in the RSK. Even if we make allowances for exaggerations in the above descriptions, it seems clear that the leaders of the Serb insurgence lacked the will, the ability, or the means—or all of this—to create a functional state able to provide its citizens with a modicum of order and security.

Moreover, when the state so flagrantly failed to deliver the goods, the population, which initially seems to have supported the rebellion, lost faith in it within a year or two. It seems safe to conclude that Operation Storm merely administered the *coup de grâce* to this de facto state, which was already crumbling rapidly from within. Why, then, had the state not collapsed even earlier? An important reason seems to have been the deployment of UN peacekeepers, which contributed to freezing the military situation.

Returning to the five points identified at the beginning of this article as necessary for sustaining a de facto state, we can note the following:

(1) *Military power.* The support of the Yugoslav army was clearly an important reason why it was possible for the RSK to break loose from Croatia in 1991. In addition, the statelet was defended by often quite war-seasoned Serbian volunteer paramilitaries. By the same token, however, growing tensions between the army leadership and civilian RSK leaders, as well as the unruly behaviour of the increasingly less disciplined paramilitaries and the general disorganization at the front, all contributed massively to the downfall of the de facto state.

(2) *External patron.* Initially, RSK did enjoy crucial support from the Milošević regime. However, this patronage proved unreliable: in order not to lose it, the Serb insurgents would have to be willing to accept all the vicissitudes of Milošević's policies. They misinterpreted the strength of Milošević's commitment to their state project and refused to become puppets of Belgrade, thereby cutting themselves off from their most vital source of sustenance. It would be wrong, however, to conclude that RSK at any point made a conscious decision to go it alone. It was Belgrade that turned its back on Knin—not the other way around. To the RSK leaders, the vision of all Serbs living in one state remained fundamental to the very end. When Milošević for all practical purposes abandoned this idea, the RSK leaders clung to the hope that at the very least—and as a first step towards full unification—they could create a common state with Republika Srpska in Bosnia (Barić, 2005, p. 477).

(3) *Weakness of parent state.* The period between the disintegration of one state and the consolidation of a successor state is almost by definition a time of weak state control and potential social upheaval, and as such an ideal moment for aspiring secessionists to act (Posen, 1993). Indeed, all de facto states in Europe and Eurasia, extant as well as defunct, were established in the tumultuous years of regime collapse in the USSR and the SFRJ in the early 1990s. In Croatia, however, Tuđman and his entourage systematically rebuilt the state structures and established a rather centralized, authoritarian control regime that brooked little dissent. After some five years, the initially weak parent state had become a formidable challenger to the RSK, intent on recapturing lost territories.

(4) *Role of the international community.* The UN and EU tried to act as impartial arbiters, but it is clear that the deployment of UN peacekeepers in Krajina at a time when the secessionists had managed to secure control over the territory of the future RSK de facto state would inevitably contribute to a cementing of the status quo. Although these major international organizations never fundamentally deviated from their assumed role of neutral conciliators, a crucial change took place in the attitude of

the US administration. Sympathy with the Croatian cause was on the rise in Washington, and the US embassy in Zagreb cleared Operation *Oluja* in advance.
(5) *Nation-building.* The RSK leadership could present its population with an image of a
    common external enemy. Large segments of the population no doubt believed that the
    Croatian state represented a lethal threat to Serbs, and an image of ethnic Croats as a
    genocidal nation was cultivated (Kljakić, 1991; Đurić & Zorić, 2009). Another impor-
    tant precondition for successful nation-building—an ethnically homogeneous popu-
    lation—was certainly in place. As a result of fear-induced flights of non-Serbs as
    well as direct ethnic cleansing in 1990–1991, the population of Krajina had
    become nearly homogeneous in ethnic terms: one official RSK report from July
    1992 gave 88% Serbs, 7% Croats and 5% others, of a total population of 400,000
    (*Republika Hrvatska*, Book 6, pp. 82–83).

The RSK leaders, however, neglected the task of nation-building. In no way did they try to
instil in the population a feeling of a separate Krajina identity, as distinct from a common
Serb identity. Although they did create some national symbols for their new state, they also
signalled that the state identity and its symbols should not really be taken seriously. These
were meant as temporary arrangements only, pending the establishment of a common
national state for all Serbs. When that happy day arrived, the RSK would be dismantled
again.

Knin never managed to establish anything resembling a sustainable economy or a law-
governed state with a law-abiding citizenry. Perhaps the second failure was a function of
the former: the industrial and agricultural collapse in the statelet made it impossible for
people to earn a decent living by honest means—they were drawn towards shady or down-
right criminal business such as smuggling and black marketeering simply in order to
survive. However, it would be wrong to conclude from this that the criminalization of
the RSK economy and RSK society was 'inevitable'. To claim that, one would have to
demonstrate that the RSK leaders made serious attempts to try to prevent their country's
downward slide into a criminal badland—instead, they led the way.

The experience of Abkhazia, Somaliland and some other weak but long-existing de
facto states indicates that a population who identify with a secessionist regime are
willing to put up with harsh living conditions (Bradbury, 2008; O'Loughlin *et al.*,
2011), but the case of the RSK would seem to show that there is a lower limit to their
patience and loyalty. The people will reject their de facto state if they feel that its
leaders, instead of building and strengthening the state, are wrecking it through asset-strip-
ping, lining their own pockets with the little of value that can be found there.

Closer examination of other now-extinct de facto states such as Ichkeria (Chechnya) and
Tamil Eelan would probably show that most of the factors highlighted in this article have
also been crucial in other instances of abortive state-building. Both Ichkeria and Tamil
Eelan were confronted by a strong parent state intent on recapturing the lost region.
With regard to external patrons, Ichkeria had none, whereas Tamil Eelam forfeited the
support of its patron, India, when a Tamil suicide bomber killed former Indian prime
minister Rajiv Gandhi in 1991. Initially, both statelets enjoyed substantial support from
their own populations but squandered most of it by ruthless authoritarian rule in Tamil
Eelan (see Pegg, 1998, pp. 66–81), and in Ichkeria through growing anarchy, not dissim-
ilar to the RSK case (Tishkov, 2004).

This study appears to confirm earlier research that protracted de facto statehood today is indeed possible, albeit quite precarious. Key factors are felicitous international circumstances and determined statesmanship. Deprived of the scaffolding provided by international recognition, the de facto states find themselves thrown back into the Hobbesian jungle and have to fend for themselves. If they neglect the tasks of nation-building and state-building, allow military capacities to crumble and/or fail to secure the support of a strong patron, their demise seems inevitable.

Acknowledgements

The authors would like to thank Nina Caspersen and Vjeran Pavlaković for valuable comments on draft versions of the article.

Funding

This article emanates from the research project 'Symbolic Nation-building in West-Balkan States: Intents and Results', which was funded by the Research Council of Norway (project number 203356).

Notes

1. It is unfortunate that such a small field of research as this should be ridden by a high degree of semantic confusion, and efforts should be made to agree on a common designation for these unruly entities. There are, it seems, only two claimants to that throne: 'unrecognized states' and 'de facto states'. Of these we favour 'de facto states', which today is preferred also by active scholars who earlier used other terms, such as 'pseudo-states' (O'Loughlin, Kolossov) and 'quasi-states' (Kolstø). O'Loughlin *et al.* (2011, p. 2) argue that this is 'the most appropriate and most neutral' term.
2. This seems to be the case with South Ossetia, for instance. Author's interviews in Tskhinvali, 2006.
3. Public International Law and Policy Group (2000, p. 27) for Nagorno Karabakh, and Montevideo Convention and Pridnestrovie's Statehood for Transnistria, both accessed in September 2006. (Both articles were later removed from the Internet.)
4. Its forerunner, the Turkish Federated State of Cyprus, was established in 1975, but formal independence was proclaimed only in 1983.
5. The easternmost part of Eastern Slavonia survived until 1998, when it was reincorporated peacefully.
6. For example, Mile Dakić, *Krajina kroz vijekove* (Belgrade: Vedes, 2002), contains some documents also published in books used in this article.
7. In this Assembly, the municipalities of Knin, Benkovac, Gračac, Donji Lapac, Obrovac and Titova Korenica were included. According to the document, other municipalities outside the region of Dalmatia and Lika may join the Community in the future.
8. The Last Constitution of Yugoslavia from 1974 stated the right of peoples (*narodi*) to secede, but also that they exercise their sovereign rights within the Republics, which were defined as states of the constituent peoples and nationalities. In any case, the Arbitration (Badinter) Commission in its opinion on the Serbia question in January 1992 stated that the right to self-determination cannot lead to changes of republican borders if an agreement is not reached between the affected republics. If no such agreement is achieved, these borders become state borders protected by international law (Degan, 2002, pp. 336–339).
9. Serb rebels blocked the roads leading into their area by felling trees over them.
10. For example, Sekulić (2001, p. 284). In his testimony before the ICTY in The Hague, Babić in confrontation with Milošević said that the war started in Belgrade, and that Milošević later turned his back on them (Žunec, 2007, p. 498).
11. The penultimate article of the RSK Constitution, Article 123, reads: 'Republika Srpska Krajina, together with the other parts of the Serb people in the territory of Yugoslavia and their states, will establish strong

connections among themselves with the aim of creating a common state for the Serbian people. As confirmed by this Constitution, Republika Srpska Krajina will then transfer a part of its authority to this common state as part of a treaty on the future arrangement of Yugoslavia.' The entire text of the constitution is reprinted in Pauković (2005, pp. 114–131); this quotation is on p. 131.

References

Bahcheli, T., Bartmann, B. & Srebrnik, H. (2004) *De Facto States: The Quest of Sovereignty* (London: Routledge).

Banac, I. (1992) Post-communism as post Yugoslavism: the Yugoslav non-revolutions of 1989–1990, in: I. Banac (Ed.), *Eastern Europe in Revolution* (Ithaca, NY: Cornell University Press).

Barić, N. (2005) *Srpska pobuna u Hrvatskoj* (Zagreb: Golden Marketing-Tehnička knjiga).

Berg, E. & Toomla, R. (2009) Forms of normalization in the quest for de facto statehood, *The International Spectator*, 44(4), pp. 27–45.

Blakkisrud, H. & Kolstø, P. (2011) From secessionist conflict towards functioning state: processes of state- and nation-building in Transnistria, *Post-Soviet Affairs*, 27(2), pp. 178–210.

Blakkisrud, H. & Kolstø, P. (2012) Dynamics of de facto statehood: the South Caucasian de facto states between secession and sovereignty, *Southeast European and Black Sea Studies*, 12(2), pp. 281–298.

Bradbury, M. (2008) *Becoming Somaliland* (Oxford: James Currey).

Caspersen, N. (2007) Belgrade, Pale, Knin: kin-state control over rebellious puppets?, *Europe-Asia Studies*, 59(4), pp. 621–641.

Caspersen, N. (2010) *Contested Nationalism: Serb Elite Rivalry in Croatia and Bosnia in the 1990s* (New York: Berghahn).

Caspersen, N. (2012) *Unrecognized States* (Cambridge: Polity).

Caspersen, N. & Stansfield, G. (2011) *Unrecognized States in the International System* (London: Routledge).

Degan, V.Ð. (2002) *Hrvatska država u Međunarodnoj zajednici* (Zagreb: Nakladni zavod Globus).

Đurić, I. & Zorić, V. (2009) Foreclosing the other, building the war: a comparative analysis of Croatian and Serbian press discourses during the conflict in Croatia, in: P. Kolstø (Ed.), *Media Discourse and the Yugoslav Conflicts: Representations of Self and Other* (Farnham: Ashgate).

Fabry, M. (2010) *Recognizing States, International Society and the Establishment of New States since 1776* (Oxford: Oxford University Press).

Geldenhuys, D. (2009) *Contested States in World Politics* (Basingstoke: Palgrave Macmillan).

Jackson, R.H. (1990) *Quasi-states: Sovereignty, International Relations and the Third World* (Cambridge: Cambridge University Press).

Jović, B. (1996) *Poslednji dani SFRJ, Izvodi iz dnevnika* (Belgrade: Politika).

Kimitaka, M. (2008) From belligerent to multiethnic democracy: domestic politics in unrecognized states after the Ceasefires, *Eurasian Review*, 1, pp. 95–119.

King, C. (2001) The benefits of ethnic war: understanding Eurasia's unrecognized states, *World Politics*, 53, pp. 524–552.

Kingston, P. & Spears, I. (2004) *States-within-states: Incipient Political Entities in the Post Cold War Era* (New York: Palgrave Macmillan).

Kljakić, S. (1991) *A Conspiracy of Silence: Genocide in the Independent State of Croatia* (Belgrade: Ministry of Information of the Republic of Serbia).

Kolossov, V. & O'Loughlin, J. (1999) Pseudo-states as harbingers of a new geopolitics: the example of the Transdniestr Moldovan Republic (TMR), in: D. Newman (Ed.), *Boundaries, Territory and Postmodernity*, pp. 151–176 (London: Frank Cass).

Kolstø, P. (2006) The sustainability and future of unrecognized quasi-states, *Journal of Peace Research*, 43(6), pp. 723–740.

Kolstø, P. (2011) The Serbian–Croatian controversy over Jasenovac, in: S. Ramet & O. Listhaug (Eds), *Serbia and the Serbs in World War Two*, pp. 225–246 (New York: Palgrave Macmillan).

Kolstø, P. & Blakkisrud, H. (2008) Living with non-recognition: state- and nation-building in South Caucasian quasi-states, *Europe–Asia Studies*, 6, pp. 483–509.

Kolstø, P. & Blakkisrud, H. (2012) De facto states and democracy: the case of Nagorno-Karabakh, *Journal of Communist and Post-Communist Studies*, 45, pp. 141–151.

Lynch, D. (2002) Separatist states and post-Soviet conflicts, *International Affairs*, 78(4), pp. 831–848.

Marijan, D. (2008) *Slom Titove armije. Jugoslavenska narodna armija i raspad Jugoslavije 1987–1992* (Zagreb: Golden Marketing-Tehnička knjiga).

Matsuzato, K. (2008) From belligerent to multi-ethnic democracy: domestic politics in unrecognized states after the ceasefires, *Eurasian Review*, 1, pp. 95–119.

Milosavljević, O. (2002) Jugoslavija kao zabluda, in: N. Popov (Ed.), *Srpska strana rata. Trauma i katarza u Istorijskom pamćenju*, Vol. 1 (Belgrade: Republika).

Montevideo Convention and Pridnestrovie's Statehood, originally online at: http://pridnestrovie.net/montevideo_convention.html

Mønnesland, S. (2013) *National Symbols in Multinational States: The Yugoslav Case* (Oslo: Sypress Forlag).

O'Loughlin, J., Kolossov, V. & Toal, G. (2011) Inside Abkhazia: survey of attitudes in a *de facto* state, *Post-Soviet Affairs*, 27(1), pp. 1–36.

Pauković, D. (2005) *Uspon i pad 'Republike Srpske Krajine'—Dokumenti* (Zagreb: Centar za Politološka iztraživanja).

Pauković, D. (2008) Konstrukcija neprijatelja: HDZ u Politikinoj rubrici 'Odjeci i reagovanja' 1989/91, *Srpsko-hrvatski odnosi u 20. Veku, Prošlost i Perspective* (Novi Sad: Grafo Marketing).

Pavlaković, V. (2013) Symbols and the culture of memory in Republika Srpska Krajina, *Nationalities Papers*, 41(6), pp. 893–909.

Pegg, S. (1998) *International Society and the De Facto State* (Aldershot: Ashgate).

Pegg, S. (2000) The 'Taiwan of the Balkans'? The de facto state option for Kosova, *Southeast European Politics*, 1, pp. 90–100.

Posen, B. (1993) The security dilemma and ethnic conflict, *Survival*, 35(1), pp. 27–47.

Protsyk, O. (2009) Representation and democracy in Eurasia's unrecognized states: the case of Transnistria, *Post-Soviet Affairs*, 25(3), pp. 257–281.

Public International Law and Policy Group (2000) *The Nagorno Karabagh Crisis: A Blueprint for Resolution, A Memorandum*, originally online at: http://www.armeniaforeignministry.com/fr/nk/blueprint.html

Republika Hrvatska i domovinski rat 1990–1995 Dokumenti (Zagreb: Hrvatski memorijalno-dokumentacijski centrar Domovinskog rata).

Sekulić, M. (2001) *Knin je pao u Beogradu* (Bad Vilbel: Nidda).

Sokol, S. & Smerdel, B. (1995) *Ustavno Pravo* (Zagreb: Školska knjiga).

Šiber, I. (1991) Nacionalna, vrijednosna i ideologijska uvjetovanost stranačkog izbora, *Hrvatska u izborima 90'* (Zagreb: Naprijed).

Tishkov, V. (2004) *Chechnya: Life in a War-torn Society* (Berkeley, CA: University of California Press).

von Steinsdorff, S. & Fruhstorfer, A. (2012) Post-Soviet de facto states in search of internal and external legitimacy, *Communist and Post-Communist Studies*, 45(1–2) pp. 117–121.

Vrcelj, M. (2002) *Rat za Srpsku Krajinu 1991–1995* (Belgrade: Srpsko kulturno društvo 'Zora').

Žunec, O. (2007) *Goli život, socijetalne dimenzije pobune Srba u Hrvatskoj*, Vol. I (Zagreb: Demetra).

Ethnopolitics, 2014
Vol. 13, No. 4, 328–354, http://dx.doi.org/10.1080/17449057.2014.888213

Ethnic Alliances Deconstructed: The PKK Sanctuary in Iraqi Kurdistan and the Internationalization of Ethnic Conflict Revisited

HANNES ČERNY

University of Exeter, UK

ABSTRACT   This article presents a critique of how the dominant paradigms in international relations (IR)—neo-realism, neo-liberalism and systemic constructivism—approach and explain ethnic conflict. It deconstructs one of the most prominent explanatory frameworks that mainstream IR has contributed to the analysis of the internationalization of ethnic conflicts, the ethnic alliance model, and demonstrates theoretically and empirically, by way of a case study of the Kurdistan Workers' Party sanctuary in Iraqi Kurdistan, the epistemological and ontological deficiencies of this approach. Furthermore, by dissecting the inherent 'groupism' of this model and related frameworks, it problematizes how scholars as co-protagonists of ethnic conflicts substantialize and reify the ethnicized discourse and politics of ethnic division, and thus contribute to the construction of a normativist and essentialist 'reality' of the conflicts that they set out to describe.

Introduction

Arguably, international relations (IR) more than any other discipline is prone to what Rogers Brubaker (2004, p. 38) calls 'groupism' and a 'clichéd constructivism' when dealing with identity politics in the social sciences, a constructivism in name only (limited to the introductory section or expressed in customary yet seemingly perfunctory disclaimers), but the main analysis, at large, continues to be done under essentialist and substantialist presumptions of ethnic identities, often bordering a primordialism slipping in through the back door. Despite advances to the contrary in sociology and anthropology, and two generations of critical theory scholarship, the three dominant schools of thought in IR—neo-realism, neo-liberalism, and systemic constructivism—still tend to treat ethnic groups as organic, static, substantive, distinct, homogeneous and bounded units and largely equate conflicts between said groups with conflicts between states. In examining this tendency, this article is first and foremost understood as a critique of how mainstream

Correspondence Address: Hannes Černy, Exeter Centre for Ethno-Political Studies, University of Exeter, Stocker Road, Exeter EX4 4ND, UK. Email: ja280@exeter.ac.uk

© 2014 The Editor of Ethnopolitics

IR approaches, understands and explains ethnic conflict, in particular the internationalization of ethnic conflict. Here, on the question of how ethnic violence diffuses or can spread
across borders, and why states may be dragged into ethnic conflicts in the neighbourhood,
IR has made two major theoretical contributions: Barry Posen's (1993) extension of the
classic neo-realist 'security dilemma' to ethnic groups, and David Davis and Will
Moore's (1997, 1998) application of the logic of alliance formation to ethnic conflicts. I
argue that both models get their unit of analysis wrong, yet despite their flawed ontology,
not only do they dominate how mainstream IR makes sense of ethnic conflicts, but also,
their misleading representations are widely reproduced in the media and by political
decision-makers. While Posen's ethnic security dilemma has received its fair share of
debate,[1] this article will interrogate Davis and Moore's ethnic alliance model and
related theoretical frameworks, which I take not just to represent the 'groupism' and
'clichéd constructivism' identified by Brubaker but to epitomize the misguided presumptions and flawed ontologies that dominate mainstream IR's approach to ethnic conflict at
large. This deconstruction of the ethnic alliance model and related frameworks will be pre-
ceded by a brief overview of how mainstream IR makes sense of ethnic conflict, a detailed
summary of the ethnic alliance model, and references to how it continues to influence
recent analyses, in particular new global data sets and prominent large-*n* studies on
ethnic conflict. For I shall argue that the systemic constructivism these studies are based
on, despite the paradigm's focus on agency rather than structure, shares similar meta-nar-
ratives with the ethnic alliance model about the internationalization of ethnic conflicts.

While not attempting to put deconstruction in a nutshell—for 'one might even say that
cracking nutshells is what deconstruction is' (Caputo, 1997, p. 32)—'a deconstructive
approach' for the purposes of this article means 'critically examining the discursive processes of materialization that produce settlements; such as the idea of pre-given subjects—
upon which the criteria for judgement are based' (Campbell, 1998, p. 30). In other words,
'the question asked is not, "what does [the text] mean?" but "what does it presuppose?"'
(Edkins, 1999, p. 74). What mainstream IR presupposes in how it makes sense of ethnic
conflict is 'groupness', for ethnicity to be the pre-eminent, determining variable in
relations between and within assumed ethnic groups, and to equate ontologically those
presupposed ethnic groups with states in their analyses of the internationalization of
ethnic conflicts. This deconstructive approach highlights why certain key concepts—in
this case the ethnic group—are no longer serviceable within the paradigms in which
they were originally developed, yet at the same time, somewhat paradoxically, instead
of being replaced they continue to be used in their now deconstructed form (Hall, 1995,
1996). 'By means of this double, stratified, dislodged and dislodging writing', in the
words of Derrida (1981, p. 42), 'we must also mark the interval between inversion,
which brings low what was high, and the eruptive emergence of a new "concept", a
concept that can no longer be and never could be, included in the previous regime'. Consequently, the aim of deconstruction is never to develop new meta-theories, models, or frameworks that replace the ones that have been identified as no longer serviceable, that is,
'the production of [truer] positive knowledge' (Hall, 1996, p. 1), but, after *herausarbeiten*
(in the sense of 'highlighting the essence of') the social context and discourse in which
they were generated, to continue operationalizing them with the caveat of the insights
deconstruction has yielded with regard to their production and utilization. In other
words, deconstruction should be understood as a moment of passage from one concept
to another (*ibid.*), in which, in lieu of a 'better' concept, the concept 'under erasure'

(Derrida, 1981) is still used until a new one has been developed—which cannot be the task of deconstruction, as to do so would violate its very principles, that is, its inherently critical attitude to any kind of meta-theory.

All this is not to say that ethnic groups do not exist. They very much exist in the hearts and minds of the respective people and as ethnonationalist ideology in the public and political discourse. This attempt at deconstruction of 'groupism' should therefore not be misunderstood as efforts to invalidate these public perceptions or to vilify the ethnonationalist elites employing such 'strategic essentialisms' (Spivak, 1987). To do so is part of their job description, for them maintaining the pretence of group cohesion and unity is the single most important goal and interest that constitutes and defines a nation or ethnic community, and their leadership often depends on how well they do in it. Yet for us social scientists demands should be different. Accordingly, this article is to be understood as a critique of how well IR scholars are doing their job as analysts when subscribing unquestioningly to these strategic essentialisms, and by doing so reproducing their logic and reifying the politics of ethnic division they set out to describe—a tendency the ethnic alliance model and related frameworks explaining the internationalization of ethnic conflicts from a mainstream IR perspective typify. By explaining ethnic conflict through presupposed 'groupism', *scholars*, like ethnonationalist elites, construct an ethnicized 'reality' in the scholarly, public and political discourse. When faced with this dynamic, the least, I would argue, that critical scholarship can do is to raise awareness about our role as co-protagonists in ethnic conflicts.

The case study of the relations, from the early 1980s to the present, between the Kurdistan Workers' Party (PKK) and the Iraqi-Kurdish ethnonationalist parties, the Kurdistan Democratic Party (KDP) and the Patriotic Union of Kurdistan (PUK), was chosen for several reasons. The so-called 'Kurdish Question' constitutes the most internationalized ethnic conflict in the Middle East, affecting four nationalizing states[2]—Turkey, Iraq, Iran and Syria—in one of the world's most strategically and economically important regions. Also, and for our purposes most significantly, the PKK sanctuary in Iraqi Kurdistan is routinely referred to in the literature as a textbook example of common ethnicity determining the conflict behaviour of actors in the internationalization of an ethnic conflict, i.e. forming an ethnic alliance. This renders it a case study ideally suited to deconstructing the model claiming to represent it and to illustrate empirically the theoretical flaws in this approach identified here.

It goes without saying, however, that a single case study is hardly sufficient to disprove an entire set of established theories; as a matter of course, likewise, to disprove these theories by way of several case studies analysed in the necessary depth would go beyond the scope of an article. Bearing these limitations in mind, I understand the case study of PKK–KDP/PUK relations as an 'extroverted case study with generic concepts', an approach introduced by Richard Rose, who, referring to Toqueville's *Democracy in America* as a classic example, calls it 'the most frequent form of analysis in comparative politics'. The crucial point here is that such a case study 'is not explicitly comparative, but comparable' (Rose, 1991, p. 454), if it is intended and possible to come to theoretical or conceptual generalizations from a single case study that can be applied to other cases. Or in the words of Peters (1998, p. 62), 'the purpose of the extroverted case-study then becomes to explore fully this one case with the existing theory in mind, with the expectation of elaborating or expanding that body of theory with the resulting data'. What I set out to achieve with this article, though, is to go beyond just expanding a body of theory but, after first having applied a deconstructive reading of the theories in question, to use the extroverted case study to substantiate empirically this deconstruction of the theory. In other words, and as stated above, I would hope for this article to be understood as an invitation for further intellectual exchange about the issues raised and as prompting analyses of additional case studies, to stimulate reflection and discussion within IR about our epistemologies of ethnic conflict and our role as knowledge producers in these discourses, where we, through our epistemologies and ontologies, run the risk of reifying and reproducing the narratives and politics of ethnic division we set out to describe.

Mainstream IR and the Internationalization of Ethnic Conflict

'Theories of international relations offer useful tools and insights in the study of ethnic conflict and conflict settlement', Karl Cordell and Stefan Wolff (2009, p. 14) state in arguing for a primacy of IR, together with theories of ethnicity and inter-ethnic relations, in explaining the dynamics of ethnic conflict. More than any other discipline, they continue, 'IR theory is primarily concerned with issues of war and peace' in the international arena, and state behaviour has a significant impact on the origins, development and duration of ethnic conflicts—whether causal, escalating or mitigating—as do norms, values, practices, institutions, legislations, and forms of governance at the local, regional and international level (*ibid.*, pp. 9–14).[3] Although the reasons they offer for IR's primacy in explaining the complex dynamics of ethnic conflict appear compelling, others would argue that IR is not particularly well-equipped for the analysis of identity conflicts.[4] Zalewski & Enloe (1995, p. 297) sum it up aptly when concluding 'all three paradigms [neo-realism, neo-liberalism, systemic structuralism] are too restricted ontologically, methodologically, and epistemologically, and in ways which ultimately render them unable to theorize or think adequately about identity'.[5] Yet think and theorize they do, but perhaps in sound self-awareness of their own limitations confined to what they understand to be their very own domain: conflict in the international arena, or in our case, the internationalization of ethnic conflict. It is here, on the question of how ethnic violence diffuses and can spread across borders, and why states may get dragged into ethnic conflicts in the neighbourhood, that mainstream IR theory has made its three main contributions to our understanding of ethnicity-based identity conflicts: Posen's ethnic security dilemma, Davis and Moore's ethnic alliance model, and a rather strict application of instrumentalism that ultimately results in the assertion that ethnicity is merely a political tool of elite manipulation and therefore has no explanatory value in itself.

The ethnic security dilemma and the ethnic alliance model clearly display what Brubaker (2004, p. 38) has come to identify as a 'clichéd constructivism' when dealing with identity politics in the social sciences, a constructivist caveat to which the main analysis pays only lip service while largely continuing under essentialist and substantialist presumptions of ethnic identities. In neo-realist and neo-liberal IR's approaches to ethnicity these essentialist and substantialist presumptions manifest themselves on two levels: (1) operationalizing ethnicity as the independent variable and therewith according it with pre-eminent explanatory power; and (2) ontologically equating ethnic groups with states. As will be shown throughout this article, both levels and the inherent presumptions that inform them lead to the reification of ethnicized discourses, politicized ethnicity, ethnic divisions, and of the 'us versus them' dichotomies that often form the basis of ethnicized discourses. In the words of Brubaker, they follow, reproduce and reify the logic of 'groupism':

['Groupism' is] the tendency to take discrete, bounded groups as basic constituents of social life, chief protagonists of social conflicts and fundamental units of social analysis; ... the tendency to treat ethnic groups, nations, and races as substantial entities to which interests and agency can be attributed; ... the tendency to reify such groups, speaking of ... [them] as if they were internally homogeneous, externally bounded groups, even unitary collective actors with common purposes. (Brubaker, 2004, p. 8)

Concurrent with or instigated by Brubaker's critique, scholars (Laitin & Posner, 2001; Fearon, 2003; Posner, 2005; Brown & Langer, 2010) have problematized the quantification of ethnicity in large-n studies on intra-state and/or inter-state conflicts—usually based on record sets such as Ted Robert Gurr's (1993) *Minorities at Risk* (MAR) project or the *Ethno-linguistic Fractionalization* (ELF) data set—that operationalize the ethnic group as their unit of analysis as if it were a substantial entity and not a sociopolitical construct, and in consequence explain its actions as derivative of the fact that ethnicity is the element defining and cohering the group. In both cases, the ethnic security dilemma and the ethnic alliance model, the action of the respective parties, antagonistic or collaborative (the dependent variable), is a function of their being part of an ethnic group (the independent variable) and follows and reifies the same ethnicized logic: a logic of presupposed internal homogeneity, cohesion, solidarity, unity and common purpose in opposition to the constructed 'Other', that is, groups of the same qualities yet of a different ethnic ascription. In the case of the ethnic security dilemma, the coherence and solidarity of one group is presumed to be perceived as a threat by others. In the case of the ethnic alliance model, contingents of one ethnic group, although separated by international borders, are suspected to form an alliance, and unite across factitious divides such as international borders as a result of group cohesion, group solidarity and against a common enemy. What is particularly conspicuous here is that these simplistic and essentialist approaches that operationalize ethnicity as the independent variable in explaining ethnic conflicts and, in our case their internationalization, by implication accept the conversion of ethnicity as the independent into the determining variable; that is, ultimately, if 'groupist'-think is brought to its tautological conclusion, ethnic conflicts are explained with ethnicity. An illustration of such flawed and potentially harmful reasoning would be the infamous 'ancient hatreds' Robert Kaplan (1994) claims to have identified as the root cause for the conflicts of the 1990s in the Balkans.

The second dimension of 'groupism' and the selection of the ethnic group as the unit of analysis in the study of ethnic conflict is belief in the unitary actor. Naturally, for ethnonationalist elites, homogeneity, group cohesion and solidarity and the undivided allegiance of their members to the nationalist principle are as much defining criteria as the polarizing principles of identity formation based on 'us versus them' dichotomies. Such 'strategic essentialisms', in the terminology of Gayatri Spivak (1987), are understandable, even normal. The use of an essentialized version of oneself—individual or group—although not without internal and external controversy, for the sake of self-representation in order to achieve political gains, is part of their job description. In the eyes of ethnonationalist elites, unity, or at least maintaining the pretence of it, is the single most important goal and interest that constitutes and defines a nation or ethnic community. Yet, for social scientists, requirements, like aims, should be different. When we uncritically accept the rhetoric of ethnonationalist elites, we run the risk of becoming complicit in their attempts to ethnicize the discourse. If we, as scholars, rather than calling it into question, adopt their strategic essentialism as the basis of our enquiries or take on '*categories of ethnopolitical practice as our categories of social analysis*' (Brubaker, 2004, p. 10, italics in original), we contribute to the reification and substantialization of the ethnonationalist elites' primordialism and to the reproduction of its logic (Brubaker, 1996, 2004, 2009; Fenton, 2004; Gagnon, 2004). In sum, and not to put too fine a point on it, both ethnonationalist elites and IR scholars studying them are protagonists of ethnic conflicts; yet while they, by essentializing the group they claim to represent, are acting within the confines of their supposed social roles, we scholars, by subscribing to their claims without challenging these strategic essentialisms, I would argue, fail in our duty to analyse them critically—and it is this failure that is the main point of critique of this article.

It is to the credit of constructivists such as Brubaker that they caution against taking '*categories of ethnopolitical practice as our categories of social analysis*' (Brubaker, 2004, p. 10, italics in original) and remind us that ethnicity has no 'independent explanatory power' (Steinberg, 2001, p. XIV), either as the determining variable to measure group consciousness and solidarity or to explain the nature of ethnicized political conflict (Bowen, 1996, Banton, 2000, Gilley, 2004)—'ethnicity is not the ultimate, irreducible source of violence in such cases' (Brubaker & Laitin, 1998, p. 425). Neither should we attribute ethnic groups with agency and interests. They are not the protagonists of ethnic conflict but rather the organizations and 'their empowered and authorised incumbents' (Brubaker, 2004, p. 14) who frame and code the discourse ethnically, and with it the conflict, i.e. they construct, instrumentalize and reinforce imagined boundaries. Rejecting the false idols of the detached scientific objectivism of positivism, we researchers also have to acknowledge our role as co-protagonists of ethnic conflicts, the ways in which we are taking part in the discourse that categorizes, constructs and constitutes ethnic identities, and our performance that produces and reifies them. In the case of mainstream IR scholars, their supposedly observing conflict from a detached distance, by adopting the strategic essentialisms of an ethnicized discourse as categories for the analysis of ethnic conflict, gets them in fact quite actively involved in these conflicts. Ultimately, their scholarship, by reproducing and reifying the divisions along the ethnic lines they set out to describe, runs risk of, deliberately or not, legitimizing the role and politics of ethnonationalist elites to an external audience. Whether those elites are the leaders of separatist national liberation movements (NLMs) or of the assimilationist states repressing diversity and plurality within their borders, their performance amounts to an unsettling tendency, which, for our case study, will be revealed via a critical reading of the mainstream IR literature on ethnic conflict in general and the PKK sanctuary in Iraqi Kurdistan in particular.

Considering neo-realists, then, for them, not unlike primordialists and ethnonationalist elites, one may say, in admittedly simplified terms, national cohesion is supposed to be a given not questioned further. Domestic politics rarely matter, and sovereign nation states are perceived and treated like a 'black box' (Singer, 1961, p. 81), as unitary, rational actors in an anarchic international system. With neo-liberalism, matters are not as clear-cut. As for neo-realists the sovereign nation state in the anarchic international system is the main unit of analysis for scholars in the neo-liberal tradition, yet unlike neo-realists the importance of the domestic decision-making process is acknowledged. As has been pointed out though,[6] this acknowledgement amounts to very little because domestic pluralism is confined to a homogenizing corset of hierarchical decision-making that, in the end, has the state speaking with one voice in the international arena in the rational pursuit of its national self-interest; the state may not be a unitary actor but its policies are ultimately unitary. 'Despite their willingness to rely on domestic level explanations and a more inclusive set of actor types than realists do, most neoliberals also tacitly adhere to a reified approach to agency' (Cederman, 1997, p. 20). Whether states or ethnic groups at the unit of analysis level, neo-realism and neo-liberalism in IR treat both as rational, unitary—or unitarily acting—agents in pursuit of self-interests in a predominantly hostile international system. In the case of ethnic groups, the internationalization of ethnic conflict is explained through the lens of 'groupism', that is, group cohesion, group solidarity and the portrayal of the ethnic group, like a state, as a unitary actor. Kenneth Bush observes:

> Communal groups are *represented* as the functional equivalent of states: unitary, power-seeking ... actors in a Hobbesian world. In other words, communal groups are viewed as being analogous to the state epistemologically and ontologically. Like states, such groups are seen to constitute stable and unified entities, and to act as coherent and separate totalities. (Bush, 2003, p. 5, italics in original)

Drawing on the famous billiard ball analogy, originally coined by Arnold Wolfers (1962), which illustrates how mainstream IR theory has focused exclusively on the 'third image', the international system, at the expense of the 'second image', the domestic composition of states (in a billiard game what matters are not the individual properties of the balls, which essentially are the same, but their external dimension, their interaction with each other), Bush (2003) and Bush & Keyman (1997) argue that mainstream IR theory in its analysis of ethnic conflict has simply made the new unit of analysis fit its already existing epistemological and ontological framework.

> Thus, the billiard ball model, which is based on relations between separate states as unified entities, now includes interethnic group relations, each of which constitutes a unified and separate totality—that is, self-contained and self-propelling entities. In effect, realism simply adds the notion of ethnic identity to its basic assumption that the position of a collectivity, whether it be a state or a group, in an anarchical system is the primary causal variable in the area of security. (Bush & Keyman, 1997, p. 313)

The example of Posen's ethnic security dilemma or Davis and Moore's ethnic alliance model attests to this presumption: 'we contend that it is useful to conceptualise ethnic linkages among people across state boundaries as functionally equivalent to alliances between states' (Davis & Moore, 1998, p. 93), and 'these alliances should behave much as alliances between states have been hypothesized to behave in international relations' (*ibid.*, p. 92). Before discussing the ontologies and epistemologies of the ethnic alliance model in more detail, though, a cursory historical backgrounder on the case study is required.

The Historical Legacies of Kurdish Ethnonationalism

As will be seen, the case of the PKK sanctuary in Iraqi Kurdistan is one of the widest quoted, almost textbook examples of the internationalization of an ethnic conflict, its diffusion across state borders, drawing in regional and global powers, and its potential to escalate to a wider regional conflagration, and, often by implication, of an ethnic alliance. It seems, therefore, ideally suited as a case study to deconstruct this model and its related frameworks.

Since the Gulf War of 1991 sparked global interest in their fate, most writers, scholarly and popular, have cited the approximately 30 million Kurds as the world's largest ethnic group without a state.[7] Historically, the Kurds inhabited the border region of the Ottoman, Safavid and Qajar empires, a peripheral frontier status that on the one hand invited attempts by imperial rulers to use them as pawns in their power struggles,[8] yet on the other hand allowed the Kurdish emirs a degree of relative autonomy in conducting their domestic affairs (van Bruinessen, 1992; O'Shea, 2004). Today, the lands with Kurdish majority population straddle one of the most geo-strategically contested and natural resource-rich regions in the world, which again has seen them used by regional and great powers, but concomitantly had Kurdish nationalist leaders harness those powers' interests for their own ends (see Figure 1).

Figure 1. Map of the Kurdistan region of Iraq (Creative Commons Generic License).

The scope of this article does not allow for an overview of the genesis of Kurdish eth-nonationalism in the twentieth century. Instead, I refer readers to standard works on the subject,[9] yet want to stress four basic tenets, elaborated elsewhere in more detail,[10] and crucial to following the key arguments made here.

First, one should bear in mind that before World War I Kurdish nationalism was largely limited to cultural societies and literati circles in Istanbul, developing and becoming salient when the borders of the nationalizing states of Turkey, Iraq, Iran and Syria were already drawn. As a consequence thereof, the process of Kurdish identi-fication has been oriented towards varying constitutive 'Others' and has been shaped by the political, social and economic contexts in the respective countries and societies. Also, pan-Kurdish ethnic consciousness and solidarity is most salient among the dia-spora; in the Kurdish 'homelands', as a result of 90 years of separation and a lack of a distinct prior feeling of communality, they are mostly an ever-present yet rarely politi-cally acted on sentiment, save political rhetoric of ethnonational elites to justify and legitimize actions *ex post*. Finally, of all major Kurdish ethnonationalist insurgencies, the PKK is the only contemporary Kurdish NLM that has ever pursued a secessionist or irredentist agenda,[11] while all others fought for national self-determination within the borders of the existing nationalizing states and—although often under severe con-straint—in dialogue with the respective governments, that is, they sought to enforce a negotiated solution, a degree of political autonomy. To put it less abstractly, while Kurds in Turkey were confronted by an effectively and ideologically strong nationaliz-ing state that denied them their very identity, Kurds in Iraq faced a notoriously weak state that lacked any coherent national legitimization, torn apart by legion internal divisions. Consequently, while Kurds in Turkey became the victims of a cataclysmic ethnocide before their national consciousness became salient, Kurdish ethnonationalism in Iraq blossomed along and often in collaboration with the manifold currents of (pan-)Arab eth-nonationalism, which, until the second half of the 1970s, frequently bestowed upon Kurdish leaders the role of kingmakers in inner-Iraqi power struggles. This role was exacerbated by Iraq—unlike Turkey—becoming an early battlefield of superpower riv-alries during the Cold War, which had its Kurdish parties enjoy the dubious privilege of serving as their proxies. Ultimately, whereas in Turkey the traditional Kurdish elites were either shattered early on, or largely co-opted by the nationalizing state, traditional societal structures in Iraq not only prevailed, but also, tribal leaders often formed the vanguard of the Kurdish ethnonationalist movement. In light of these different trajec-tories it then appears justifiable to conclude with Martin van Bruinessen, the only scholar who has conducted extensive ethnographic field work in all major parts of Kur-distan, 'it might, in fact, be more apt to consider the Kurds not as one, but as a set of ethnic groups' (van Bruinessen, 2000, p. 14), and to speak of Kurdish ethnonationalisms in plural rather than a singular implying an ethnic group defined by cross-border unity, communality and solidarity. Yet it is such presupposed cross-border unity and commun-ality by which the internationalization of the so-called 'Kurdish conflict' is explained by the ethnic alliance model.

The Ethnic Alliance Model

Symptomatic of what has been criticized in the first section, Davis & Moore (1997, 1998), in two articles on dyads, or a pair of states with transnational ethnic ties, of which the first was pointedly titled 'Ethnicity Matters', contend that 'transnational ethnic alliances serve as a conduit for conflict behaviour' (Davis & Moore, 1997, p. 172). They hold that 'it is useful to conceptualise ethnic linkages among people across state boundaries as functionally equivalent to alliances between two states', and second, purport that 'conflict between a state and an ethnic group will escalate to the international level when other elite members of that same ethnic group play a role in policy making in another state and that state finds the first state to be politically relevant' (Davis & Moore, 1998, p. 93). In other words, the likelihood of violent conflict between two neighbouring states increases if in one state (A) (in this case Turkey) a disenfranchised ethnic minority fights state oppression, while in the other state (B) (in this case Iraq, then the Iraqi Kurdish de facto state, and after 2003 the Kurdish Autonomous Region in Iraq) a co-ethnic group of said minority holds considerable power or dominates the political structure. The policies of A via its minority then not only constitute part of B's Politically Relevant International Environment (PRIE) (Maoz, 1997), but also determine its actions via A. As a consequence, Davis and Moore claim that B and the oppressed minority in A will form an ethnic alliance against state A, and the internal conflict within state A will diffuse to the point where the likelihood of it escalating to the international level rises. The authors test this hypothesis by contrasting three dependent weighted variables—conflict, cooperation and net interaction between the dyadic states—from the *Conflict and Peace Databank* of Edward Azar (1982), which measures levels of interaction between states with data from the *Minorities at Risk* set of Ted Robert Gurr (1993) with individual ethnopolitical groups as its unit of analysis. Notably, they at first caution that 'we do not believe that the ethnic composition of the dyads is the most critical determinate of such [cooperative or conflictual] behaviour' (Davis & Moore, 1997, p. 174), and come themselves to the conclusion that the ethnic composition of dyads matters only 'at the margins' (*ibid.*, p. 181).[12] Then, however, in a rather difficult to comprehend attempt at creative reinterpretation, and trusting that future quantitative research with more extensive data will prove their hypotheses, they maintain 'the impact of ethnic alliances is not spurious' (Davis & Moore, 1998, p. 100).

Karen Petersen (2004) re-examined Davis and Moore's model and, after modifying some variables with an improved measure of the foreign policy behaviour of the original dyads and adjusting control variables, discovered a slightly stronger amplitude towards conflict and decreased net interaction between dyads of states with one ethnic group in common, which led her to allege that 'ethnic alliances do in fact matter' and 'may not operate at the margins' (*ibid.*, p. 39).[13] Her findings concur with Saideman's, whose more nuanced utilization of the *Minorities at Risk* data set and actual application of his hypotheses to three empirical case studies show that 'a group with kin dominating a nearby state is at least 10 percent more likely to receive support' (Saideman, 2001, p. 181). He too, admits, though, that generally speaking 'we cannot say with confidence that the particular identity of a group causes it to get more or less support' (*ibid.*). Yet, despite only marginal empirical evidence for such presumptions, scholars of the neo-realist/neo-liberal tradition seem never to tire of working the bogeyman of ethnic alliances forming against the status quo and ethnic minorities with irredentist aspirations acting as 'fifth columns' for the territorial ambitions of neighbouring states. Although not specifically called an ethnic alliance, the notions of common ethnicity, bounded and homogeneous ethnic groups and presupposed group solidarity are also at the core of the approaches to the internationalization of ethnic conflict of Cetinyan (2002), Woodwell (2004), Jenne (2006, 2010) and Salehyan (2007, 2008, 2009), among others. Here a picture is presented in which 'ethnically intermixed areas are magnets for kin state inter-ventions' (Jenne, 2010, pp. 123–124), and 'potential rescuers' will be tempted 'to jump through any windows of opportunity that may arise … to rescue the diaspora now by force' (van Evera, 1994, p. 20). Salehyan (2009), for example, not only lists the case of the PKK presence in Iraqi Kurdistan as an archetype of common ethnicity determining the conflict behaviour of actors in the internationalization of an ethnic conflict, but also actually begins his monograph on transnational insurgencies with a three-page description of the PKK sanctuary in Iraqi Kurdistan. In political practice, the myth of the PKK as a 'fifth column' without legitimate cause and controlled by foreign elements in pursuit of a region-wide pan-Kurdish secessionism was used for decades prior to 2007 by the Turkish nationalizing state to justify addressing the so-called 'Kurdish Question' in Turkey by violent means and for countless military interventions in Iraq (Lundgren, 2007).

At first sight the Kurdish case, one of the most prominent examples of an internationa-lized ethnicized conflict, and in particular the PKK sanctuary in Iraqi Kurdistan, seem to fit this pattern of ethnic alliance formation as if taken from a textbook and consequently is routinely cited as a model case for these dynamics (Gurr & Harff, 1994; Kaufmann, 1996; Kirisci & Winrow, 1997; Byman, 1998; Freij, 1998; Helsing, 2004; Husain & Shumock, 2006; Milton-Edwards & Hinchcliffe, 2008; Rear, 2008; Salehyan, 2009). Of the countless instances of banditry, pillaging raids, minor insurrections, insurgencies and rebellions, one or another self-proclaimed Kurdish NLM has been involved in the border region of Iran, Turkey, Iraq and Syria since World War I; hardly any has not had an international dimension or has not escalated to the international level, that is, sought shelter across the border, shared intelligence, received logistical support and arma-ments, and joined forces on a temporary basis. All major Kurdish rebellions have been supported and sustained by affiliated or temporarily allied Kurdish NLMs from the border-ing state and many of these rebellions have escalated to regional conflagrations that dragged in regional and super powers such as the USSR, Israel and the US during the Cold War.[14]

Consequently, and to counter these supposedly secessionist insurgencies, a 'balance of threat' (Walt, 1985, 1987) was formed by the nationalizing states. As early as 1937, Turkey signed the Treaty of Sa'dbad with Iraq and Iran 'to coordinate their defence policy' (Entessar, 1992, p. 54) against Kurdish uprisings that could spill over from one state into the others' territories; a coordination and collaboration among the three countries that was extended in the Baghdad Pact of 1955 and led to occasional joint military oper-ations against Kurdish insurgencies.[15] The latter, in particular, can be understood as an actual alliance in the political sense of the term as it established a 'mutual military assist-ance' clause against 'internal revolts liable to threaten common security' (Nezan, 1993, p. 64). After Turkish–Iraqi relations had degenerated in the aftermath of the 1958 revolu-tion, in 1983 the practice of Turkey securing from Iraq the right to pursue Kurdish insur-gents on to its territory was revived under Saddam Hussein—then too weakened by the Iran–Iraq War to control effectively the Kurdish north—and, after Saddam's downfall, was one of the first concessions the Turkish government called for from the post-2003 Iraqi government (Phillips, 2007). Given all these cross-border counter-insurgency oper-ations over the past 60 years with the single goal of keeping Kurdish separatism at bay, it might seem the 'balance of threat' of the status quo preserving nationalizing states against presupposed irredentist Kurdish claims and activities, and, in converse argument, the Kurdish ethnic alliance, has been a factual reality. However, this view is only one possible reading of the empirical data, and indeed a very superficial one. A more nuanced, less nor-mative approach that puts these data into context will show that the case for Kurdish ethnic alliances is not tenable. Instead, we might pursue an appraisal of the way the so-called Kurdish conflict has been portrayed in a large part of the literature on ethnic conflict, and here in particular the internationalization of a presupposed Kurdish secessionist struggle in mainstream IR-based approaches to ethnic conflict has reified and to a certain extent legitimized the politics of division on both sides, be it ethnic elites and leaders of Kurdish NLMs or the totalitarian propagators of homogenization and assimila-tion in the nationalizing states.

Reading the PKK Sanctuary in Iraqi Kurdistan across the Grain

The internationalization of the PKK conflict in Turkey occurred in several stages, the first of which—as we can only concern ourselves here with the PKK's relations with the Iraqi Kurdish nationalist parties—happened in late 1979 when Abdullah Öcalan arrived with a handful of followers in Lebanon as refugees from martial law in pre-*coup d'état* Turkey. In Beirut, the PUK, on order of its leader Jalal Talabani,[16] brought Öcalan in contact with the Democratic Front for the Liberation of Palestine (DLFP), one of the largest organizations within the Palestine Liberation Organization (PLO) umbrella, that over the following years allowed the PKK to co-use its camps and training facilities in the Beqaa Valley (Marcus, 2007), and provided them with arms as well as logistical and perhaps financial support. The support of the PUK and PLO not only allowed Öcalan to reassemble, enlarge and pro-fessionalize his forces; but also, equally importantly, facilitated his connection with the Syrian government. The regime of Hafez Assad had many issues with Turkey—from the contested province of Alexandretta or Hatay, to Turkey's Güneydoğu Anadolu Projesi (Southeastern Anatolia Project, GAP) dam projects disturbing the flow of the Euphrates and Tigris, to its alleged shelter of the Muslim Brotherhood after the Hama insurrection—and welcomed the PKK as a tool in dealing its more powerful neighbour minor, and if necessary deniable, blows (Olson, 1997; Çelik, 2002; Marcus, 2007).

While now the PKK enjoyed the backing of the Syrian *mukhabarat*, and Öcalan no longer had to worry about logistics, supply, or finances—he set up headquarters in Damas-cus where he resided in relative open comfort until expelled in 1998—the one strategic element the PKK was acutely lacking was direct access to the border, a safe haven-cum-launch pad for military incursions into Turkey. The Assad regime, afraid of carrying its provocations of Turkey too far, had shrewdly denied the PKK the right to launch direct military raids into Turkey from its territory. This critical defect was soon resolved, though, when KDP leader Massoud Barzani offered Öcalan the use of KDP-controlled parts of the Iraqi-Turkish border region for operations. The 'Principles of Solidarity' protocol they signed in July 1983 was the birth hour of the PKK sanctuary in Iraqi Kurdistan (Imset, 1992; Gunter, 1996), a military presence lasting until today. With this the PKK not only became a major player in Iraq and beyond, but also, without the sanctuary in Iraqi Kurdistan the PKK would not have been able to launch its historic August 1984 offensive that constituted the beginning of the civil war in Turkey. In fact, without sanctuary in Iraqi Kurdistan no PKK insurgency in Turkey would have been realizable at all.

If the collaboration of the Iraqi Kurdish parties was the decisive factor for the PKK to recover, make strides and ultimately launch its insurgency in Turkey, we need to ask what motivated this collaboration. Can we speak of an ethnic alliance here? Is common ethnicity and group solidarity the determining variable to explain relations between the PKK and the Iraqi Kurdish parties during these early stages? Needless to say, PUK and KDP used to couch their support of the PKK in terms of group solidarity, fellow kinship and pan-Kurdish solidarity. Massoud Barzani declared,

> for us, it is always a source of pride that in the regions that we have liberated with the cost of our blood, we have opened the area as a fortress for every Kurdish fighter. We signed the alliance with the PKK with this logic and for these reasons.[17]

To be sure, in the early stages of PKK–Iraqi Kurd relations, such performance via one's ethnicized constituency cannot be dismissed as mere propaganda, not least as solidarity should not be confused with altruism. The late 1970s/early 1980s were hard times for Kurdish insurgents everywhere; they had not much to lose from lending a helping hand to an ideologically related party, in particular because one could not expect the PKK to excel where all other Kurdish parties in Turkey had not even tried: challenging the Kemalist republic in a guerrilla war. The PKK's future strength was not conceivable when Talabani took up its cause, and even when Barzani opened his territory to the PKK four years later he can be excused for not having foreseen ending up with more than he bargained for. It could also be argued, as Romano (2006) and Marcus (2007) as well as many Iraqi Kurdish journalists I interviewed claim, that Talabani and Barzani saw the PKK as a vehicle to boost their pan-Kurdish credentials—an act of political performance beyond their own finite constituency in Iraq yet equally important in the wider ethnicized Kurdish discourse. Talabani had always fancied himself the international statesman he ultimately became in post-2003 Iraq, and he was understandably eager to establish himself and his newcomer PUK among ideologically related organizations. Not too much, though, should be made of the fact that PKK and PUK supposedly share a radical leftist persuasion. Their nationalism is not from the same stable.[18] Although it is true that Talabani succeeded in uniting under the PUK umbrella disgruntled former members of the KDP Political Bureau with student and youth movements swooning over then trendy Maoism, their radicalism soon turned out to be quite bourgeois. At the end of the day, the PUK was as much an elite creation as the KDP, both featuring to varying degrees tribal elements and enjoying the support of Sufi orders; the PUK gave itself a veneer of being more urbane, of greater intellectualism, worldliness and progressiveness (Romano, 2006; Tahiri, 2007; Entessar, 2009). And, although pursuing pan-Kurdish networking at a more sophisticated level, the PUK's nationalist ambitions, like the KDP's, remained limited to the borders of Iraq. The PKK's Marxist–Leninist credentials and commitment to Maoist principles of guerrilla war, on the other hand, pursued a distinctly irredentist and secessionist form of national self-determination, and its nationalism was emphatically anti-elitist (van Bruinessen, 1992; White, 2000).

Even more than the PUK, the PKK and KDP differ dramatically in composition, constituencies, ideology and political aims. The KDP is the grand doyen of Kurdish ethnonationalism, founded by the legendary Mulla Mustafa Barzani in 1946, who succeeded in wedding his clan's interests and those of affiliated tribes with budding urban nationalism, characterized by Ghareeb (1981, p. 39) as a 'a marriage of convenience, albeit with suspicion on both sides'. This mutual suspicion between progressive and conservative elements led to a split in 1964, from which the PUK ultimately emerged in 1975. Although the emergence of the PUK initially weakened the KDP, one could also see the split as a necessary adjustment (Stansfield, 2003) that rendered possible an even more dominant position of the Barzani clan and its constituencies. The PKK, on the other hand, had declared the very *aghas* and tribal leaders that emulated the KDP in Turkey their prime target.[19]

When claiming ethnic group solidarity as the key explanandum for the KDP offering the PKK its territory as sanctuary, however, we need to consider the regional context of the Iran–Iraq War and the eternal rivalry between PUK and KDP, which, I argue, strategically explains, to an extent, the latter's alliance with the PKK. For unlike the PUK, whose nationalist rhetoric on a pan-Kurdish level had always been more pronounced and for whom group solidarity and pan-Kurdish credentials may in part have informed its actions, the KDP might have been less compelled by fellow kinship and more by orders from Tehran when granting the PKK access to its territory. In the crucial summer of 1983, hoping to gain the upper hand against its arch-rival the KDP, and hoping to negotiate an autonomy status for Iraqi Kurdistan, the PUK entered the Iran–Iraq War on the side of Saddam Hussein (van Bruinessen, 1986). In return Syria, Iran's major ally, expelled the PUK, and both Damascus and Tehran encouraged their then clients, the PKK and KDP, to collaborate, in the hope of weakening the PUK in Iraqi Kurdistan. Although there is no smoking gun to give substantive evidence of the PKK–KDP alliance being concocted in Tehran and Damascus, it is the explanation supported by leading scholars,[20] and also fits the historical pattern, while the ethnic alliance model subscribes to the protagonists' strategic essentialisms by allowing ethnicity pre-eminent explanatory power and portraying the KDP–PKK alliance as a result of their allegedly shared kinship.

In the course of the Iran–Iraq War, Iraqi Kurds suffered their darkest hour when at least 100,000 civilians were killed in the genocidal Al Anfal campaign (Human Rights Watch, 1993). To belie once and for all any notions of group solidarity, we need only observe that the PKK not only watched its 'kin' being massacred from the sidelines, but also intensified its collaboration with the regime of Saddam Hussein in the immediate wake of Al Anfal in order to solidify its position in Iraq (Imset, 1992). For with KDP and PUK crushed, and the *Serhildan* of March 1990—mass public unrest in the course of the annual *Newroz* celebrations—showing the potential of turning into a public uprising seizing the whole of southeast Turkey (White, 2000; Çelik, 2002; Marcus, 2007), the PKK had reached its zenith: not only had it become the most potent Kurdish insurgency since the 1970s, but it also dominated Iraqi Kurdistan, and had shaken the mighty Turkish state to its core. Simply put, the PKK had become an actor with whom all regional players had to reckon.

In a most staggering reverse of fate, though, less than three years later KDP and PUK ruled the freest Kurdish political entity in history and the PKK had to surrender to them in humiliation. Saddam Hussein's 1990 invasion of Kuwait triggered a chain of events that would alter the power constellations in the modern Middle East dramatically, and with it rescind historical patterns that had determined Kurdish history for decades. Within weeks Iraqi Kurds found themselves alleviated from utter defeat—the *Repareen*, the 1991 spontaneous public uprising President George H. W. Bush had called for, was swiftly crushed when Kurdish hopes for US support were betrayed—to becoming the dependants of an international alliance initiated by Turkey that stopped the Iraqi assault and created an Allied fighter jet-patrolled humanitarian safe haven north of the 36th parallel (Graham-Brown, 1999; DiPrizio, 2002). There, on 19 May 1992, Iraqi Kurdistan held its first free elections for parliament, giving birth to the Kurdistan Regional Government (KRG) and the Kurdish de facto state in northern Iraq (Gunter, 1999; Stansfield, 2003; Lundgren, 2007; Tahiri, 2007).

As surprising as Iraqi Kurdistan's quasi-independence was, so too was Turkey's initial support for the embattled Iraqi Kurds, and there has been much speculation on the true motives of President Turgut Özal for his dramatic change in position (Pope & Pope, 2005; Hale, 2007; Lundgren, 2007).[21] What can be established is that Özal envisioned the Iraqi Kurdish leaders acting as mediators between him and the PKK to negotiate a political solution for the civil war in Turkey—a role Jalal Talabani took up enthusiastically (Gunter, 2010).[22] Hence, in the watershed year 1992, not only did Iraqi Kurds gain de facto independence and institute their own quasi-independent political entity, government and administration—in all of which they were *nolens volens* protected from the wrath of their 'home state' by the international community—but also Turkey, who until recently had formed regional alliances to blight any attempts at Kurdish autonomy, now had KDP and PUK open liaison offices in Ankara and permitted Barzani and Talabani to travel on Turkish diplomatic passports (Tahiri, 2007; Marcus, 2007; Lundgren, 2007; Gunter, 2010).[23] Yet these sea changes at the regional level did not entice Abdullah Öcalan to back down. On the contrary, he interpreted the rise of KDP and PUK, and in particular the new regional and international relations they cultivated, as a vital threat to the PKK. For Öcalan the ensuing confrontation came down not just to preserving the PKK supremacy and sanctuary in Iraqi Kurdistan but to which party would dominate and therewith determine the direction of the Kurdish ethnonationalist discourse. For KDP/PUK, with the survivability of their de facto state depending on 'Western' goodwill and backing, a welcome opportunity presented itself to be rid of the PKK, who continued to challenge them politically and strategically on their very home turf. When the PKK threatened to blockade the Harbur border gate with Turkey, through which two-thirds of the international aid for Iraqi Kurdistan passed, KDP/PUK took up the gauntlet, and alongside a Turkish incursion, after a month of intense fighting defeated the PKK (Laizer, 1996; Gunter, 1996).

What could have been the end of the PKK, however, turned out to be its second reprieve via the perennial KDP–PUK rivalry. Jalal Talabani anticipated that the next round of fighting would be with the KDP over supremacy in the Kurdish de facto state and intended to save the PKK from annihilation and win it as a future ally. He arranged for the PKK to surrender to the PUK—under most generous terms they kept all their weaponry and equipment, relocated to PUK camps[24]—and for Öcalan to take up Özal's initiative and declare a unilateral ceasefire in March 1993, an opportunity for peace that came to naught owing to the untimely death of Turgut Özal less than a month later. Yet for Jalal Talabani his brinkmanship paid off when in the following year hostilities with the KDP started in which he could count the PKK on his side (Laizer, 1996; Gunter, 1999; Marcus, 2007; Tahiri, 2007).

The four-year civil war that broke out between the PUK and the KDP in May 1994 was first and foremost fought over supremacy of the Kurdish polity in Iraq, pitting the KDP, backed by Turkey and once even saved by Saddam Hussein's direct intervention, against the PUK, who received support from Iran and the PKK (Laizer, 1996; Gunter, 1998, 1999; Romano, 2006; Tahiri, 2007). While the PKK sporadically collaborated with the PUK, it also acted as a spoiler throughout the civil war, deliberately attacking the KDP whenever KDP and PUK had agreed on an internationally mediated ceasefire in order to provoke a new round of fighting. The PKK had no interest in a peaceful solution for the conflict; Öcalan reasoned that in KDP and PUK wearing each other down he could achieve what had eluded him in 1992: supremacy over Iraqi Kurdistan.[25] Ultimately, though, international mediation paid off, with Barzani and Talabani signing the

Washington Agreement of September 1998 to end the civil war, a deal that was sweetened by US President Bill Clinton signing a month later the *Iraq Liberation Act* into law, bestowing on KDP and PUK millions of dollars in funding aimed at regime change in Iraq.[26]

Worse for the PKK than the settlement between KDP and PUK was that in the same month, as a result of Turkish pressure, Syria expelled Abdullah Öcalan, leading to his capture by Turkish intelligence in Kenya in February 1999 and ultimately imprisonment for life on İmralı Island. It proved to be a blow from which the PKK never recovered. Today only a shadow of its former self, an estimated 3,500 fighters—down from 15,000 active fighters at its peak in the early 1990s (Marcus, 2007; Eccarius-Kelly, 2011)—are scattered across less than a dozen camps in northern Iraq. The PKK underwent several name changes along with ideological transformations and internal power struggles that weakened it irrevocably.

What can be said in favour of the PKK in the early 2000s is that it contributed significantly to the transformation of the ethnicized discourse of the so-called 'Kurdish Question' in Turkey into a civil society discourse (*ibid.*; Gunes, 2011), yet when this development threatened to exclude it from the ensuing political dialogue, it reverted to armed struggle in 2004 and until recently undermined peace initiatives to which it was not party (Uslu, 2010). The fortunes of the KDP and PUK, on the other hand, blossomed with the autonomy of the Kurdistan Region being enshrined in the US occupation-imposed Iraqi Constitution of 2005, and it being hailed in Western media as a heaven of stability and prosperity in an otherwise war-torn country. For many in Washington, 'the Iraqi Kurdish region [became] the one unambiguous success story of the Iraq war' (Zakaria, 2006).

The pattern outlined here for the PKK sanctuary in Iraqi Kurdistan shows that the case for an ethnic alliance between the PKK and the Iraqi Kurdish NLMs is not tenable. After theoretically deconstructing the model, testing it against one of the most widely referenced examples in support of the ethnic alliance model explaining the patterns of alliance formation in internationalized civil wars illustrates the model's futility. While for the origins of strategic cooperation in the early 1980s the ethnicized rhetoric and the propagandistic value of group solidarity could have played a role in strategically essentializing pan-Kurdish solidarity—in particular between the PUK and the PKK—other, non-ethnic strategic considerations and relations were at least as decisive, most notably between the PKK and Syria and the KDP and Iran, in the latter granting the PKK access to and sanctuary on its territory. Since then all three Kurdish parties—PKK, PUK and KDP—have fought each other and entered alliances with the adversarial nationalizing states against each other as often as they have collaborated. When discussing this case study, though, it has to be acknowledged that the Kurdistan Region of Iraq today is no independent Kurdish state. Although the scope of this article does not allow for a detailed discussion of the peculiar political status of the Kurdistan Region, which I address in detail elsewhere (Černy, forthcoming a), I would like to emphasize that, according to its authors, the ethnic alliance model does not necessarily specify for the entity from where the insurgency receives support to be an independent state but only that 'elite members of that same ethnic group play a role in policy making in [that] state and that state finds the first state to be politically relevant' (Davis & Moore, 1998, p. 93). There can be no doubt that the state of Iraq finds its neighbour Turkey politically relevant, nor can there be any doubt, irrespective of the political status of the Kurdistan Region, about the central role Iraqi Kurds play in policymaking in Iraq.[27] In sum, then, irrespective of whether the post-2005 Kurdistan Region is an independent state or an autonomous region, I hold that the central tenet of my critique applies: the behaviour of PKK, PUK and KDP in the context of the PKK sanctuary in Iraqi Kurdistan cannot be explained by supposed kinship ties; common ethnicity is not the independent variable in these relations, which fails as an explanandum for the conflict dynamics or to account for its internationalization.

By Way of Conclusion: The Similar Meta-narratives of the Ethnic Alliance Model and Systemic Constructivism/Instrumentalism

All that has been discussed here so far could easily be interpreted as making a case for a constructivist or instrumentalist understanding of identity. There is considerable ambiguity in the literature as to whether instrumentalism can be considered to be related to constructivism, neo-realism, or whether it should be understood as independent from both. While Varshney (2002) lists it as a distinct approach and Christia (2012) understands her instrumentalism as originating in neo-realism, in the context of IR, as detailed elsewhere (Černy, forthcoming a), I identify it as related to what Christian Reus-Smit (2009) calls a 'systemic constructivism'. I further argue that this 'systemic' or, after one of its key theorists, Alexander Wendt, 'Wendtian constructivism' is as guilty of essentializing and of reifying the actor as its neo-realist and neo-liberal counterparts. The reason for this tendency stems from Wendt's (1999, pp. 40, 47) attempts to charter a 'media via' through the debate between what is commonly referred to in IR as 'rationalists' and 'reflectivists', to carve out for constructivism a 'true middle ground' (Adler, 1997, p. 322) between these two approaches, 'to bridge the still vast divide separating the majority of IR theorists from postmodernists' (Checkel, 1998, p. 327), by combining a positivist epistemology with a post-positivist ontology. Such an experiment in having it both ways inevitably has to fail, leading Maja Zehfuss (2006, p. 116) to conclude 'Wendt's constructivism does not work'. The crux of the problem with Wendt's understanding of identity is that he conceives of state identity as at the same time constructed and changeable but also as a pre-social, pre-given stable corporate identity, and after having spent literally hundreds of pages in *Social Theory of International Politics* (Wendt, 1999) elaborating that identities resulting from social interaction are more basic than interests, he declares that he is less interested in identity formation than in the workings of the state system (*ibid.*, p. 11), where states have essential properties 'prior to and independent from social context', thus not 'considering the constitution of states in the first place' (Zehfuss, 2002, p. 89). 'From this perspective, it is impossible to explain how fundamental changes occur, either in the nature of international society or in the nature of state identity. By bracketing everything domestic, Wendt excludes by theoretical fiat most of the normative and ideational forces that might prompt such change' (Reus-Smit, 2009, p. 224).

Unquestionably, though, at first sight there are profound merits to a constructivist reading of ethnic conflict, the most pre-eminent being that not the structure, the presupposed group, but the social agent should be the main focus of analysis. Here, in an allusion to Alexander Wendt's famous dictum that 'anarchy is what states make of it', one may say systemic constructivists and instrumentalists argue that ethnicity and ethnic groups are what ethnic elites make them to be: when strategically useful ethnicity is employed as a political tool to manipulate, sway and rally the masses behind one's temporary position, as, for example, one could argue, the PUK leadership did when it justified its alliance with the PKK in the mid-1990s as defending the 'Kurdish cause' against the KDP who had sold out and joined forces with Saddam Hussein. Yet as easily as group solidarity can be constructed by elites it can be discarded later on when no longer strategically opportune— for example, when after the KDP–PUK rapprochement, the PUK bowed to Turkish pressure and attacked the PKK in 2000 (Gunter, 2001). This instrumentalist understanding of ethnicity as merely a political tool of elite manipulation, an 'invented tradition' in the Hobsbawmian sense (Hobsbawm & Ranger, 1984), of it having no intrinsic value and in its utility as a political tool to sway the masses being as good as any other social category, be it class, gender, or religion, culminates in the Rational Choice Theory (RCT)-based understandings of ethnicity and ethnic group formation of, among others, Michael Hechter (1986, 1987, 2001) and Russell Hardin (1997). In this notion ethnic identity and group membership are a result of individual profit maximization and cost–benefit analyses, as exemplified for the study of alliance formation in civil wars by Warren & Troy (forthcoming) and Christia (2012).[28] Whether or not to strike an alliance with an insurgency of supposedly common ethnicity appears to be the result of little more than pragmatic cost– benefit analyses to maximize political gain—a calculating cynicism all three Kurdish parties have been routinely accused of by analysts and frustrated Kurdish party followers alike, who in these machinations detect the reason for Kurdish disunity and the parties' failure to deliver on the promise of self-determination (Özcan, 2006; Gunter, 2007; Tahiri, 2007).

Yet such instrumentalism and RCT-based approaches to ethnic identity often 'presuppose their findings by simply looking for and then finding their explanans and explanandum in ... assumed to be rationality, intentionality and the egoistic motives of actors. This circularity and tautology of analysis leads towards post hoc types of reasoning' (Malešević, 2004, p. 102). Cordell & Wolff (2009, p. 17) remind us that it is important 'to bear in mind that motive alone is not enough to explain ethnic conflict' or cooperation. Ethnicity as an identity narrative in an ethnicized political discourse is more than a mere tool of elite manipulation that the masses adopt out of self-interest or an instinct to maximize individual gain. To claim that it is ultimately empty of intrinsic meaning, that ethnic groups are nothing more than 'informally organized interest group[s]' (Cohen, 1974, p. 92),[29] that when power considerations call for it these ethnic 'communities and traditions will be cast aside and new ones imagined in their place' (Christia, 2012, p. 7) is too simplistic an approach to do the complexities of inter-ethnic relations justice. A strict instrumentalist and RCT-based reading of ethnicity and ethnicized discourses does not just fail to explain, for example, 'mass self-immolation of Kurds in front of Greek embassies after the capture of the PKK leader [Öcalan] in 1999' (Malešević, 2004, p. 107), or, as will be elaborated shortly, why the Iraqi Kurdish NLMs fail to rally their constituencies behind a more antagonistic line towards the PKK, systemic constructivism in IR, as Cynthia Weber and others remind us, runs the risk of again indirectly reifying the structure via the agent. Wendtian or systemic constructivism 'fails to deliver on its promise to take us beyond reification, because in order to escape the reified logic of anarchy, it reifies the state' (Weber, 2010, p. 80). Applied to ethnic identities, this sort of systemic constructivism that instrumentalism RCT and related approaches draw on, in order to escape the logic of 'groupism', reifies the ethnic elites and thus indirectly their strategic essentialisms by making them omnipotent, by, paraphrasing the title of Nicholas Onuf's (1989) famous constructivist work, rendering ethnic identity discourses a world exclusively of their making. Thus, the outcome of the challenge of such narrow constructivism to 'groupism' ironically all too often runs the risk of repeating the mistakes of neo-liberalism: the importance and plurality of internal actors is acknowledged, yet by declaring these actors omnipotent in shaping the ethnicized discourse, by reifying them and conceding to them an exclusivity of representation, those actors are portrayed again as if acting unitarily. This becomes evident, for example, in a series of recent prominent large-*n* studies based on the *Ethnic Power Relations* data set at the University of California, Los Angeles, and the related *Ethnic Armed Conflict* data set at Harvard University (Cederman & Girardin, 2007; Buhaug *et al.*, 2008; Wimmer, 2008; Wimmer *et al.*, 2009; Cederman *et al.*, 2009a, 2009b, 2010, 2013). Not only is it telling that the *GeoSim* agent-based models developed by Lars-Erik Cederman that form the core of his team's survey of ethnic conflicts were first developed to simulate inter-state relations, but similar presumptions about unitarily acting ethnic groups that form the basis of neo-realist/neo-liberal readings of ethnic conflict and group solidarity also characterize these *n*-studies' systemic constructivist understanding of ethnic identity. On the one hand the authors want ethnicity to be understood as 'a subjectively experienced sense of commonality based on a belief in common ancestry and shared culture', that is, socially constructed, but then proceed to caution 'we do not distinguish between degrees of representativity of political actors who claim to speak for an ethnic group, nor do we code the heterogeneity of political positions of leaders claiming to represent the same community' (Wimmer *et al.*, 2009, pp. 316–317). Thus the authors, like Wendt, do not just bracket the 'domestic component', i.e. the social discourse that brought about these ethnic identities, but further, their studies, like neo-realist and neo-liberal approaches, treat ethnic groups as unitary actors and indirectly equate them ontologically with states. In a nutshell, they share the same meta-narrative.[30]

One instance in which the dynamics of the construction of ethnic identity in PKK–Iraqi Kurdish relations becomes manifest particularly clearly is in post-2005 Iraqi Kurdistan. It can be argued that once the political status of the Kurdish Autonomous Region had been enshrined in the Iraqi Constitution of 2005, in order to maintain political leverage via Turkey, the KRG momentarily accepted the presence of a weakened PKK on its territory. Later expelling the PKK or exerting pressure on them to lay down arms tacitly remained an option that could be used as a bargaining tool in future negotiations with Turkey (Černy, forthcoming a, forthcoming b); also, by refusing to send the PKK to its doom, the KRG kept operating within the ethnicized discourse it had constructed, which, if not vocally proclaiming their 'free' Kurdistan as a regional champion of Kurdish self-determination, at least liked to play lip service to the image of a safe haven for Kurds persecuted in other countries. Yet from 2007/08 onwards, this narrative increasingly became a liability. With their damaged relations from the Iraq War repaired, both Washington and Ankara increasingly called on Erbil to become more active in limiting the PKK's freedom of action on the territory the KRG claimed to control (International Crisis Group, 2008; Barkey, 2010). Justifiably or not, the freedom Iraqi Kurds had enjoyed since 1992 had become a beacon of hope for Kurds in all neighbouring countries and the diaspora, yet when forced to demonstrate its supposed ethnic loyalties, the KRG had to choose between continuing to cultivate that myth or shifting to an 'Iraqi Kurdistan first' discourse that portrayed the KRG as the reliable partner of Western strategic and economic interests in the region. Those two ethnonationalist discourses the KRG had tried to cultivate simultaneously were increasingly at odds with each other, and trying to live up to the contradictory promises of each threatened to tear the fragile fabric of Kurdish autonomy in Iraq apart. For since 2005, Turkey has become Iraqi Kurdistan's biggest investor, arguably turning the Kurdistan Region into something akin to a special economic zone for Turkey (Ahmed, 2012; Černy, forthcoming b); yet what is more, in anticipation of a US troop withdrawal after the 2008 elections, Turkey appeared set to replace the US as the main political backer of Kurdish autonomy vis-à-vis the central government in Baghdad (Barkey, 2010; Černy, forthcoming a, forthcoming b). It might not be overstating the current political dynamics in Iraq to claim that the political survival of the KRG has come to depend to a significant extent on Turkey's goodwill (Černy, forthcoming a, forthcoming b). Every time Turkish fighter jets bomb PKK positions in Iraqi Kurdistan, as happened during my last stay there in October 2011, it is not just bad for business because it scares away international investors, it also has the potential to jeopardize vital KRG–Turkey relations. If, then, according to an instrumentalist interpretation of ethnicity, the Iraqi Kurdish leaders can shape the ethnicized discourse as they see fit, or in the words of Christia (2012, p. 7), no longer expedient ethnic consciousness and allegiances 'will be cast aside and new ones imagined in their place', they should have been able to denounce the PKK as a threat to the 'national interest' of the KRG, and to justify a Turkish–KRG alliance against the PKK as necessary for the survival of the Kurdish Autonomous Region. My own data from interviews with journalists, civil society groups and students at Iraqi Kurdish universities during my ethnographic field research in Iraqi Kurdistan in 2010/11, though, show that a KRG increasingly under public pressure from charges of corruption and nepotism and accused of selling out the country to foreign, mostly Turkish investors at the expense of local jobs and real estate affordability, cannot afford the negative image of Kurds fighting Kurds on Turkey's behalf (Černy, forthcoming a, forthcoming b). This is particularly true since it experienced its own version of a scaled-down 'Arab Spring' in Sulimaniyah in 2011 (Artens, 2011) and after the trauma of the devastating Kurdish infighting of the 1990s still tainting their public perception.[31]

The example of the strategic quandary in which the KRG finds itself since 2007, in conjunction with increasing public unrest over surmounting corruption and a descent into authoritarianism, shows that the discourse of Kurdish ethnonationalism over the past decade has developed beyond the ethnonationalist elites' control, and that what it means for the Iraqi Kurdish population to self-identify as Kurd cannot be altered and reconfigured as easily as an instrumentalist reading of ethnicity claims. On the one hand the KRG, unable actively to contain the PKK itself, had to acquiesce tacitly into recurring Turkish border raids in 'hot pursuit' of the PKK, recurring since 2007 (Černy, forthcoming a, forthcoming b); on the other hand, it demonstrated its own impotence in allaying the PKK into a more conciliatory position towards the so-called 'Kurdish opening' of the Erdoğan government in 2009. What is telling in this context is the limited role the KRG has played overall in recent peace initiatives between the Turkish state and the PKK,[32] a conspicuous restraint that also contradicts the ethnic alliance model. For if common ethnicity were the determining factor in KRG–PKK relations, and if the KRG would benefit from a political solution to 'Turkey's Kurdish Question', the KRG could play an important role as a mediator in these negotiations and could, if necessary, exert substantial pressure on the PKK. Yet if the historic pattern of the relations between the Iraqi Kurdish NLMs and the PKK discussed in this article clearly shows one constant denominator, it is that KDP and PUK hold little sway over the decision-making within the PKK. In conclusion then, neither the presumptions about ethnicity of the ethnic alliance model nor the presumptions of a systemic constructivism or instrumentalism can explain the continuing strategic dilemma the KRG finds itself in via the PKK and Turkey. How their relations will evolve further then depends not only on the actions of the respective ethnonationalist elites but also, to a considerable extent, on how we scholars of IR interpret and narrate these actions.

Acknowledgements

The author's thanks first and foremost go to Sarah Keeler, whose encouragement, support and intellectual input to his work in general and to this article in particular have been invaluable. The author's extensive field research and interviews in Iraqi Kurdistan, partially funded by a generous grant from the British Institute for the Study of Iraq, would have been impossible without the unwavering support of Omar Sheikhmous, to whom he owes his most profound gratitude. The author's appreciation also extends to the two anonymous reviewers of *Ethnopolitics* who provided valuable feedback to this article.

Funding

This work was partially supported by the British Institute for the Study of Iraq.

Notes

1. Posen's approach features prominently in Brown (1996), is mirrored in Wagner (1993) and van Evera (1994), and has been utilized and adapted by a myriad of scholars from such diverse schools of thought as Kaufmann (1996, 1998), Roe (1999) and Saideman (2001). It is criticized by, among others, David (1997), Kaufman (2001) and Cederman (2012).
2. Echoing Hutchinson (2005), here, rather than 'nation state', I use the term 'nationalizing state', not only to indicate that the four states in the context of this article—Turkey, Iraq, Iran and Syria—are home to more than one nation, but also to allude to the often brutal process of assimilation during their ongoing state formation.
3. A similar recent case for a primacy of IR in analysing ethnic conflicts is made in another primer by Neal Jesse and Kristen Williams (2010).
4. IR is a notorious latecomer to debates on questions of identity—the concept did not feature prominently as an eminent category in IR-specific approaches until the so-called 'Fourth Great Debate' and the post-positivist challenge of the early 1990s (Zalewski & Enloe, 1995). In slight exaggeration, John Stack (1997, p. 11) observes 'ethnicity is as alien to the study of international relations as would be Sigmund Freud's musings in *Civilization and Its Discontents*'.
5. These limitations are particularly lamentable because questions of identity (who are we as individuals, as a community and polity?) should be at the centre of our discipline, and as Hansen (2006) and Weber (2010) argue, once were—think Kenneth Waltz's original *Man, the State and War* (Waltz, 1959). Since then mainstream IR has come to neglect them, to our discipline's detriment.
6. The convergence of key positions of these two schools of thought in the 1980s, such as on the state as unitary actor, has been termed the 'neo-neo synthesis' and is discussed exemplarily in Wæver (1997).
7. Owing to the political situation in Turkey, Iraq, Iran and Syria any figures on the Kurdish population there can only be estimates. According to Gunter (2009, p. XXIX), there are '12 to 15 million Kurds in Turkey (18 to 23 percent of the population), 6.5 million in Iran (11 percent), 3.5 to 4 million in Iraq (17 to 20 percent), 1 million in Syria (9 percent)', and one to two million in the diaspora in Europe and North America.
8. Although the Treaty of Zuhab in 1639 stabilized the border between the empires after almost 150 years of intermittent wars, border disputes remained the norm in the larger Ottoman–Persian antagonism.
9. For the early stages of Kurdish ethnonationalism see Jwaideh (2006), for general overviews see Natali (2005), Romano (2006), McDowall (2007), Tahiri (2007) and Entessar (2009).

10. Partially these arguments are taken from Natali (2005) and McDowall (2007); in their entirety they are made for the first time in Černy (forthcoming a).

11. The only other instance in Kurdish post-World War II history where a case for secessionism can be made was the short-lived Republic of Mahabad in Iran in 1946/47; see Eagleton (1963) and Ghassemlou (1965).

12. They found that the presence of an 'ethnic alliance' increases conflict between dyads of states by two weighted points on a scale from zero to 60 (Davis & Moore, 1997, p. 179).

13. Petersen detected a 3.4 weighted points amplitude towards conflictual dyadic interaction on the same scale from zero to 60 (Petersen, 2004, p. 36).

14. However, the term 'internationalization' itself might be an anachronism in an inaccessible mountain terrain beyond any attempt to enforce the law, monitor and police the borders or keep taps on comings and goings. This is to say that that the concept of 'internationalization of a conflict' does not mean the same in the Kurdish mountains as at the border separating the two Koreas. Until recent advances in satellite technology generations of mountain dwellers with clan links encompassing the entire region and with the interchangeable expertise of pastoralists, smugglers, and guerrilleros have moved goods, arms, and drugs on hidden paths and hazardous tracks only known to their kin as freely as if in the Schengen Area. International borders have mostly existed on paper and in the heads of bureaucrats in the nationalizing and state-building capitals of Tehran, Ankara, Baghdad and Damascus.

15. The first military application of the alliance took place in 1956 when Iranian and Iraqi forces in joint operations crushed the uprising of Djiwanroji Kurds in Iran (Nezan, 1993, p. 64).

16. Interview with then PUK representative in Beirut, Adel Murad, Erbil, Iraqi Kurdistan, 3 September 2010.

17. Massoud Barzani in an interview with Turkish journalist Rafet Balli in 1993, quoted in Marcus (2007, p. 70).

18. Offering more detailed background on the three Kurdish parties than this article can provide are, for the KDP and PUK, Stansfield (2003), and, for the PKK, the slightly dated but excellent study of White (2000), the more recent treatments of Eccarius-Kelly (2011) and Gunes (2011) as well as the more journalistic approach of Marcus (2007), and, in German, the account of a former PKK fighter by Çelik (2002).

19. One of the signature feats of the PKK in its founding year was an assassination attempt on Kurdish MP Mehmet Celal Bucak, whose relatives had founded the KDP-T, mirrored on and enjoying cordial relations with Barzani's KDP (McDowall, 2007).

20. This was confirmed in an interview with the leading expert on Iran and its relations with its own and Iraqi Kurds, Abbas Vali, Istanbul, Turkey, 8 May 2012, as well as by Turkish scholar Doğu Ergil, interviewed in Istanbul, Turkey, 25 October 2011. Other scholars with decades of expertise on the Iraqi Kurdish nationalist parties such as Robert Olson and Michael Gunter, when asked, thought this chain of events 'absolutely plausible'; interviewed in Lexington, USA, 9 March 2011, and Cookeville, USA, 11 March 2011, respectively.

21. Özal is said to have harboured ambitions to regain the Ottoman *vilayet* of Mosul, roughly corresponding with today's Iraqi Kurdistan, for Turkey via the Iraqi Kurds (Lundgren, 2007). This argument is often used by Kurdish critics of the KRG's present dependence on Turkey, a view they believe substantiated by Jalal Talabani initially in 1991 offering Turgut Özal Iraqi Kurdistan as a Turkish protectorate (Marcus, 2007).

22. Interview with Qamran Karadaghi, the Iraqi Kurdish journalist who facilitated the first contact between Özal and Talabani, London, UK, 21 April 2011.

23. Rather than of the Turkish state it would be more correct here to speak of Özal and his closest confidants. In this mediation effort the president acted on his own initiative and against most of the Turkish politico-military establishment (Pope & Pope, 2005).

24. Interview with the PUK field commander to whom the PKK surrendered in October 1992, Mustafa Chawrash, Sulimaniyah, Iraqi Kurdistan, 31 May 2010.

25. This reading of events is supported by former PKK fighter Selahettin Çelik, interviewed 9 May 2010, San Louis, France, as well as several Iraqi Kurdish journalists I spoke to *in situ* and the scholars Michael Gunter, interviewed in Cookeville, USA, 11 March 2011, and Henri Barkey, in Bethlehem, USA, 1 February 2011.

26. Interview with then Director of Persian Gulf Affairs of the National Security Council, Kenneth Pollack, Washington, USA, 21 March 2011.

27. In both Artens (2013) and Černy (forthcoming a)—see note 31—I have portrayed the Iraqi Kurdish elites and main parties, KDP and PUK, as enjoying the role of 'kingmaker' in today's inner-Iraqi politics. As a matter of fact, Prime Minister al-Maliki would not be in power were it not for Barzani's backing after the elections of 2010.

28. In its most radical form this view led to the simplistic and equally essentializing excesses of the 'greed versus grievances' theory (Berdal & Malone, 2000; Collier & Hoeffler, 2000).

29. Since for him the term ethnic group can encompass any politically conscious status group, Cohen (1974) infamously goes so far as to identify stockbrokers as an ethnic group. This trivialization ultimately renders the social category 'ethnicity' absolutely meaningless and useless for analysis.

30. In general I am very sceptical of the suitability of quantitative analyses for capturing the complexities of ethnic conflicts. On its limitations, see an excellent symposium in *Ethnopolitics*, 7(2–3), with contributions by Shale Horowitz, Pieter van Houten, Patrick James, Stuart Kaufman *et al*. In the annotations only the article by Horowitz (2008) is referenced, but the entire exchange is to be recommended.

31. All my publications prior to 2014 appear under the name 'Hannes Artens'.

32. Interview with Huge Pope, International Crisis Group Representative in Turkey, Istanbul, Turkey, 6 May 2012. See also International Crisis Group (2012). Presumably, as is discussed repeatedly, Iraqi Kurdistan could serve as a future exile for former PKK fighters who Turkey refuses to readmit—as it already does for thousands of Kurdish political refugees from Turkey and hundreds of PKK dissenters.

References

Adler, E. (1997) Seizing the middle ground: constructivism in world politics, *European Journal of International Relations*, 3(3), pp. 319–363.

Ahmed, M. (2012) *Iraqi Kurds and Nation-building* (Basingstoke: Palgrave Macmillan).

Artens, H. (2011) Kurdistan protests could drive Iraq to the brink, *World Politics Review*, 29 March, available online at: http://www.worldpoliticsreview.com/articles/8340/kurdistan-protests-could-drive-iraq-to-the-brink

Artens, H. (2013) Iraqi Kurdistan elections cement Barzani's role as regional powerbroker, *World Politics Review*, 30 September, available online at: http://www.worldpoliticsreview.com/articles/13256/iraqi-kurdistan-elections-cement-barzani-s-role-as-regional-powerbroker

Azar, E. (1982) Conflict and Peace Databank (COPDAB), 1948–1978, 2nd release, *Study No. 7767* (Ann Arbor: Interuniversity Consortium for Political and Social Research), available online at: http://www.icpsr.umich.edu/icpsrweb/ICPSR/studies/07767

Banton, M. (2000) Ethnic conflict, *Sociology*, 34(3), pp. 481–498.

Barkey, H. (2010) Turkey's New Engagement in Iraq: Embracing Iraqi Kurdistan, United States Institute for Peace, *Special Report 237*, available online at: http://carnegieendowment.org/files/USIP_SR_Turkey_Iraq.pdf

Bengio, O. (2012) Will the Kurds get their way?, *The American Interest*, November/December issue, available online at: http://www.the-american-interest.com/article.cfm?piece=1323

Berdal, M. & Malone, D. (2000) *Greed and Grievance: Economic Agendas in Civil Wars* (Boulder: Lynne Rienner).

Bowen, J. (1996) The myth of global ethnic conflict, *Journal of Democracy*, 7(4), pp. 3–14.

Brown, G.K. & Langer, A. (2010) Conceptualizing and measuring ethnicity, *Oxford Development Studies*, 38(4), pp. 411–436.

Brown, M. (Ed.) (1996) *The International Dimensions of Internal Conflict* (Cambridge, MA: Center for Science and International Affairs).

Brubaker, R. (1996) *Nationalism Reframed: Nationhood and the National Question in the New Europe* (Cambridge: Cambridge University Press).

Brubaker, R. (2004) *Ethnicity without Groups* (Cambridge, MA: Harvard University Press).

Brubaker, R. (2009) Ethnicity, race, and nationalism, *Annual Review of Sociology*, 35, pp. 21–42.

Brubaker, R. & Laitin, D. (1998) Ethnic and nationalist violence, *Annual Review of Sociology*, 24, pp. 423–452.

Buhaug, H., Cederman, L.E. & Rød, J.K. (2008) Disaggregating ethno-nationalist civil wars: a dyadic test of exclusion theory, *International Organization*, 62(3), pp. 531–551.

Bush, K. (2003) *The Intra-group Dimensions of Ethnic Conflict in Sri Lanka: Learning to Read between the Lines* (Basingstoke: Palgrave Macmillan).

Bush, K. & Keyman, F. (1997) Identity-based conflict: rethinking security in a post-Cold War world, *Global Governance*, 3(3), pp. 311–328.

Byman, D. (1998) The logic of ethnic terrorism, *Studies in Conflict and Terrorism*, 21(2), pp. 149–169.

Campbell, D. (1998) *National Deconstruction: Violence, Identity and Justice in Bosnia* (Minneapolis: University of Minnesota Press).

Caputo, J. (1997) *Deconstruction in a Nutshell: A Conversation with Jaques Derrida* (New York: Fordham University Press).

Cederman, L.E. (1997) *Emergent Actors in World Politics: How States and Nations Develop and Dissolve* (Princeton: Princeton University Press).

Cederman, L.E. (2012) Nationalism and ethnicity in international relations, in: W. Carlsnaes, T. Risse & B. Simmons (Eds), *Handbook of International Relations*, 2nd edn, pp. 531–554 (London: Sage).

Cederman, L.E. & Girardin, L. (2007) Beyond fractionalization: mapping ethnicity onto nationalist insurgencies, *American Political Science Review*, 101(1), pp. 173–185.

Cederman, L.E., Buhaug, H. & Rød, J.K. (2009a) Ethno-nationalist dyads and civil war: a GIS-based analysis, *Journal of Conflict Resolution*, 53(4), pp. 496–525.

Cederman, L.E., Girardin, L. & Gleditsch, K.S. (2009b) Ethno-nationalist triads: assessing the influence of kin groups on civil wars, *World Politics*, 61(3), pp. 403–437.

Cederman, L.E., Wimmer, A. & Min, B. (2010) Why do ethnic groups rebel? New data and analysis, *World Politics*, 62(1), pp. 87–119.

Cederman, L.E., Gleditsch, K.S., Salehyan, I. & Wucherpfennig, J. (2013) Transborder ethnic kin and civil war, *International Organization*, 67(2), pp. 389–410.

Çelik, S. (2002) *Den Berg Ararat versetzen. Die politischen, militärischen, ökonomischen, und gesellschaftlichen Dimensionen des aktuellen kurdischen Aufstands* (Frankfurt/Main: Zambon).

Černy, H. (forthcoming a) Performing Ethnicity, Enacting Sovereignty: The Kurdistan Region of Iraq between Group Solidarity and Statecraft, PhD Thesis, University of Exeter.

Černy, H. (forthcoming b) The Kurdish Rapprochement: From Securitization to De-securitization to 'Neo-Ottomanism' in Turkey's Relations with the Kurdistan Region of Iraq, Conflict, Security and Development.

Cetinyan, R. (2002) Ethnic bargaining in the shadow of third-party intervention, *International Organization*, 56(3), pp. 645–677.

Checkel, J. (1998) The constructivist turn in international relations theory, *World Politics*, 50(2), pp. 324–348.

Christia, F. (2012) *Alliance Formation in Civil Wars* (Cambridge: Cambridge University Press).

Cohen, A. (1974) *Two-Dimensional Man: An Essay on the Anthropology of Power and Symbolism in Complex Society* (London: Routledge).

Cohen, A. (1981) *The Politics of Elite Culture* (Berkeley: University of California Press).

Collier, P. & Hoeffler, A. (2000) Greed and Grievance in Civil War, *World Bank Policy Research Paper 2355*, available online at: http://economics.ouls.ox.ac.uk/12055/1/2002-01text.pdf

Cordell, K. & Wolff, S. (2009) *Ethnic Conflict: Causes, Consequences, and Responses* (Cambridge: Polity Press).

David, S. (1997) Internal war: causes and cures, *World Politics*, 49(4), pp. 552–576.

Davis, D. & Moore, W. (1997) Ethnicity matters: transnational ethnic alliances and foreign policy behaviour, *International Studies Quarterly*, 41(1), pp. 171–184.

Davis, D. & Moore, W. (1998) Transnational ethnic ties and foreign policy, in: D. Lake & D. Rothchild (Eds), *The International Spread of Ethnic Conflict: Fear, Diffusion, and Escalation*, pp. 89–104 (Princeton: Princeton University Press).

Derrida, J. (1981) *Positions* (London: Athlone Press).

DiPrizio, R. (2002) *Armed Humanitarianism: U.S. Interventions from Northern Iraq to Kosovo* (Baltimore: Johns Hopkins University Press).

Eagleton, W. (1963) *The Kurdish Republic of 1946* (London: Oxford University Press).

Eccarius-Kelly, V. (2011) *The Militant Kurds: A Dual Strategy for Freedom* (Santa Barbara: Praeger).

Edkins, J. (1999) *Poststructuralism and International Relations: Bringing the Political Back In* (Boulder: Lynne Rienner).

Entessar, N. (1992) *Kurdish Ethnonationalism* (Boulder: Lynne Rienner).

Entessar, N. (2009) *Kurdish Politics in the Middle East*, revised edn (Lanham: Lexington Books).

Fearon, J.D. (2003) Ethnic and cultural diversity by country, *Journal of Economic Growth*, 8, pp. 195–222.

Fenton, S. (2004) Beyond ethnicity: the global comparative analysis of ethnic conflict, *International Journal of Comparative Sociology*, 45(3–4), pp. 179–194.

Fenton, S. (2010) *Ethnicity*, 2nd edn (Cambridge: Polity Press).

Freij, H.Y. (1998) Alliance patterns of a secessionist movement: the Kurdish nationalist movement in Iraq, *Journal of Muslim Minority Affairs*, 18(1), pp. 19–37.

Gagnon, V.P. (2004) *The Myth of Ethnic War: Serbia and Croatia in the 1990s* (Ithaca: Cornell University Press).

Ghareeb, E. (1981) *The Kurdish Question in Iraq* (Syracuse: Syracuse University Press).

Ghassemlou, A.R. (1965) *Kurdistan and the Kurds* (Prague: Czechoslovak Academy of Science).

Gilley, B. (2004) Against the concept of ethnic conflict, *Third World Quarterly*, 25(6), pp. 1,155–1,166.

Graham-Brown, S. (1999) *Sanctioning Saddam: The Politics of Intervention in Iraq* (London: I.B. Tauris).

Gunes, C. (2011) *The Kurdish National Movement in Turkey: From Protest to Rebellion* (London: Routledge).

Gunter, M. (1996) Kurdish infighting: the PKK–KDP conflict, in: R. Olson (Ed.), *The Kurdish Nationalist Movement in the 1990s: Its Impact on Turkey and the Middle East*, pp. 50–64 (Lexington: University of Kentucky Press).

Gunter, M. (1998) Turkey and Iran face off in Kurdistan, *Middle East Quarterly*, 5(1), pp. 33–40.

Gunter, M. (1999) *The Kurdish Predicament in Iraq: A Political Analysis* (Basingstoke: Macmillan).

Gunter, M. (2001) The bane of Kurdish disunity, *Orient*, 42, pp. 615–616.

Gunter, M. (2007) The modern origins of Kurdish nationalism, in: M. Gunter & M. Ahmed (Eds), *The Evolution of Kurdish Nationalism*, pp. 1–17 (Costa Mesa: Mazda Press).

Gunter, M. (2009) *The A to Z of the Kurds* (Lanham: Scarecrow Press).

Gunter, M. (2010) Turgut Özal and the Kurdish Question, in: M. Casier & J. Jongerden (Eds), *Nationalisms and Politics in Turkey: Political Islam, Kemalism and the Kurdish Issue*, pp. 85–100 (London: Routledge).

Gurr, T.R. (1993) *Minorities at Risk* (Washington, DC: United States Institute for Peace).

Gurr, T.R. & Harff, B. (1994) *Ethnic Conflict in World Politics* (Boulder: Westview Press).

Hale, W. (2007) *Turkey, the U.S. and Iraq* (London: Saqi).

Hall, S. (1995) Fantasy, identity, politics, in: E. Carter, J. Donald & J. Squires (Eds), *Cultural Remix: Theories of Politics and the Popular*, pp. 63–69 (London: Lawrence & Wishart).

Hall, S. (1996) Introduction: who needs 'identity'?, in: S. Hall & P. du Gay (Eds), *Questions of Cultural Identity*, pp. 1–18 (London: Sage).

Hansen, L. (2006) *Security as Practice: Discourse Analysis and the Bosnian War* (London: Routledge).

Hardin, R. (1997) *One for All: The Logic of Group Conflict* (Princeton: Princeton University Press).

Hechter, M. (1986) Rational choice theory and the study of ethnic and race relations, in: J. Rex & D. Mason (Eds), *Theories of Ethnic and Race Relations*, pp. 264–279 (Cambridge: Cambridge University Press).

Hechter, M. (1987) *Principles of Group Solidarity* (Berkeley: University of California Press).

Hechter, M. (2001) *Containing Nationalism* (Oxford: Oxford University Press).

Helsing, J. (2004) The regionalization, internationalization and the perpetuation of conflict in the Middle East, in: S. Lobell & P. Mauceri (Eds), *Ethnic Conflict and International Politics: Explaining Diffusion and Escalation*, pp. 133–164 (Basingstoke: Palgrave Macmillan).

Hobsbawm, E. & Ranger, T. (1984) *The Invention of Tradition* (Cambridge: Cambridge University Press).

Horowitz, S. (2008) Mapping pathways of ethnic conflict onset: preferences and enabling conditions, *Ethnopolitics*, 7(2–3), pp. 307–320.

Human Rights Watch (1993) Genocide in Iraq: The Anfal Campaign against the Kurds, *Middle East Watch Report*, available online at: http://www.hrw.org/reports/1993/iraqanfal/

Husain, M.Z. & Shumock, S. (2006) Kurdish ethnonationalism: a concise overview, in: S. Saha (Ed.), *Perspectives on Contemporary Ethnic Conflict: Primal Violence or the Politics of Conviction*, pp. 269–294 (Lanham: Lexington Books).

Hutchinson, J. (2005) *Nations as Zones of Conflict* (London: Sage).

Imset, I. (1992) *The PKK: A Report on Separatist Violence in Turkey* (Ankara: Turkish Daily News Publications).

International Crisis Group (2008) Turkey and Iraqi Kurds: Conflict and Cooperation?, *Middle East Report 81*, available online at: http://www.crisisgroup.org/en/regions/middle-east-north-africa/iraq-iran-gulf/iraq/081-turkey-and-iraqi-kurds-conflict-or-cooperation.aspx

International Crisis Group (2012) Turkey: The PKK and a Kurdish Settlement, *Europe Report 219*, available online at: http://www.crisisgroup.org/~/media/Files/europe/turkey-cyprus/turkey/219-turkey-the-pkk-and-a-kurdish-settlement.pdf

Jenne, E.K. (2006) *Ethnic Bargaining: The Paradox of Minority Empowerment* (Ithaca: Cornell University Press).

Jenne, E.K. (2010) Ethnic partition under the League of Nations: the cases of population exchanges in the interwar Balkans, in: E. Chenoweth & A. Lawrence (Eds), *Rethinking Violence: States and Non-state Actors in Conflict*, pp. 117–140 (Cambridge, MA: MIT Press).

Jesse, N. & Williams, K. (2010) *Ethnic Conflict: A Systematic Approach to Cases of Conflict* (Washington: CQ Press).

Jwaideh, W. (2006 [1960]) *The Kurdish National Movement: Its Origins and Development* (Syracuse: Syracuse University Press).

Kaplan, R. (1994) *Balkan Ghosts: A Journey through History*, 2nd edn (New York: St. Martin's Press).

Kaufman, S. (2001) *Modern Hatreds: The Symbolic Politics of Ethnic War* (Ithaca: Cornell University Press).

Kaufmann, C. (1996) Possible and impossible solutions to ethnic civil wars, *International Security*, 20(4), pp. 136–175.

Kaufmann, C. (1998) When all else fails: ethnic population transfers and partitions in the twentieth century, *International Security*, 23(2), pp. 120–156.

Kirisci, K. & Winrow, G. (1997) *The Kurdish Question and Turkey: An Example of a Trans-state Ethnic Conflict* (London: Frank Cass).

Laitin, D. & Posner, D. (2001) The implications of constructivism for constructing ethnic fractionalization indices, *American Political Science Association—Comparative Politics Newsletter*, 12(1), pp. 13–17.

Laizer, S. (1996) *Martyrs, Traitors and Patriots: Kurdistan after the Gulf War* (London: I.B. Tauris).

Lundgren, A. (2007) *The Unwelcome Neighbour: Turkey's Kurdish Policy* (London: I.B. Tauris).

Malešević, S. (2004) *The Sociology of Ethnicity* (London: Sage).

Maoz, Z. (1997) Domestic political change and strategic response: the impact of domestic conflict on state behaviour, 1816–1986, in: D. Carment & P. James (Eds), *Wars in the Midst of Peace: The International Politics of Ethnic Conflict*, pp. 116–147 (Pittsburgh: University of Pittsburgh Press).

Marcus, A. (2007) *Blood and Belief: The PKK and the Kurdish Fight for Independence* (New York: New York University Press).

McDowall, D. (2007) *A Modern History of the Kurds*, 3rd edn (London: I.B. Tauris).

Milton-Edwards, B. & Hinchcliffe, P. (2008) *Conflicts in the Middle East since 1945*, 3rd edn (London: Routledge).

Natali, D. (2005) *The Kurds and the State: Evolving National Identity in Iraq, Turkey, and Iran* (Syracuse: Syracuse University Press).

Nezan, K. (1993) Kurdistan in Turkey, in: G. Chaliand (Ed.), *A People without a Country: The Kurds and Kurdistan*, 2nd edn, pp. 38–71 (London: Zed Press).

Olson, R. (1997) Turkey–Syria relations since the Gulf War: Kurds and water, *Middle East Policy*, 5(2), pp. 168–193.

Onuf, N. (1989) *World of Our Making: Rules and Rule in Social Theory and International Relations* (Columbia: University of South Carolina Press).

O'Shea, M. (2004) *Trapped between the Map and Reality: Geography and Perceptions of Kurdistan* (London: Routledge).

Özcan, A.K. (2006) *Turkey's Kurds: A Theoretical Analysis of the PKK and Abdullah Öcalan* (London: Routledge).

Peters, G. (1998) *Comparative Politics: Theory and Methods* (New York: New York University Press).

Petersen, K. (2004) A research note: reexamining transnational ethnic alliances and foreign policy behaviour, *International Interactions*, 30, pp. 25–42.

Phillips, D. (2007) Disarming, Demobilising, and Reintegrating the Kurdistan Workers' Party, Policy Paper, National Committee on American Foreign Policy.

Pope, N. & Pope, H. (2005) *Turkey Unveiled* (London: Gerald Duckworth).

Posen, B. (1993) The security dilemma and ethnic conflict, in: M. Brown (Ed.), *Ethnic Conflict and International Conflict*, pp. 104–124 (Princeton: Princeton University Press).

Posner, D. (2005) The implications of constructivism for studying the relationship between ethnic diversity and economic growth. Paper delivered at the *2004 Annual Conference of the American Political Science Association*, available online at: http://www.sscnet.ucla.edu/polisci/wgape/papers/7_Posner.pdf

Raer, M. (2008) *Intervention, Ethnic Conflict, and State-building in Iraq: A Paradigm for the Post-colonial State* (London: Routledge).

Reus-Smit, C. (2009) Constructivism, in: S. Burchill & A. Linklater (Eds), *Theories of International Relations*, 4th edn, pp. 212–236 (Basingstoke: Palgrave Macmillan).

Roe, P. (1999) The intrastate security dilemma: ethnic conflict as a 'tragedy'?, *Journal of Peace Research*, 36(2), pp. 183–202.

Romano, D. (2006) *The Kurdish Nationalist Movement: Opportunity, Mobilization and Identity* (Cambridge: Cambridge University Press).

Rose, R. (1991) Comparing forms of comparative analysis, *Political Studies*, 39(3), pp. 446–462.

Saideman, S. (2001) *The Ties that Divide: Ethnic Politics, Foreign Policy, and International Conflict* (New York: Columbia University Press).

Salehyan, I. (2007) Transnational rebels: neighbouring states as sanctuary for rebel groups, *World Politics*, 52(2), pp. 217–242.

Salehyan, I. (2008) No shelter here: rebel sanctuaries and international conflict, *Journal of Politics*, 70(1), pp. 54–66.

Salehyan, I. (2009) *Rebels without Borders: Transnational Insurgencies in World Politics* (Ithaca: Cornell University Press).

Singer, J.D. (1961) The level of analysis problem in international relations, *World Politics*, 14(1), pp. 77–92.

Spivak, G. (1987) *In Other Worlds: Essays in Cultural Politics* (New York: Methuen).

Stack, J. (1997) The ethnic challenge to international relations theory, in: D. Carment & P. James (Eds), *Wars in the Midst of Peace: The International Politics of Ethnic Conflict* (Pittsburgh: University of Pittsburgh Press).

Stansfield, G. (2003) *Iraqi Kurdistan: Political Development and Emerging Democracy* (London: Routledge).

Steinberg, S. (2001) *The Ethnic Myth: Race, Ethnicity, and Class in America*, 3rd edn (Boston: Beacon Press).

Tahiri, H. (2007) *The Structure of Kurdish Society and the Struggle for a Kurdish State* (Costa Mesa: Mazda Press).

Uslu, E. (2010) Resolution of Turkey's 'Kurdish Question' in critical stage as PKK threatens to end peace initiatives, *Jamestown Foundation Terrorism Monitor*, 8(7), available online at: http://www.jamestown.org/single/?no_cache=1&tx_ttnews[tt_news]=36063

Van Bruinessen, M. (1986) The Kurds between Iran and Iraq, *MERIP Middle East Report*, 141, pp. 14–27.

Van Bruinessen, M. (1992) *Agha, Shaikh and State: The Social and Political Structures of Kurdistan* (London: Zed Books).

Van Bruinessen, M. (2000) *Kurdish Ethno-nationalism versus Nation Building States* (Istanbul: Isis Press).

Van Evera, S. (1994) Hypotheses on nationalism and war, *International Security*, 18(4), pp. 5–39.

Varshney, A. (2002) *Ethnic Conflict and Civic Life: Hindus and Muslims in India* (New Haven: Yale University Press).

Wæver, O. (1997) The rise and fall of the inter-paradigm debate, in: S. Smith, K. Booth & M. Zalewski (Eds), *International Theory: Positivism and Beyond*, pp. 149–185 (Cambridge: Cambridge University Press).

Wagner, R.H. (1993) The causes of peace, in: R. Licklider (Ed.), *Stopping the Killing: How Civil Wars End*, pp. 257–263 (New York: New York University Press).

Walt, S. (1985) Alliance formation and the balance of world power, *International Security*, 9(4), pp. 3–43.

Walt, S. (1987) *The Origins of Alliances* (Ithaca: Cornell University Press).

Waltz, K. (1959) *Man, the State, and War: A Critical Analysis* (New York: Columbia University Press).

Warren, C. & K. Troy (forthcoming) The logic of intra-ethnic conflict: group fragmentation in the shadow of state power, *Journal of Conflict Resolution*.

Weber, C. (2010) *International Relations Theory: A Critical Introduction*, 3rd edn (London: Routledge).

Wendt, A. (1999) *Social Theory of International Politics* (Cambridge: Cambridge University Press).

White, P. (2000) *Primitive Rebels or Revolutionary Modernizers? The Kurdish Nationalist Movement in Turkey* (London: Zed Books).

Wimmer, A. (2008) The making and unmaking of ethnic boundaries: a multilevel process theory, *American Journal of Sociology*, 113(4), pp. 970–1,022.

Wimmer, A., Cederman, L.E. & Min, B. (2009) Ethnic politics and armed conflict: a configurational analysis of a new global dataset, *American Sociological Review*, 74(2), pp. 316–337.

Wolfers, A. (1962) *Discord and Collaboration: Essays on International Politics* (Baltimore: Johns Hopkins University Press).

Woodwell, D. (2004) Unwelcome neighbours: shared ethnicity and international conflict during the Cold War, *International Studies Quarterly*, 48(1), pp. 197–223.

Zakaria, F. (2006) Rethinking Iraq: the way forward, *Newsweek*, 5 November, available online at: http://www.thedailybeast.com/newsweek/2006/11/05/rethinking-iraq-the-way-forward.html

Zalewski, M. & Enloe, C. (1995) Questions about identity in international relations, in: K. Booth & S. Smith (Eds), *International Relations Theory Today*, pp. 279–305 (Cambridge: Polity Press).

Zehfuss, M. (2002) *Constructivism in International Relations: The Politics of Reality* (Cambridge: Cambridge University Press).

Zehfuss, M. (2006) Constructivism and identity: a dangerous liaison, in: S. Guzzini & A. Leander (Eds), *Constructivism and International Relations*, pp. 93–117 (London: Routledge).

Ethnopolitics, 2014
Vol. 13, No. 4, 355–376, http://dx.doi.org/10.1080/17449057.2014.894175

The Awakening of a Latent Diaspora: The Political Mobilization of First and Second Generation Turkish Migrants in Sweden

BAHAR BASER

University of Warwick, UK

ABSTRACT   This paper explores how political developments in a host country catalyse the awakening of a latent diaspora and lead to the activation of a transnational community that previously consisted of loose and scattered networks. It also draws attention to the generational continuation of identity politics in a diaspora context through analysing a second generation's abrupt interest in homeland politics. By using the Turkish community in Sweden as a case study and by basing its main arguments on extensive research and fieldwork, it suggests that inter-diaspora rivalries and group competition may help to gain a better understanding of the interest that diasporans show in the promotion of homeland politics. It also suggests that although the diasporic discourses are based on contested political issues in their home country, the framing process takes place with regards to the host country context. The paper suggests that there were two significant transformative and triggering factors in Sweden that motivated the Turkish diaspora to participate actively in efforts to affect policymaking mechanisms in Sweden: Kurdish diaspora activism in general and the passage of the Armenian Genocide Bill by the Swedish Parliament on 11 March 2010.

Introduction

'We had to respond to the Kurds in some way', responded one of the Turkish interviewees when I asked the reason behind his interest in Turkish politics, 'they are ruining our [Turkish] image here in Sweden'. He was a young Swedish citizen of Turkish origin who was born in the suburbs of Stockholm. He had recently been active in one of the main Turkish organizations and was dynamically participating in discussions on blogs and in chat rooms that were formed to raise awareness against the passage of the Armenian Genocide Bill on 11 March 2010 at the Swedish Parliament. He was also among the participants at the rally, which for the first time gathered approximately 3,000 members of the Turkish community in the main square in Stockholm to protest in the name of their homeland.[1] According to him, the image of the Turks in Sweden was 'damaged' because of the

---

Correspondence Address: Bahar Baser, Politics and International Studies Department, Social Sciences Building, Coventry CV4 7AL, UK. Email: mailto:bahar.baser@gmail.com

© 2014 The Editor of Ethnopolitics

'Kurdish diaspora lobby against Turkey', and the passage of the Genocide Bill, which 'passed due to this lobby', could be interpreted as the 'last straw'. In his words, it was an 'eye-opener' for the Turkish community to become part of a counter-political mobiliz-ation process and 'act as a diaspora'. He stated, 'We have to do something as we are already too late'.

The testimony above was surely not exceptional; on the contrary, this interviewee was one of many second generation Turks who started to show a sudden interest in homeland politics and became engaged in political mobilization efforts in order to affect policymak-ing mechanisms in Sweden. Since the Swedish Parliament approved a resolution recogniz-ing the mass killing of Armenians under the rule of the Ottoman Empire in 1915 as genocide, there has been a visible increment in Turkish political activism in Sweden. This is a highly contested issue in both Turkey and in the international arena due to the Turkish state's refusal to define the atrocities (forced deportations, massacres and disap-pearances) of 1915 as genocide. This has caused significant nationalistic reactions in Turkey and among Turkish migrant populations in Europe.

Countries such as France, Greece and Belgium have already recognized the atrocities of 1915 as genocide. In Sweden the bill won the support of five of the seven Swedish parlia-mentary parties, which mainly represented the left side of the political spectrum, and was passed after highly contentious debates among parliamentarians before and after 11 March.[2] The fact that the passage of the bill was supported by various Kurdish organiz-ations as well as Kurdish-origin members of parliament caused dismay and enhanced the widespread Turkish bitterness towards Kurdish activism in Sweden in general. Some members of the Turkish community in Sweden responded to the decision with a strong sense of frustration; for instance, some Turkish members of the Social Democrat Party, which voted in favour of the passage of the Genocide Bill, resigned en masse in Gothenburg to protest against their parties' approach to this sensitive issue.[3] What was interesting about these developments was that, strikingly, the second generation's reaction was evidently stronger than the reaction of the first generation.

According to Adamson (2012, p. 33), 'the first step in the creation of a diasporic com-munity is the activation of a transnational constituency from the mass of entangled and messy social networks'. At this point, diaspora elites play a big role and channel these scat-tered small group efforts into one collective narrative. The aim is to create 'coherent cat-egories, discourses and symbols that can merge dispersed social networks under a single diasporic category' (Adamson, 2012, p. 33). The push for the creation of a diasporic com-munity usually comes from a critical juncture that occurs in the home country, but, as will be argued in this paper, sometimes the circumstances in the host country may also catalyse this activation process. Over recent years, despite their intra-group ideological differences, the Turkish transnational community has been slowly but surely forming a diasporic struc-ture that could act as the 'Turkish Voice' by bringing together the sporadic and weak net-works of various ideological clusters and collecting them under an alliance that aims at 'protecting the reputation of Turkey in the eyes of the Swedish public'.[4]

Members of the Turkish community who belong to opposite camps in Turkish politics came together to demonstrate against the decision of the Swedish Parliament and form a diasporic space that channels the grievances of the Turkish community into a collective narrative. The reason behind this effort was the accumulated resentment of the Turkish community against Kurdish activism in Sweden, as well as Sweden's welcoming approach towards non-militant Kurdish activism on its soil (Baser, 2012). The second generation is particularly active in this newly emerging mobilization. This is largely due to the political developments in the host country and because they perceive Sweden's approach to Turkey's political matters to be a threat to their own image and status as a minority group in Sweden. Contingent alliances are made between other groups who are considered as 'co-ethnics' or 'ethnic cousins', such as the Azerbaijanis and the Uyghurs, and diasporic battle fronts are being formed that reflect the enmities back in Turkey. What we can see today is that from a transnational community that had predominantly economic and cultural ties with the homeland, a diaspora with solid political projects is being born.

In this case at hand, the political developments in Sweden have triggered an urge to form a coherent stance, but coincidentally enough, this diasporic awakening has coincided with the homeland's new trajectory of strengthening the Turkish diaspora and its co-ethnics abroad. For the last couple of years, the Turkish state, which used to perceive Turkish migrants abroad as 'remittance machines' (Østergaard-Nielsen, 2003) rather than robust political agents representing Turkey abroad, has started formulating strategies to utilize effectively Turkish migrants' transnational potential for its own benefit (Baser, 2013). This neo-liberal approach required more contact with the Turkish communities abroad and a specific unit was formed by the Turkish state called the Presidency for Turks Abroad and Kin Communities. Yet, the phenomenon of a diaspora's political activism is far more complicated than a simple response to 'homeland calling' (Demmers, 2007, p. 14). One can observe that the interactions between the Turkish diaspora actors have been enhanced over the past few years, but it does not mean that this newly established link between the homeland and the diaspora elites can become an alternative explanation for the diasporic awakening of the Turkish community in Sweden. The centre of gravity of motivations and initiatives for mobilization still came from the Turkish community in Sweden itself and the new diaspora strategy of the Turkish state officials could play only a complementary role rather than constituting the fundamental explanation behind these recent developments.

The current paper seeks to provide a deeper understanding of these newly embraced political mobilization efforts of the Turkish transnational community in Sweden. The main questions asked here can be listed as the following. What triggers an interest in diaspora mobilization in the hostland? Why and how do the second generation employ transnational identity politics as a policy tool (Shain & Barth, 2003 p. 462)? First, the paper addresses how political developments in a host country affect a transnational migrant community, which can lead to the formation of a diaspora that actively mobilizes for policy change in the host country. Second, it explores the generational continuation in a diaspora context through a second generation's interest in mobilizing for homeland politics. It argues that although the diasporic discourses of the Turkish community are based on contested political issues in their home country, the frames they use for their discourses are related to the host country's context and the awakening process occurs due to the political state of affairs in Sweden. The aim is not to analyse profoundly the long-standing issues revolving around the Turkish–Kurdish question or the recognition of the Armenian genocide, but instead to use these empirical findings to understand better the mobilization processes of diasporas, the generational continuation of diasporic activism and the intra-group rivalries and contingent alliances among diaspora groups in a given hostland.

The focus on the Turkish diaspora activism is important in the sense that there is insufficient academic work on the Turkish community and its engagement with Turkish politics so far, apart from that of a few authors who worked on the media practices (Akin, 2006) and organizational behaviour (Akis & Kalaylioglu, 2010) of the Turkish migrants in Stockholm. Other Turkish migrant groups in Germany or the Netherlands have been largely investigated, but the Turks in Sweden remain an unexplored topic for researchers. Analysing the Swedish case shows that home states unevenly distribute their attention to their constituencies abroad and the diasporization process of an ethnic community occurs asynchronously in each hostland context depending on various factors, such as the existence of diaspora elites, the composition of migrants, the hostland's political environment as well as the home state's reach to those communities.

Theoretical Approaches to Diaspora and Mobilization for Homeland Politics

Over the last few decades, diasporas have become one of the most popular subjects among scholars and there is a growing literature analysing the role of diaspora groups as non-state actors. Broadly defined as migrant communities dispersed outside a homeland's borders, which keep certain social, economic and political attachments to the homeland and mobilize under a collective identity that is ideological, ethnic or religious, diaspora groups all around the world are attracting the attention of numerous scholars, specialists, journalists and policymakers. Many authors argue that the opportunities facilitated by globalization enable diasporas to influence directly their homelands, as well as to lobby the host country governments for their homeland's benefit (Shain & Barth, 2003; Østergaard-Nielsen, 2003; Lyons & Mandaville, 2010a; Adamson, 2012), and they try to understand further the galvanizing factors behind their mobilization.

Existing studies usually focus on the experience of the first generation and their attachments to their homeland to explain the causes of diaspora mobilization for a collective aim. From this perspective, a diaspora's connection to their homeland is their principal motivation for political action, both in their hostland and transnationally. Diaspora mobilization practices such as voting abroad, sending remittances or promoting homeland politics (Østergaard-Nielsen, 2003; Nell, 2008) are cited as examples to demonstrate its importance. Surely, diaspora–homeland relations are an incontestable part of the diaspora mobilization process; however, the promotion of homeland-related issues does not solely explain why interest in diaspora formation within a transnational community is triggered. Some authors also point to the hostland context to analyse the impact of the hostland's political environment on the evolution of diasporic identities. Many authors argue that the scope of the political transnationalism practised by diaspora groups depends on the transnational opportunity structures (Koopmans & Statham, 2001; Ögelman et al., 2002; Nell, 2008). An abundance of research is available on the experiences of exclusion, segregation, limited economic, political and social opportunities as well as how they strengthen a transnational migrant community's retention of their ethnic ties. The emphasis on the host country's context usually revolves around integration issues, which are useful but limited in explaining diasporic identity formation. Diaspora mobilization and their related political aims are more complex than they appear and are affected by a combination of exogenous and endogenous factors that need further attention by scholars. More precisely, 'diasporans' intervention in matters concerning the homeland depends on interests and obligations rooted in the host society as well as the homeland' (Brinkerhoff, 2009, p. 7). While having strong ties to their homeland is one of the main components in the definition of a diaspora, it does not mean that diasporas are neutral to the political developments in their hostland.

Research in diaspora studies often emphasizes a specific framework in homeland–diaspora relations that depicts diasporas as groups dedicating their time and energy solely to benefit the homeland, undermining the fact that the promotion of the homeland's interests sometimes coincides with the interests of the diaspora groups. This approach, which perceives the diaspora as an altruistic entity, is highly prominent in current studies. For example, the work of Saideman *et al.* (2011, pp. 6–13) summarizes the current perspectives on the motivational and capacity theories of mobilization and finds in both theories that the homeland is central and diasporas are perceived as romantic pursuers of long-distance nationalism, or tools of their home states. They are accepted as individual actors in some cases, but use this energy on homeland interests, assuming they have no interests of their own. For example, how diasporas form a counter-stance against other rival groups within a given context is largely neglected in the literature. By criticizing this approach, Saideman *et al.* argue that diasporas may function in a similar way as interest groups, such as making a material and non-material 'cost–benefit mobilizational calculus' before they act on a certain issue. In other words, the idea behind diaspora mobilization cannot be explained solely by 'emotional fulfilment' (Sheffer, 2003). Kenny (1998) further suggests, 'support for diasporan nationalism is strategically adopted by particular groups within the immigrant community as a means of generating support for their own local goals in the host society'. He argues that once these elite groups are absent, it is hard to find support for homeland-related political issues and/or mobilization levels are much lower (Kenny, 1998, p. 1). In parallel with these arguments, this paper contends that it should not be taken for granted that diasporas prioritize their homeland's agenda first and a diaspora's own interests and its status within the host country are also to be considered part of the puzzle.

Understanding the Peculiarities of Diaspora Mobilization

Some argue that the emergence of diaspora groups can be explained by an essentialist point of view, as a natural and automatic result of migration, exile or dispersion. However, this perspective ignores the mobilization factor in the diasporization process and runs the 'risk of moving towards essentialising diaspora as an ethnic label rather than a framework of analysis' (Butler, 2001, p. 190). This paper, in accordance with Fiona Adamson (2008, p. 7), builds on the constructivist approach, which perceives diasporic identity as a social construction of transnational networks and identities. Not all the members of an ethnic and religious community in a hostland constitute a diaspora. Diasporic identity is formed as a result of a combination of experiences both in the homeland and in the hostland. Based on this approach, diaspora is not simply a dispersed ethnic group but rather an identity constructed by the mobilization efforts of certain elites in the hostland context. Political engagement also constitutes one of the central characteristics of a diaspora group. As Lyons & Mandaville (2010b, p. 126) argue, diasporas are not 'given, pre-existing social actors' but instead they are 'generated by politics'. Not every migrant who retains a sense of belonging to the homeland is a member of the diaspora, therefore 'diasporas include only those who are mobilised to engage in homeland political processes' (Lyons & Mandaville, 2010b, p. 126).

Based on the argument that diasporas are *not* a natural outcome of migration but are political entities, one should ask the question: 'Why does a diaspora discourse arise among a certain group of people?' (Sökefeld, 2006). Many explain the motivations for diaspora mobilization by referencing an experience of traumatic dispersal or exile (Jewish and Armenian examples are the most common). However, this definition excludes many other migrant groups that act as a diaspora or define themselves as such. How, then, can we explain the diasporic mobilization of the transnational migrant communities who migrated for purely economic reasons? According to Kenny (1998, p. 1), 'In most cases support for homeland nationalism may be a social norm, but it requires at most no-cost lip service support. Successful nationalist mobilization entails arriving at a situation in which the issue of the homeland is seen by at least some immigrants as a high priority issue requiring high-cost active support'. What then causes this behavioural shift? Safran (2007) argues that 'diaspora consciousness may be revived after a special event, such as a revolutionary struggle or a tragic experience that brings back the importance of the kinship connection'. Demmers (2007, p. 8) adds to the discussion the phenomenon of a 'diasporic turn', which transnational community members might experience after specific events that trigger diaspora identification. These kinds of argument help us to understand why a transnational community might, over time, give birth to a diasporic segment. However, there is a tendency to assume that this shift followed by diaspora formation will occur due to critical developments or changes only in the homeland. Several examples exist along these lines, such as the Croatian diaspora's reaction to the disintegration of Yugoslavia or the support of Kosovo Albanians from former Yugoslavia in the struggle for Greater Albania (Faist, 2004, p. 349).

This paper argues that diaspora mobilization can also occur as a result of certain political developments in the hostland, such as changes in the bilateral relations between the homeland and hostland political actors or a sudden divergence in a hostland's foreign policy priorities towards the homeland. These events can induce significant changes in how a transnational community shapes its political stance towards homeland politics within the political and social contexts of a hostland. They can pave the way for a loosely bonded transnational community to combine scattered actions into a unified and solid act. In some cases, diaspora groups may feel that their status as an ethnic minority in the host society is threatened, and then seek assistance from homeland actors in reaction to these changes. As Kenny suggests, members of a transnational community may mobilize for homeland-related issues not through failing to integrate into the host society or because they have emotional attachments to their ancestral land, but because promoting homeland interests will also advance their position in the host country (Kenny, 1998, p. 3). Their motivations may arise from 'social reinforcement or pride' (Brinkerhoff, 2008, p. 243) or their material and non-material interests as a collective group within the hostland. Diaspora mobilization should not be associated solely with the 'homeland calling'. In today's world the reverse is possible; diasporization of a transnational community may cause a 'diaspora calling' situation. For example, the diaspora elites could actively seek synchronization on particular issues with the homeland discourses, policies and politics in order to have more say in their hostland political spheres.

Homeland nostalgia is not the sole catalyst for transnational communities to mobilize as diaspora groups. Interest-based politics and rational anticipation could also explain why certain groups transform into collectively organized, politically active networks. Especially when there is competition between several ethnic groups in the homeland, cost–benefit calculations and concerns about their status in the hostland become much more prominent for the diaspora elites. Political or social tensions in the homeland can be imported to the host country's context and from time to time surface rivalries among groups within the hostland may arise. Achieving a certain position in the eyes of the host society may trigger competition and tension between two adversary diaspora groups. If one group enjoys less media attention or believes its discursive opportunities are more limited owing to the host country's support of the other group(s), then it could be motivated to take action. In the case of state-linked diaspora groups, the elites may seek assistance from homeland actors better to influence hostland politics. They may also synchronize their own narratives with the pre-existing homeland discourses on a certain issue. For these groups, building an alliance with the homeland is not a precondition for mobilization. They may act on their own, with or without seeking the material and non-material support of their homeland, on issues relating to homeland politics. In these cases, contingent alliances between diaspora elites and homeland actors are conceivable. In other cases involving stateless diasporas, the elites of these groups might adjust their actions according to the given situation to focus more on bringing about policy change in the host country or in building alliances with non-governmental organizations and civil society organizations.

Mobilization of the Second Generation for Homeland Politics

There is still a huge gap in terms of understanding how diasporas mobilize and how the generational continuation of political activism takes place. Scholars are not in agreement about whether the second generation has as strong transnational ties as the first generation. Authors such as Portes & Rumbaut (2001) argue that the second generation has fewer ties with the homeland and that those transnational ties are a 'one-generation phenomenon'. Other authors argue that the second generation maintains ties with the homeland of their parents; however, this attachment cannot be measured solely by statistics, such as remittances or frequency of visits to the homeland (Levitt & Waters, 2002). Today, more and more scholars argue that some second generation members maintain a sense of belonging towards their country of residence, despite being unable to speak the native language, having never visited that 'imagined' homeland, and having no intention to move there.

Glick-Schiller (2004, p. 578) argues that the offspring of migrants, even those who have obtained citizenship in their new country of residence, may embrace long-distance nationalism as a response to the racism and negative stereotyping that they encounter in the hostland. She offers the example of Turkish youths whose families have resided in a country for several generations and yet are denied full citizenship rights and, thus, need to look for a homeland transnationally. However, experiences of exclusion in the host country cannot solely explain diasporic mobilization among the second generation members of the community. As Perlmann (2002, pp. 218–219) argues: 'the answer can hardly be that the host society is uniformly hostile'. It is important to look at the positive incentives and opportunities that the host societies provide for the following generations. For instance, multicultural policies and encouraging diversity could be one of the main reasons that the second generation establishes symbolic ties with their ancestor's homeland.

Most important is the fact that the second generation establishes transnational networks and practices yet their repertoires of action are not always identical to the actions and strategies of the first generations. As Lyons & Mandaville (2010b, p. 137) state, 'loyalties can remain high across generations whereas the most important frames shift'. The following generations have different attitudes towards homeland issues owing to their socialization in the host country and their symbolic ties to their ancestors' homeland. Therefore, they frame their dissent or endorsement of particular issues differently from previous generations.

Data Gathering and Fieldwork in Sweden

The paper focuses on those Turks who have an interest in and influence upon homeland politics. To borrow Brubaker's terms, only the members of the Turkish transnational community who take a 'stance' or have a 'claim' (Brubaker, 2005) about the political issues in Turkey have been included in the sample. The interviewees were active in protest events or other types of political demonstration and action, constantly followed the political developments in Turkey and tried to get involved in the political projects constructed by the diaspora elites. Rather than reifying a whole ethnic group and homogenizing them to one cluster of a diaspora community, the diaspora is accepted as a subset of a transnational community (Bauböck, 2010) that is formed outside the borders of a defined or imagined homeland and whose members sustain attachments to the homeland economically, culturally and politically and as a result feel part of a collective movement that has solid political engagements to the homeland (Lyons & Mandaville, 2010a). The diaspora is not taken for granted as being representative of a whole ethnic group, but instead diaspora is perceived as a combination of various individuals and groups who *claim to represent* a certain ethnic group.

While selecting the interviewees, Shain & Barth's (2003, p. 452) categorization of diaspora members into three groups was highly useful:

(1) *Core members* are the organizing elites, intensively active in diasporic affairs and in a position to appeal for mobilization of the larger diaspora.
(2) *Passive members* are likely to be available for mobilization when the active leadership calls upon them.
(3) *Silent members* are a larger pool of people who are generally uninvolved in diasporic affairs but who may mobilize in times of crises.

The sample consisted of core and passive members of the Turkish diaspora in Sweden. Those who are assimilated into Swedish society or show no interest in homeland politics were not interviewed. Therefore, this paper does not represent the entire Turkish-origin population in Sweden, but, rather, tries to present a comprehensive study about first and second generation Turks who have a politicized ethnic consciousness and are transnationally part of a broader ideological or political collective movement. The interviewees were members of the Turkish community who act as lobby groups, engage in political mobilization efforts and seek to affect policymaking and carry their causes to the political platforms in Sweden.

The findings are based on an ethnographic research study that combines methods such as direct and participant observation, semi-structured group and individual interviews, as well as casual conversations. Various web pages of diaspora organizations, documents, leaflets and other social media sources were also utilized to gather more information. The participants were reached through migrant organizations, blogs, discussion forums and protest events. Among the interviewees were public intellectuals, authors, politicians, bloggers, organization leaders and members. For the purposes of this study, 30 Turkish participants who were born in Sweden (all were born after 1975) and 20 Turkish first generation participants were interviewed over a total period of six months between 2008 and 2011 in several cities in Sweden, including Stockholm, Malmo, Uppsala and Gothenburg.[5]

Turkish Transnational Community in Sweden

Apart from a number of leftist activists who fled Turkey for political reasons in the 1970s and 1980s, Turkish migration to Sweden was the result of labour migration in the 1960s, and these labour migrants came predominantly from a specific region, which made them a relatively homogenous group compared with Turkish migrant communities in other European countries. The majority of these immigrants came from a small district called Kulu (Konya) and they were of peasant origin, with a low educational background.[6] The sense of belonging and the loyalties they harbour also revolve around this regional identity, as family ties and regional attachments are particularly strong (Westin, 2003, p. 991).

Currently, the number of Turkish citizens residing in Sweden is estimated to be 100,000.[7] Large flows of Turkish migration happened between 1966 and 1973, until Sweden closed its doors to labour migrants (Akin, 2006, p. 33). The composition of migrants shifted with the arrival of asylum seekers (mostly Assyrians and Kurds) who came to Sweden after the 1971 military intervention in Turkey. Another wave of migration began after the military coup in 1980 and on this occasion the asylum seekers were mostly of Kurdish origin as the ongoing Kurdish conflict in Turkey between the Turkish state and the Kurdistan Workers Party (PKK) paved the way for more migration flows of Kurdish refugees and asylum seekers to Sweden.

The composition of migrants and their profiles reflect the organizational structure of the Turkish groups in Sweden. Unlike other groups from Turkey, such as Kurds and Assyrians, which were politically active and mobilized in a sustained manner, the Turkish organizations have, until very recently, distanced themselves from political action and focused solely on migration-related issues and the preservation of Turkish culture. The organizations serve as hometown associations, which enable Turkish people to gather and interact without a specific political agenda. Most of the associations define their agenda as more Sweden-oriented rather than Turkey-oriented.[8] The main organizations were founded to act as a bridge between the Swedish policymakers and the rivalries between them are also contextual towards their situation in Sweden rather than ideological or religious divisions imported from Turkey (Akis & Kalaylioglu, 2010). The first Turkish organization, Turkiska Riksförbundet (TRF), assumed a leading role among the Turkish population for two decades. During the 1990s, second generation Turks who wanted to surpass the TRF directive and follow a more 'integration-oriented' and 'Sweden-oriented' agenda formed a second Turkish umbrella organization called Svensk-Turkiska Riksförbundet (STRF). This organization also followed a non-partisan programme and, until very recently, refrained from Turkish politics in order to focus on the social situation of Turkish migrants in Sweden. The STRF also cooperated with a youth association called Turkiska Ungdomsförbundet (TUF). Besides these three umbrella organizations, Turkiska Student och Akademiker Föreningen (TSAF) is another youth association that recently became active among university students.

The vast majority of the Turkish community members were from a conservative background and inclined to support parties with nationalist agendas; however, their party loyalties did not result in a mobilized network in Sweden.[9] As Akis & Kalaylioglu (2010, p. 13) observed, 'in respect of their political interests, Turkish associations in Sweden display a considerably different character in comparison to other Turkish associations in Europe' where 'the associational life of Turks has taken shape in line with the basic political divisions and ideological fault lines of Turkish politics'. Instead in Sweden, 'political divisions were not decisive in the development of Turkish associations'. These organizations support different Swedish parties and their activities vary; yet, when it comes to issues regarding homeland politics, they usually present a united front during protests and campaigns that are about 'condemning terrorism', 'supporting the territorial integrity of Turkey' or 'protecting the image of Turkey in Sweden', and they claim to represent a collective 'Turkish Voice' in these matters.

Diaspora groups are not homogenous entities, therefore surely they consist of various groups that pursue different agendas or have diverse interests. The Turkish diaspora also suffers from intra-group rivalries and ideological or religious divides. During the recent Gezi protests in Turkey, it was evident that there are tensions within the Turkish community in terms of supporting or criticizing the Turkish government,[10] yet when it comes to targeting policy change in Sweden, different Turkish diaspora members with diverse interests could come together. In other words, the divisions are not sharp enough to divide them on matters related to the well-being of the Turkish community in Sweden or the image of Turkey on international and Swedish platforms. Another reason is that there are no actively mass-mobilized political groups who can be perceived as the branches of political movements in Turkey. For example, movements such as the ultra-nationalist Grey Wolves[11] are large migrant networks in Germany with connections to political parties in Turkey. However, there are no groups (except for small associations that have no significant mass support) that could be counted as satellite institutions of these movements in Sweden. The political activism of Turkish leftist groups could be sporadically observed until the end of the 1980s (Akin, 2006; Akis & Kalaylioglu, 2010, p. 14), but this is not the case today and they do not have a strong foothold in Turkey.

Whereas the Turkish community remained detached from active engagement in homeland politics and kept a low profile for a couple of decades, Kurdish diaspora members were very active in establishing associations and speaking out about matters related to the Kurdish situation in Turkey. In the early 1980s, an umbrella organization for all Kurdish organizations was formed and officially recognized by the Swedish government. Sweden has been very supportive towards the cultivation of the Kurdish identity by supporting civil society organizations and other similar migrant associations. Sweden tends to host a comparatively well-educated Kurdish intelligentsia consisting of journalists, authors, academics, artists and directors. It became a safe haven for Kurds who fled oppression in Turkey. This gave them the opportunity to cultivate their culture through the preservation of their traditions and the survival of their mother tongue, which was potentially endangered in Turkey. Van Bruinessen (1999, p. 10) emphasizes that Kurdish writers found Sweden 'a much more stimulating environment for developing Kurdish into a modern literary language than they would have found back in Turkey, even if the language had not been banned there'. The Swedish government has also financed the publication of books in Kurdish and, in the early 1980s, it was the only country that offered such opportunities for the Kurdish cause. The Kurdish elite lobbied

Swedish political parties on issues related to the Kurds in Turkey and the Middle East. The Kurdish diaspora is highly visible in the Swedish media and there are a significant number of Kurdish-origin politicians in Sweden who carry the Kurdish issue to Swedish political platforms (Baser, 2012).

Kurdish activism in Sweden greatly agitated some members of the Turkish community, leading to reactionary responses through time.[12] Although no violence was recorded between the two communities, such as the street fights that occurred between Turkish and Kurdish nationalist groups in Germany (Østergaard-Nielsen, 2003), there was apparent tension and growing social distance between the two communities. This dissociation also reflected on the social, economic, political and media practices of migrants from Turkey, and the escalation of the Turkish–Kurdish conflict in Turkey had repercussions on the diaspora spaces (Akin, 2006; Baser, 2012). In the following, the reasons behind the activation of a diasporic identity among the Turkish community in Sweden are analysed with the aim of understanding the sudden interest in the promotion of homeland-related politics. With the assumption that diasporic identities can remain active and dormant according to political and social circumstances as well as individual reasons and can be revived again under various circumstances, in Sweden two transformative and triggering factors can be observed: Kurdish diaspora activism and the passage of the Armenian Genocide Bill in the Swedish Parliament. The first factor is a more sustained one, which galvanized interest in homeland politics gradually, and the latter became the triggering event that catalysed activation and combined the scattered networks together.

Kurdish Activism as a Transformative Factor

Saideman *et al.* (2011, p. 14) suggest that 'we should expect greater diaspora activism if there is significant political competition within the diaspora organization(s)'. Diasporas make cost–benefit calculations and mobilize to ameliorate their perceived status within a given hostland. If there are pre-existing tensions between two diaspora groups imported from the homeland, it is possible that the two groups will monitor each other's political movements in the host country to maintain the upper hand in discourses related to contested issues. Competition with other groups may indeed cause a behavioural shift and awaken interest and the will to mobilize and affect policymaking mechanisms, and the diaspora groups 'stop seeing the issue of homeland as a low priority' (Kenny, 1998, p. 1).

Certainly each member of the Turkish migrant community had a political stance, supported a political party/figure back in Turkey and had an individual interpretation of the state of affairs both in Sweden and in Turkey. However, the proliferation of these political stances in a collective manner coincides with the ascending Kurdish activism in Sweden that started in the 1980s. Based on the participant observations as well as testimonies given in the interviews, it can be said that the Turkish community's mobilization developed to protect the 'Turkish image' in the face of a (perceived) threat by other ethnically politicized groups in the host country. Mobilization was gradual and born as a response to a specific situation in Sweden when the Turkish elite recognized that they were losing a *discursive battle* over the Kurdish issue. The second generation interviewee accounts in particular reveal that mobilization for homeland-related political issues only started being discussed in migrant organizations during the last decade. According to the majority of the interviewees, the reason they became interested in promoting homeland politics was that they gradually developed a reflexive nationalist discourse because 'when Turks were silent, Kurds seized the opportunity to raise their voice'. Putting homeland politics on the agenda is strongly related to the Turkish community feeling neglected by the Swedish authorities and their need to intervene in a 'worsening situation', in the words of one interviewee.

During the course of the interviews, the majority of Turkish respondents listed similar grievances: 'the Swedish state is partial when it comes to the Kurdish question and supports the Kurds by all means'; 'whatever the Turks have to say about the Kurdish question is badly received'; 'Turks are disappointed by the Swedes' behaviour and feel discriminated'; and 'the Turks feel the need to be involved in politics at an organisational level only because the Swedish state takes sides in this conflict'. Their assertions regarding the existence of the 'Kurdish lobby' and its alliance with other groups pushed them into a reactionary and politicized restructuring of their associations. Almost all of the participants had an openly negative stance towards the PKK and agreed that, although the PKK is on the terror list in EU countries, Sweden has a loosely tolerant policy towards it. Many others also mentioned that they feel frustrated in Sweden with regards to the Kurdish question, stating that they have no chance of 'defending Turkey or themselves' because they are labelled as the 'bad guys' by the Swedish authorities and Swedish society. They also stated that the Swedish authorities and media silenced their voices and they are not given sufficient opportunity to express themselves.

Another fieldwork observation was that although the participants were economically and socially well integrated within Swedish society, they strove to be more active than their parents in terms of influencing the Swedish decision-making processes regarding Turkish political issues. This is not because they are more radical than their parents in terms of interpreting homeland politics, but instead it is because they relate these issues to Swedish politics and their reactions are framed in the Swedish context rather than the Turkish one. To the second generation, Kurdish activism as well as the passage of the Genocide Bill is not interpreted as Turkish politics but it is a domestic issue that they need to deal with in Sweden. The second generation members act because these developments affect their lives in Sweden. The following testimony demonstrates that the homeland issues became a high priority for them not because of their interest in a policy change in Turkey but because of their concerns about their own status vis-à-vis the other ethnic minority groups in Sweden:

> Every day they were protesting in Sergels Torg[13] ... When we passed by, we saw it ... and we thought: what would the Swedes think about us, the Turks? We had to show them we were not as bad as the Kurds were trying to show us to be. (Interview)

Another testimony from a TUF member also shows that the Turkish community acted like a typical dormant state-linked diaspora until a political juncture in Sweden that galvanized an interest in counter-mobilization:

> At first I thought we did not have to organise ourselves against the Kurds ... we are brothers. It is just a handful of extremists engaging in separatist propaganda. I told myself, we have our state, army, intelligence service, and embassy in Sweden ... it is not our job to respond to these Kurds. But after the Genocide Bill, I changed my mind. I realised that we are on our own and we will have to bear the consequences if we do not act.

These reactions against Kurdish activism did not unite the Turkish community instantly but laid the foundation for an established diasporic structure. More and more Turkish members started writing blogs on a regular basis dealing with the issues related to Kurdish activism in Sweden and their support for 'terrorist groups' in Turkey. Increasingly, one could see commentaries in numerous newspaper articles related to Turkey condemning Sweden for 'letting the Kurdish diaspora show open support for the PKK', which was considered a 'terrorist organisation'. The chat rooms of websites that publish articles about the political conundrum in Turkey became a venue for Turkish and Kurdish politically active youth to have virtual fights and provocations. For instance, one of the most famous blogs is called 'The Anatolian Voice', which was founded by a second generation Turk with the motto of 'a reaction to the incitement campaign against Turkey'.[14] These individual attempts did not have a big impact on how Swedish policymakers perceived Turkish unease about what is going on in Sweden but they surely helped to show the Turkish community that these are not solely individual grievances but that there are many people out there who share similar views about the Kurdish diaspora activism. Diaspora nationalism started spreading within the Turkish community as a reactionary response to their perceived pecking order of ethnic groups in Sweden.

Therefore, these reactions signal the initial motivations that raised interest in homeland politics. They began importing official homeland discourses to the hostland political sphere and strengthening ties with the Turkish state and its political actors. In 2007, various Turkish organizations led by TRF and TUF organized a meeting, which was titled 'No to Terror!', and there were more than 1,000 people gathered in Stockholm to protest against the Kurdish organization PKK and its actions in Turkey.[15] With the responses to Kurdish activism, the first sparks of the diaspora mobilization process were born. These meetings gained continuous momentum and were repeated almost every year. Another 'anti-PKK' meeting was organized in 2011 by the main Turkish umbrella organizations.[16]

The Armenian Genocide Bill as a Triggering Event

The interviewee accounts indicate that the real push to mobilize was the Genocide Bill of 2010, which came as a shock to the Turkish community. They believe it stigmatized the Turkish community in Sweden and worried about its consequences. For example, the Turkish community raised concerns about the genocide-related issues being taught in schools in history classes and memorials in remembrance of the genocide being erected in Sweden. They found this to be an 'unfair' representation of the Turkish community. Even though the members of the Turkish community had different opinions about the Armenian genocide, the majority of the members united around one idea: 'the decision of the parliament was discriminatory'. There are diaspora members who admit that the genocide occurred, but they disagreed with the Swedish Parliament's role in condemning Turkey. There are others who deny the existence of Armenian genocide and blame foreign powers for generating a 'lie' to damage Turkey's reputation. Finally, there are groups who think that both the Armenians and Turks committed crimes against each other and only historians can decide their fate. There are diverse perspectives about what happened in 1915, but what united and eventually mobilized the Turkish-Swedes were their common concerns regarding the consequences of this bill for their status in Sweden.

The Genocide Bill also increased antagonism towards the Kurdish diaspora as the majority of the interviewees claimed that the bill was passed because the Kurdish diaspora lobbied for it. It is true that several Kurdish groups supported the passage of the bill by holding demonstrations before and after the process as well as by publishing declarations in favour of it. Moreover, several politicians from Kurdish backgrounds gave speeches in the Swedish Parliament regarding this issue. These acts were proof for the Turkish community that a 'Kurdish lobby' had played a significant role. The Turkish association leaders and their members felt a sense of isolation throughout the entire process of passing the Genocide Bill. It was also apparent that diaspora nationalism was evolving rapidly, particularly among the Turkish youth. During the interviews, I asked why they perceived the Genocide Bill to be the 'last straw' considering that Kurdish activism had always existed in Sweden. Several interviewees argued that the Genocide Bill was the first time that the Swedish state had been openly involved in a contentious issue among supposedly antagonistic ethnic groups and showed its bias 'officially'. Their answers revealed that the Turkish reaction was in response to a long-held complaint about Sweden's attitude towards Turkish politics and was very much contextual.

The initial reaction to the genocide resolution was an attempt to prevent it, later followed by protests and petitions. Before the vote in parliament, some Turkish groups came together to form a small organization called 'Fakta forum Turkiet'.[17] Their aim was to inform the Swedish public about Turkish history and politics, from their perspective, in order to 'correct' current information about Turkey circulating in the Swedish public and media. To support their claims they referenced the official Turkish discourse, which consisted of Turkish and foreign scholars' works that deny the existence of genocide and several websites that belong to the Foreign Ministry of Turkey. The seminar organized by STRF, with the participation of Prof. Justin McCarthy, who argues that the atrocities of 1915 were not a genocide and who is frequently referred to in Turkish official discourses, is an important example which shows that the diaspora discourse was being synchronized with the homeland's official narrative of this highly sensitive issue. They issued a press release in February 2010 stating that the decision as to whether the 1915 events were an act of genocide should be the responsibility of historians—not parliamentarians. They also noted that the Social Democrats' decision would cause political division among migrant communities from Turkey.[18] Additionally, some organization members sent emails to the Social Democrat Party members, which included the reactions and concerns of the Turkish community in Sweden.[19]

Shortly after the resolution was passed, the Swedish Turkish Workers Federation, the Swedish-Turkish Federation, the Swedish Turkish Youth Federation, the Kemalist Thought Association and the Turkish Women's Association organized a joint protest in Sergels Torg to condemn the parliament's decision. It was one of the few occasions when Turkish associations gathered more than 3,000 people together for a protest. The Turkish association members carried banners accusing Sweden of 'being unfair towards Turks' or 'distorting historical facts for political reasons'. The Turkish elite who spoke at the protest highlighted the 'unfairness' of the resolution for the Turkish community, the worsening relations between Armenia and Turkey, and the discriminatory consequences for the next generation. These protest events were mainly organized by the diaspora elites, not by the Turkish Embassy or any other official party. According to the leader of STRF, the embassy did not actively get involved in any stage of these events, but they could feel its moral support. When asked about the importation of the official discourse in order to represent the Turkish discourse, he responded that these methods had been chosen not because the embassy projected it on them but because it was 'practical'.

The TUF published an article on the Turkish community's concerns about the resolution itself and the monuments possibly being erected in recognition of the resolution where Turkish, Kurdish or Assyrian people live. Most of the people who were interviewed for the article were disturbed by the decision and said that the monuments would only increase tension between ethnic groups.[20] One of the leaders of the Turkish association said:

> They will raise monuments throughout Sweden, put this in the school books—our children will have to study it at school. Then they will come home and ask if our ancestors had committed such a crime. We don't want this to happen. It is a problem for us, for young people and for our future children.

Sökefeld (2006, p. 275) argues that critical events in the home or host country are a necessary condition for diaspora mobilization but they do not evoke diasporic consciousness all at once. As he states, 'Events are only critical when they are perceived and framed in a particular way. Actors are needed to articulate that such events require new forms of action, discourse and ways of conceptualising the world'. It is usually the elites who initiate such actions, as is the case for the Turkish community in Sweden. Immediately following the passing of the Genocide Bill, the diaspora elite developed new strategies to accelerate the mobilization process and to turn 'all the spontaneous reactions into one collective action', as one of the interviewees described. Many interviewees from different organizations highlighted their focus on the following aims: (1) forming special lobby groups to support Turkish interests and to ameliorate the image of Turkey in the eyes of the Swedish public and parliament; (2) convincing young people (in particular) to learn about Turkish politics by organizing seminars, inviting scholars from Turkey to speak, providing workshops on Turkey for Swedish politicians and scholars, etc.; (3) maintaining close relations with the Swedish political parties and being actively involved in Swedish politics; and (4) inviting Turkish authorities into the process and striving for greater cooperation between Turkey and Sweden to benefit the Turkish community in Sweden. As one association member stated:

> This all happened because we remained silent. We didn't see what was coming. Now, all we need to do is to start from scratch. As the Turkish Youth in Sweden, we need to inform ourselves about Turkish politics in order to be able to respond to others when necessary. We will work on mobilising the young people first.

Another one agreed:

> We cannot ignore the fact that the image of Turkey becomes our image here. We cannot just say I don't care. Whatever happens in Turkey comes and finds us here in Sweden.

The participants also commented on their engagement with Swedish political parties. For instance, almost all of them said they would never vote for the Leftist Party, as it is very partial in its support of the Kurdish community in Sweden. They were also reticent about the Social Democrats, which, for years, had the support of Turkish migrants. The interviewees said that after the Genocide Bill had been passed the Social Democrats should 'forget about Turkish votes' because this action had ignored the Turkish community in Sweden. Another participant from the TUF indicated that no party in Sweden 'likes' Turkish people and as a Swedish citizen of Turkish origin, she feels under-represented in Sweden. Because members of the Turkish community felt isolated by left-wing parties who voted in favour of the Bill, they sought an unofficial tacit alliance with the centre-right Moderate Party, which criticized the bill and commented adversely on the passing of the bill. Turkish associations organized petitions and campaigns to condemn the parliamentary decision but also to persuade the Turkish community to vote for the Moderate Party. Facebook and YouTube were utilized to encourage votes for the Moderate Party for the national elections that were held on 19 September 2010. Group emails were also sent to inform people about the voting process and about the importance of opposing the leftist block. Not only did the Turkish diaspora elite encourage an alliance with the Moderate Party in order to counterbalance Kurdish diaspora activism and the support it receives from left-wing parties, but also the Moderate Party began acknowledging the 'Turkish Voice' and the Turkish diaspora as a monolithic body and started addressing them as such. For instance, for the 2010 elections, the Moderate Party prepared postcards that were sent to Turkish voters with the following messages: 'Show your reaction to the leftist block which declared you as genocide perpetrators. Vote for the Moderate Party!' or 'End this dirty game! Vote for the Moderate Party who supports the Turks' (Baser, 2013, p. 269). Even this changing attitude of a political party demonstrates that the perception of the Turkish community as an awakening diaspora was widening to political circles in Sweden. As shown, the Genocide Bill remarks on the bourgeoning of diasporic activities as well as the changing perceptions and self-perceptions of the Turkish community in a Swedish context.

Was it a One-off Reaction?

Almost four years since the Genocide Bill was passed, there have been significant developments in Turkish diasporic spaces related to homeland and hostland politics. First, clear signs of political mobilization are evident: new websites, blogs and Facebook pages exist, encouraging Turks to unite in transnational cyberspace, as well as actual protest events, seminars and parliamentary visits. New online newspapers have been established by second generation diaspora members to draw attention to politics in Turkey. For example, TUF members established a website called gazete.se[21] to inform Swedish society, as well as the Turkish community in Sweden, about controversial politics in Turkey. On their website, their stated aim is 'to provide news in a balanced way and to pay attention to news and topics that may not be given adequate coverage in the traditional media'. Headlines have included 'The Cyprus Question', 'The Kurdish Question', 'The Occupation of Azerbaijan' and 'What Happened in Anatolia in 1915'. The links have been prepared in a question–answer format, which coincides with the official Turkish discourse on these issues. *Harbi Gazete*, which is published by Turkish diaspora members in Sweden, added a separate section to its website under the title of 'Genocide' where they regularly publish articles that are related to what they call 'so-called Armenian Genocide' and how Sweden and other European countries approach this issue.[22] Young Turks published articles on TRF's website, calling for members of the Turkish community to 'unite' and 'surmount' the legacy of this event.[23]

In addition to online social networking, Turkish migrant organizations, in collaboration with young Turkish activists, have organized several lobbying trips to Brussels and Turkey. In their opinion, Turkish membership to the EU is the key to solving the many problems that Turkey faces today. Therefore, a small committee consisting of 25 individuals organized a trip to the European Parliament in Brussels to lobby for Turkish membership of the EU.[24] The diaspora newspapers and websites highlight the Turkish community's efforts in Sweden to ameliorate the image of Turkey in Sweden and Europe.

Conferences have been jointly organized by Azeri and Turkish associations in order to form a strategy of counter-mobilizing against the antagonistic diaspora groups. On the anniversary of the Genocide Bill's ratification, 12 Turkish associations, in collaboration with the Azeri, Uygur and Kazak associations in Sweden, organized a protest in Stockholm. The protestors laid a black wreath, as a sign of their discontent, and presented a letter to the Swedish Parliament. The members of the associations not only complained about the worsening image of the Turks but also referred to the image of Muslims.[25] During the protests, the leader of TRF, the biggest Turkish umbrella organization in Sweden, stated the following: 'It is difficult to fight with a Christian issue in a Christian country. This is how most Christian countries including Sweden perceive the Armenian issue'.[26] This brought a different dimension to the discussions around the status of Turks within Swedish society. Their protest, as part of the diasporic narrative, combined their dissent about the worsening image of the Turkish community in Sweden with the generally worsening image of Muslims. Protesting on the anniversary of the passing of the bill became an annual event for various Turkish organizations in Sweden, and in 2013 there was a protest in front of Riksdag,[27] thus it seems these reactionary mobilizations will take a sustained and systematic form in the coming years.

Interactions with Turkey and Turkish Political Actors

In the literature, there are numerous examples of homeland governments that are interested in creating a diaspora abroad as leverage in hostland policymaking processes. Therefore, diasporas are not simply a product of hostland elites but can be the result of homeland government efforts (Bauböck, 2010, p. 316), and homeland political actors might expect diaspora groups to lobby host country governments for their 'cause' (Østergaard-Nielsen, 2003, p. 211). The literature on homeland–diaspora relations touched on the homeland's involvement in diasporization; however, there is still a huge gap regarding how the homeland decides to mobilize which diaspora group in a certain hostland. As Harutyunyan (2012, p. 7) suggested: 'the diaspora–homeland relationship is often seen from the perspective of the so-called Solar System, where the diaspora is viewed as a periphery connected and belonging to one center, namely the homeland'. Yet the following questions remain. Which diaspora groups attract more attention from homeland actors? Does it relate to territorial proximity or bilateral relations between the homeland and the hostland? It is not within the scope of this paper to answer these questions. However, the case of the Turkish community in Sweden clearly shows that some diaspora groups attract more attention from homeland actors than others. For a very long time, the Turkish community in Sweden remained outside the scope of the Turkish state's diaspora formation project. Compared with other countries, such as Germany or the Netherlands where many homeland political actors actively seek to build transnational networks, we see the Turkish

migrants in Sweden suffering from the uneven distribution of attention of the Turkish policymakers (Baser, 2013).

The leading members of TUF and STRF mentioned that the consulate had a passive
policy with the Turkish community that started with the first wave of migration to
Sweden. They felt that Turkey abandoned them in Sweden and the embassy did not
work to sustain a strong connection. Some members expected the first mobilization initiatives to come from the embassy, while others argue that the organizations should take the
lead. However, drawing from the interviewee accounts, it is clear that especially during the
last decade, relations between the Turkish community and the Turkish Embassy improved.
There were also several significant official visits from Turkey. The prime minister, Tayyip
Erdoğan, visited Sweden in 2008 and held meetings with the leaders of Turkish associations. In his speech, Erdoğan emphasized the Swedish-Turks' duty to be involved in
Turkish politics because they had been granted voting rights in Turkey.[28] This kind of
encouragement increased after the genocide resolution and continues today. The vast
majority of the interviewees repeated their expectation of continued Turkish state
support and contact with Turkish authorities regarding their lobbying activities. Organizations such as STRF and TUF also visited Ankara to strengthen relations and to offer suggestions about how to lobby in Sweden. The foreign minister, Ahmet Davutoğlu, and the
minister responsible for Turks abroad, Faruk Çelik, met with those groups to discuss how
to organize better the Swedish-Turks in support of Turkey's accession to EU membership
and other political issues.[29] When President Abdullah Gul visited Sweden, he made a
speech addressing the Turkish migrants in Sweden. Referring to the Genocide Bill, he
ordered the Turkish diaspora members to take a more active role in Sweden with
regards to homeland-related politics:

> You should act like ambassadors of your motherland, Turkey, which you should rep-
> resent here in the best way. You should protect and defend Turkey's image, as there
> could be anti-Turkish propaganda. Turkey's realities are much more different from
> such propaganda indeed.[30]

These initiatives, however, have not yet met the expectations of the Turkish community.
Newly achieved, closer cooperation does not mean that the Turkish state suddenly turned
the immigrant organizations in Sweden into proxy actors in the hostland. Diasporization
projects by the homeland actors require further effort to achieve such a dramatic
change. In reality, it will be difficult for the homeland political actors to diffuse into the
already existing organizational structures. Therefore, the current mobilization in
Sweden is a call for collaboration from the diaspora elites to the homeland actors and it
might lead to a reciprocal bonding between the homeland and the diaspora. It is important
to note that the vast majority of diaspora elite members expressed their aim to build contingent alliances on certain issues, rather than taking direction from the Turkish Embassy
or homeland actors. The leaders of both STRF and TRF emphasized seeking 'partners not
patrons'.

Conclusion

The purpose of this paper was twofold: to enhance our theoretical knowledge on how
latent diasporas turn into active diasporas, while at the same time contributing to empirical

knowledge on the Turkish political mobilization in Sweden. It has argued that diasporic awareness can be triggered by political developments in the host country, despite the issues possibly relating to homeland politics. The second generation members of the transnational community can be affected by these developments, which could make them the forerunners of diasporic mobilization. Especially at times when their interests are at stake they may align themselves with home state institutions or import discourses from home country policymakers. Their political actions do not always focus on policy change in their home country but they may use homeland-related politics in the host country to influence host country politics.

Diasporic awareness does not evolve overnight but is the result of the accumulation of grievances and common interests over time. This, in combination with the elite members' strategies, can bring a community together for a collective aim. In the case of Sweden, the reactions of the Swedish-Turkish community were not against the Kurdish movement in Turkey per se, but to losing a discursive battle against the Kurdish diaspora in Sweden. In the same way, Turkish reactions to the Genocide Bill were not against the Armenian claims per se but mostly against the loss of prestige in the eyes of Swedish society. What concerned the Turkish first and second generations more was the consequences of this bill for their community and what it indicated about their status in comparison with other ethnic communities in Sweden. The passing of the Genocide Bill had a more enduring impact on the Turkish community because the Turkish community felt targeted and stigmatized by the parliament's decision. It marked community members seeing the issue of homeland politics as high priority for the first time. Consequently, it strengthened the Turkish community's pre-existing connection with Turkey. The Turkish community in Sweden presents several noticeable trends in displaying diasporic behaviour, such as having stronger ties with the Turkish Embassy and other political actors, forming lobbying strategies, and elite members' efforts to mobilize young people within the Turkish community. Diaspora nationalism is on the rise and it is the second generation who are taking the lead in converting a Turkish transnational migrant community into an active Turkish diaspora.

Notes

1. 'Isvec'teki Turkler Soykirim Yasasini Protesto Etti', *Hurriyet*, 11 March 2010, available online at: http://www.hurriyet.com.tr/dunya/14180087.asp?gid=200 (last accessed 23 January 2013).
2. 'Sweden to recognize the Armenian genocide', *The Local*, 11 March 2010, available online at: http://www.thelocal.se/25468/20100311/ (last accessed 23 January 2013).
3. 'Isvec'teki Turkler Soykirim Yasasini Protesto Etti', *Hurriyet*, 11 March 2010, available online at: http://www.hurriyet.com.tr/dunya/14180087.asp?gid=200 (last accessed 23 January 2013).
4. Interview with the former president of the Turkish Youth Association, June 2010.
5. The interviews were conducted in Sweden as part of the author's PhD research at the European University Institute in Florence, Italy, between 2008 and 2012. The article was written during her employment as a postdoctoral fellow, and member of the ERC Project 'Diasporas and Contested Sovereignty' at the University of Warwick between 2012 and 2013.
6. Kurdish groups were among the immigrants from Kulu. Today, some define themselves as Turkish and take part in the activities of the Turkish community, while others have rediscovered their Kurdish identity and joined the Kurdish political movement.
7. The Ministry of Labour and Social Security Official Website, available online at: http://www.csgb.gov.tr/csgbPortal/diyih.portal?page=yv&id=1#_ftn8 (last accessed 30 May 2012).
8. Interview with the president of the Turkish association and with the former president of the Turkish Youth Association, June 2010.

9. Interview with the president of the Turkish association, June 2010.
10. Author's observation of chat rooms and Turkish associations' web page discussions during and after the Gezi events in Turkey between June and December 2013.
11. The Grey Wolves are the youth branch of an ultranationalist political party, MHP, in Turkey. They are mobilized in several European countries and are occasionally involved in fights with Turkish leftist groups, PKK followers or neo-Nazis.
12. Interview with the president of the Turkish association and with the former president of the Turkish Youth Association, June 2010.
13. Sergels Torg is the central public square in Stockholm, Sweden, where many different groups organize protests.
14. www.anatolianvoice.blogspot.co.uk
15. 'Isvec ve Avusturya'da Terore Hayir Yuruyusu', *Milli Gazete*, 29 October 2007, available online at: http://www.milligazete.com.tr/haber/Isvec_ve_Avusturya39da_terore_hayir39_yuruyusu/59631#.UtVKchbbdUQ (last accessed December 2013).
16. 'Isvec'teki Turkler Teroru Protesto Etti', *Sabah*, 28 August 2011, available online at: http://www.sabah.com.tr/Gundem/2011/08/28/isvecteki-turkler-teroru-protesto-etti (last accessed December 2013).
17. 'Fakta Forum Turkiet Toplanti Cagrisi', available online at: http://www.tuf.nu/index.php?option=com_content&task=view&id=1263&Itemid=99999999&lang=tr (last accessed 23 January 2013).
18. *Yeni Birlik Magazines* can be reached via http://www.trf.nu/yenibirlik/
19. *Vizyon Magazine*, Speech of the leader of the Turkish Association in Gothenburg.
20. 'Sozde Soykirim Anitlari Yolda, Turkler Tepkili', available online at: http://www.tuf.nu/index.php?option=com_content&task=view&id=1498&Itemid=1203 (last accessed 23 January 2013).
21. 'Vad hände 1915?', available online at: http://gazete.se/index/index.php/Fragor-Svar/vad-haende-1915.html (last accessed 23 January 2013).
22. *Harbi Gazete*, available online at: http://www.harbigazete.com/haberler/soykirim/ (last accessed 23 December 2013).
23. 'Sorunlarimizin Ustesinden Gelmenin Tek Yolu Birlik Olmak', TRF website, available online at: http://www.trf.nu/sorunlarimizin-ustesinden-gelmenin-tek-yolu-birlik-olmak.html (last accessed 13 January 2014).
24. 'İsveçli Türkler Avrupa Parlamentosu'nda Türkiye'nin önemini anlattılar', available online at: http://www.tuf.nu/index.php?option=com_content&task=view&id=1728&Itemid=1203 (last accessed 23 January 2013).
25. 'İsveç Meclisi Siyah Çelenkle Protesto Edildi', available online at: http://www.trf.nu/isvec-meclisisiyah-celenkle-protesto-edildi.html (last accessed 23 January 2013).
26. 'Turkish diaspora accuses Sweden of double standards', available online at: http://news.az/articles/11350 (last accessed 23 December 2013).
27. 'Isvec Ucuncu Kez Protesto Edildi', *Harbi Gazete*, available online at: http://www.harbigazete.com/haber/795/isvec-3-kez-protesto-edildi.html (last accessed 23 December 2013).
28. 'Stockholm'de 23 Nisan Kutlamasi', available online at: http://www.kuluhaber.net/haber_detay.asp?haberID=170 (last accessed 23 January 2013).
29. *Vizyon Magazine*, page 24.
30. Presidency of the Republic of Turkey Official Webpage, available online at: http://www.tccb.gov.tr/news/397/85377/gul-pays-the-first-state-visit-from-turkey-to-sweden.html (last accessed December 2013).

References

Adamson, F. (2008) Constructing the diaspora: diaspora identity politics and transnational social movements. Paper presented at the *Annual Meeting of the ISA's 49th Annual Convention, Bridging Multiple Divides*, San Francisco Hilton, San Francisco, CA.

Adamson, F. (2012) Constructing the diaspora: diaspora identity politics and transnational social movements, in: *Politics from Afar: Transnational Diasporas and Networks* (New York: Columbia University Press).

Akin, A. (2006) Ethnic Minority Media from Producers' perspective: Case of Turkish Broadcasts in Swedish Public Service Radio (SR), Masters' Thesis for Journalism Masters' Programme, JMK, Stockholm University.

Akis, Y. & Kalaylioglu M. (2010) Turkish Associations in Metropolitan Stockholm: Organizational Differentiation and Socio-political Participation of Turkish Immigrants, *Working Paper No. 5*, The Stockholm University Linnaeus Centre for Integration Studies.

Baser, B. (2012) Inherited Conflicts: Spaces of Contention between the Turkish and Kurdish Second-generation Diasporas in Sweden and Germany, PhD Thesis, European University Institute, Italy.

Baser, B. (2013) *Diasporada Turk–Kurt Sorunu: Isvec ve Almanya'da Ikinci Kusak* (Istanbul: Iletisim Yayinlari).

Bauböck, R. (2010) Cold constellations and hot identities: political theory questions about transnationalism and diaspora, in: R. Bauböck & T. Faist (Eds), *Diaspora and Transnationalism: Concepts, Theories and Methods*, pp. 295–322 (Amsterdam: Amsterdam University Press).

Brinkerhoff, J. (2008) Exploring the role of diasporas in rebuilding governance in post-conflict societies, in: R. Bardouille, M. Ndulo & M. Grieco (Eds), *Africa's Finances: The Contribution of Remittances*, pp. 239–262 (Newcastle upon Tyne: Cambridge Scholars Publishing).

Brinkerhoff, J. (2009) *Digital Diasporas: Identity and Transnational Engagement* (New York: Cambridge University Press).

Brubaker, R. (2005) The 'diaspora' diaspora, *Ethnic and Racial Studies*, 28(1), pp. 1–19.

Butler, K.D. (2001) Defining diaspora, refining a discourse, *Diaspora*, 10(2), pp. 189–219.

Demmers, J. (2007) New wars and diasporas: suggestions for research and policy, *Journal of Peace, Conflict and Development*, 11, pp. 1–26.

Faist, T. (2004) Towards a political sociology of transnationalization: the state of the art in migration research, *European Journal of Sociology*, 45(3), pp. 331–366.

Glick-Schiller, N. (2004) Long distance nationalism, in: M. Ember, C.R. Ember & I. Skoggard (Eds), *Encyclopaedia of Diasporas: Immigrant and Refugee Cultures around the World*, Vol. I: Overviews and Topics; Vol. II: Diaspora Communities, XXXII. New York: Kluwer Academic/ Plenum Publishers.

Harutyunyan, A. (2012) Challenging the Theory of Diaspora from the Field, *Working Papers des Sonderforschungsbereiches 640, Nr. 1/2012*, Humboldt University.

Kenny, J. (1998) Mobilizing diasporas in nationalist conflicts. Comparing American immigrant groups, 1870–1920. Paper prepared for presentation at the *CASPIC MacArthur Scholars' Conference*, Wilder House, Chicago, IL, 17–18 January.

Koopmans, R. & Statham, P. (2001) How national citizenship shapes transnationalism: a comparative analysis of migrant claims-making in Germany, Great Britain and the Netherlands, *Revue Européenne de Migrations Internationales*, 17(2), pp. 63–100.

Levitt, P. & Waters, M.C. (2002) *The Changing Face of Home: The Transnational Lives of the Second Generation* (New York: Russell Sage Publications).

Lyons, T. & Mandaville, P. (2010a) Diasporas in global politics, *Policy Brief*, George Mason University, Centre for Global Studies.

Lyons, T. & Mandaville, P. (2010b) Think locally, act globally: toward a transnational comparative politics, *International Political Sociology*, 4, pp. 124–141.

Nell, L.M. (2008) Transnational Migrant Politics in the Netherlands: Historical Structures and Current Events, PhD Thesis, University of Amsterdam.

Ögelman, N., Money, J. & Martin, P.L. (2002) Immigrant cohesion and political access in influencing host country foreign policy, *SAIS Review*, 22(2), pp. 145–165.

Østergaard-Nielsen, E. (2003) *Transnational Politics: Turks and Kurds in Germany* (London and New York: Routledge).

Perlmann, J. (2002) Second-generation transnationalism, in: P. Levitt & M.C. Waters (Eds), *The Changing Face of Home: The Transnational Lives of the Second-Generation*, pp. 216–220 (New York: Russell Sage).

Portes, A. & Rumbaut, R.G. (2001) *Legacies: The Story of the Immigrant Second Generation* (Berkeley: University of California Press).

Safran, W. (2007) Concepts, theories, and challenges of diaspora: a panoptic approach. Prepared for presentation at the workshop on *Dispersione, Globalizzazione e Costruzione dell'alterità: Diaspore et Migrazioni nel Bacino del Mediterraneo et Oltre*, xix–xx secc., sponsored by University of Pisa, Department of History, Marsala, Italy.

Saideman, S.M., Jenne, E.K. & Cunningham, K. (2011) Diagnosing diasporas: understanding the conditions fostering or blocking mobilization, preliminary analyses. Paper prepared for presentation at the *Annual Meeting of the American Political Science Association*, Seattle, Washington, 31 August–4 September.

Shain, Y. & Barth, A. (2003) Diasporas and international relations theory, *International Organization*, 57(3), pp. 449–479.

Sheffer, G. (2003) *Diaspora Politics: At Home Abroad* (Cambridge: Cambridge University Press).
Sökefeld, M. (2006) Mobilizing in transnational space: a social movement approach to the formation of diaspora, *Global Networks*, 6, pp. 265–284.
Van Bruinessen, M. (1999) The Kurds in Movement: Migrations, Mobilisations, Communications and the Globalisation of the Kurdish Question, *Working Paper No. 14*, Islamic Area Studies Project, Tokyo, Japan.
Westin, C. (2003) Young people of migrant origin in Sweden, *International Migration Review*, 37(4), pp. 987–1,010.

Ethnopolitics, 2014
Vol. 13, No. 4, 377–395, http://dx.doi.org/10.1080/17449057.2014.896571

Shifting Dynamics of the Insurgency and Counter-insurgency in the North Caucasus

ROLAND DANNREUTHER

University of Westminster, London, UK

ABSTRACT   This paper seeks to provide an explanation of the shifts and trends in the insurgency and Russian counter-insurgency strategy in the North Caucasus. The article first identifies the multiple factors that initially contributed to the radicalization and Islamization of the conflict in Chechnya and how this fostered increased instability in the North Caucasus by the late 1990s, representing a serious threat to the security and integrity of the Russian state. The subsequent section sets out how the incoming prime minister and then president Vladimir Putin seized on the growing crisis in the North Caucasus to develop and refine a new strategy that not only gained the support of the general Russian public, but also was a critical factor in cementing his personal popularity. The strategy also had some notable successes, not least in the relative pacification of Chechnya and the start of the reconstruction of the war-damaged republic. However, the strategy also had its less successful and more negative consequences, which have revived and changed the nature of the insurgency towards a more Islamist and diffuse character and presented new challenges for Russia's counter-insurgency strategy. The final section makes a division between the social, economic and political factors and the religious and ideological factors that are driving the insurgency and argues that greater weight should be accorded to the religious and ideological factors than is often accorded by analysts.

Introduction

In October 2007, Doku Umarov, the Emir and President of the Chechen Republic of Ichkeriya, announced the formation of the Islamic Emirate of the North Caucasus.[1] This declaration, which signalled a significant shift in strategic objectives from a Chechen national liberation struggle to a pan-Caucasian struggle for an Islamist state, represented the culmination of two trends. The first is the long-term and gradual shift from an ethnonationalist and secular struggle in the Chechen Republic in the early 1990s to a military confrontation with an increasingly Islamo-nationalist Chechen dimension in the latter part of 1990s, and then in the 2000s to the growing domination of radical Islamist jihadists who reject ethnic affiliation as anti-Islamic and who promote a generalized jihad linking the struggles in the North Caucasus with those in Iraq, Afghanistan, Somalia and Palestine. The insurgency has thus

Correspondence Address: Roland Dannreuther, University of Westminster, 309 Regent Street, London W1B 2HW. Email: R.Dannreuther@westminster.ac.uk

© 2014 The Editor of Ethnopolitics

shifted increasingly over the two decades from a particularist nationalist to a more general-ized Islamist conflict or, as in Olivier Roy's (2004) terms, from an Islamo-nationalist to a neo-fundamentalist struggle. The second long-term trend is the shift of the locus of the con-flict from Chechnya to its neighbouring North Caucasus republics. During most of the 1990s and 2000s, the conflict was centred on Chechnya and the other North Caucasus republics remained generally loyal to Moscow and the political situation was reasonably stable. However, by the late 2000s it was Chechnya which was notably more quiet and conflict-free than its immediate neighbouring republics of Dagestan, Ingushetiya and Kabardino-Balkaria. In 2012, it is estimated that of the 571 attacks perpetrated during this period, almost two-thirds of these were in Dagestan, resulting in 3003 killed and 478 wounded, with Kabardino-Balkaria and Ingushetiya as the next most conflict-ridden republics and with Chechnya being the relative laggard (Hahn, 2013). It is thus now Dagestan, not Chech-nya, which is the epicentre of the insurgency in the North Caucasus (Hahn, 2013).

This article seeks to provide an explanation of these shifts and trends in the insurgency and Russian counter-insurgency strategy in the North Caucasus. The following section identifies the multiple factors that initially contributed to the radicalization and Islamiza-tion of the conflict in Chechnya and how this fostered, by the late 1990s, increased instabil-ity in the North Caucasus, representing a serious threat to the security and integrity of the Russian state. The subsequent section sets out how the incoming prime minister and then president Vladimir Putin seized on the growing crisis in the North Caucasus to develop and refine a new counter-insurgency strategy that not only gained the support of the general Russian public, but also was a critical factor in cementing his personal popularity. The strategy also had some notable successes, not least in the relative pacification of Chechnya and the start of the reconstruction of the war-damaged republic. However, the strategy also had its less successful and more negative consequences that have revived and changed the nature of the insurgency towards its more Islamist and diffuse character and presented new dilemmas for determining a countervailing strategy. The final section makes a division between the social, economic and political factors and the religious and ideological factors that are driving the insurgency and argues that greater weight should be accorded to the religious and ideological factors than is often accorded by analysts.

Separating these differing factors in such a way is not to deny the need to incorporate multicausality when understanding such a complex phenomenon as the insurgency in the North Caucasus. Neither strictly material and political factors nor religious and ideational factors are sufficient explanatory variables on their own and it is a combination of such factors that is necessary to provide an overarching explanatory framework. There is also inevitably certain artificiality in separating material and ideational causes from each other. Nevertheless, there is a tendency in the policy and academic literature to place greater causal weight on material and political factors for explaining the continued conflict, most notably through highlighting the corrosive mix of economic poverty, perva-sive corruption, ethnonational and clannish politics, and the Kremlin's centralizing dynamics for understanding the root causes of the conflict. Relatively less attention is given to the primarily intra-Caucasian religio-theological struggle over what it means to be a loyal and true Muslim and which has increasingly split apart not only religious believ-ers and communities but also different generations and ethnic groups, and even has divided families among the peoples of the North Caucasus. It is, though, this religio-theological struggle over the very identity of the modern North Caucasus, and where the issue of Russian control is almost a secondary issue, which gives the insurgency its particular dynamic and durability and which makes it particularly problematic for Moscow to resolve.

Chechnya and Islamic Radicalization in the 1990s

The North Caucasus has always been one of the most conflictual and problematic regions for Russia, even though there has been almost continual contact and engagement between Russia and the region since the sixteenth century.[2] It was in the nineteenth century that the conflict became most intense as Russia expanded southwards so as to contain Ottoman and Persian imperial penetration into the Caucasus. In the early nineteenth century, loyal Russian protectorates were established in the southern Caucasus, in modern day Georgia, Armenia and Azerbaijan, which generally involved existing rulers of well-established polities shifting their allegiance to Moscow. However, there were no such established political institutions in the regions north of the Caucasus mountains owing to the cultural and social fragmentation of the inhospitable highland territory. As a consequence, there were frequent local challenges to the leaders promoted by Moscow, which resulted in Russian forces being involved in the ensuing civil wars, the most notable being the extensive guerrilla campaign by the highland leader Imam Shamil, which continued from the early 1830s until his capture in 1859 and which eventually petered out in the mid-1860s.[3]

There are two features of this military confrontation that have provided a lasting legacy. The first is the collective memory of the brutality of the wars where Russian forces adopted tactics such as punitive raids, the destruction of villages thought to be harbouring the guerrillas and the clearing and destruction of much of the forests, hills and upland villages where the highlanders found sanctuary (King, 2008, pp. 73–77).[4] The cruelty inflicted by the Russian forces was as often matched by the reprisals of the North Caucasus rebels. Among Russians, the perception that the peoples of the North Caucasus are unreliable and potentially treacherous has remained a continuing theme. In the 1920s, Bolsheviks engaged in a brutal campaign to subjugate resistance in Chechnya and in other parts of the Caucasus. During World War II, almost half a million people from the North Caucasus were forcibly deported to Central Asia, including Chechens, Ingush, Balkars and Karachais. To the present day, the Russian hostility and discrimination to Caucasians are rooted in a deeply embedded fear of the 'alien' or 'other' as an internal threat (Moore, 2006). For many Caucasians, such hostility only entrenches a sense of Russia's continuing traditions of brutality and repression.

The second legacy is the central role played by Islam as a mobilizing and unifying ideology to bring together the various communities in the North Caucasus into an effective resistance force. Shamil was himself a Sufi adherent of the Naqshbandi-Khalidi *tariqa* and his fighting forces were not only inspired by but also socially connected through the Naqshbandi Sufi networks. Sufism and Islam did, in this way, provide a vital ideological and resource for the uprisings. There is, though, an extensive academic debate about whether Sufism provided, in itself, a consistent and continuing source of anti-Russian opposition in the North Caucasus or whether the connection was more incidental and that Sufi shaykhs could support collaboration as much as resistance.[5] However, what is certainly the case is that Shamil's principal identity was as a committed Muslim whose mission was as much to bring other Muslims in the North Caucasus back to a strict interpretation of the Qur'an and to the full imposition of *shari'a* law as to resist

Russian imperial penetration (Kemper, 2002). As King (2008, p. 82) notes, the 'fight against the Russians appears as a by-product of the struggle to purify Islam'. This has a significant resonance with the contemporary Islamist insurgency where, as with Shamil, the concern is as much with *munafiqs* (those Muslims who collaborate with non-Muslims) as with *kafirs* (non-Muslims).[6]

Despite this history of conflict, brutality and Islamic-inspired resistance, there was no inevitability that these 'ancient grievances' would lead to a brutal war in Chechnya after the break-up of the Soviet Union. Nationalities in the Caucasus other than the Chechens who had similar histories of Russian injustice and oppression and could also be expected to have seized the opportunity for secession, such as the Circassians or the Ingush or the Dagestanis, remained loyal to the post-Soviet Russian Federation. Chechnya was, in this sense, the exception rather than the rule in the North Caucasus. Moreover, the declaration of the independence of the Chechen Republic of Ichkeria in 1991 by Jokhar Dudayev was only following a precedent that had been set in various parts of the Soviet Union from Lithuania to Georgia. Within the Russian Federation, Chechnya's demands were not significantly different from those made in Tatarstan. Dudaev was also initially committed to the development of a secular state, as he made clear when he warned that 'if religion takes priority over an institutional secular system, a more striking form of the Spanish inquisition and Islamic fundamentalism will emerge' (*Literaturnaya gazeta*, 12 August 1992).

What then transformed Chechnya's far from unusual claim, in the context of the collapse of the Soviet Union, for sovereignty and independence into a violent bloody conflict was primarily the consequences of the decision of Yeltsin and his coterie of advisers to wage war and not negotiate with the Chechens in 1994. There was no inevitable 'clash of civilisations'. It was, in particular, the brutality of the war and the indiscriminate tactics used by the Russian forces, most notably the bombing of civilian targets in Chechnya and the wide-scale destruction and suffering that this caused, which radicalized the Chechens behind an anti-Russian nationalism that inevitably incorporated a strong Islamic dimension.[7] During the first Chechen war from 1994 to 1996, Islam was principally a unifying force against a clearly defined enemy. It was the Sufi Mufti of Chechnya, Akhmad Kadyrov, who legitimated the call for *gazawat* or jihad against the Russian forces in 1995 and there was a significant degree of common purpose between Sufi and more radical Islamic orientations.

It was the aftermath of the first Chechen war that resulted in the fragmentation of the Chechen resistance, increasing divergences between differing Islamist identities, and spreading the growth of Islamist radicalism beyond the North Caucasus. There were three main factors behind this. First, there were the growing political divisions within the Chechen insurgency, which were in part due to the very success of the insurgency securing a humiliating withdrawal of Russian forces from Grozny and negotiating an agreement at Khasavyurt in 1996 that gave the Chechen republic de facto independence. The subsequent presidential election in 1997 was won by Aslan Maskhadov, a moderate nationalist, who, however, defeated the more radical and militant Shamil Basayev (Sokirianskaia, 2008, pp. 118–119). Basayev's disappointment with this result led him to assume a more radical salafist Islamist position, gathering together a loose and complex alliance of Chechen Islamist ideologues, such as Zelimkhan Yandarbiev and Movladi Udugov, militant warlords such as Salman Raduyev and Arbi Barayev, and foreign jihadis associated with Shaykh Ali Fathi al-Shishani, such as al-Khattab and Abu Walid (Moore & Tumelty, 2009). The failure of Maskhadov to counter the growing influence of a stricter Salafist movement, with its links to foreign Islamist groups, only led to alienating more traditionalist and Sufi-oriented Chechens. As Sokirianskaia notes, it was in 1997 that Ahmad Kadyrov, the Mufti of Chechnya who had previously supported the jihad, decisively shifted against the new government and towards Russia, due to the fear of the growing radical islamization and instability inside Chechnya (Sokirianskaia, 2008, pp. 123–124).

The second factor was how developments in Dagestan increasingly influenced and affected developments in Chechnya, particularly in terms of the broader phenomenon of the radicalization of the anti-Russian opposition. Part of this was undoubtedly due to the influence of foreign fighters and foreign influences as the Chechen war brought the North Caucasus to the attention of the wider Muslim world and the war becoming part of the 'landscape of global jihad', to use Faisal Devji's phrase (Devji, 2005). However, the internal roots of radicalization are more significant than these foreign connections.[8] The search for a more pure and radical Islam, challenging existing practices in the Caucasus, had even existed in the Soviet period and was wrongly identified by the security forces at that time as 'Wahhabism' as this current of religious thought was part of a longer indigenous inter-Muslim debate rather than a Saudi ideological import.[9] In the context of the disintegration of the Soviet Union, it was in Dagestan and particularly through the figure of Akhmad Akhtaev that an alternative and more radical form of Islam challenged the Sufi-dominated traditionalist approach. In terms of Islamist movements, Akhtaev was closer ideologically to the Muslim Brotherhood than to Saudi-inspired Wahhabism and articulated the need for Islam, purified from such deviations as Sufism and other traditionalist practices, to promote the economic modernization of Dagestan and the region more generally. His version of an Islamic regeneration was, though, moderate in the sense that it did not involve the call for jihad against Russia and he believed that this transformation needed to be pursued through existing political structures and institutions (Ware & Kisriev, 2010, pp. 96–97).

It was the suspicious death of Akhtaev in 1998 that brought an end to the moderate and more cerebral form of political Islam. His place was taken up by Bagauddin Kebedov, who had been ally of Akhtaev in the early 1990s but increasingly began to compete with him through adopting more hard line and uncompromising stances. On one occasion, he claimed that Sufism deviated from *shari'a* law in over 100 places (Makarov, 2000, p. 15).[10] He violently opposed any form of cooperation or compromise with officials in Dagestan, was fiercely hostile towards Russia and sought to create an Islamic state that would span all of the Caucasus. In the process, he not only alienated the Sufi-influenced traditionalist Muslim authorities in Dagestan but also empowered these traditionalists against the more secularist state officials, adding a further set of social cleavages (Gammer, 2008, pp. 187–188). He also inspired and oversaw the rise of an Islamic 'jamaat' in his home village of Kadar and the neighbouring villages of Karamakhi and Chabanmakhi. This generated a series of increasingly violent conflicts between the so-called 'Wahhabis' and the traditionalists in these villages, which succeeded in effectively excluding the secular authorities from the region, making it a de facto autonomous zone from 1996 to 1999 (Bobrovnikov, 2006). After his party and his activities had been banned in 1997, Kebedov fled to Chechnya, where he was welcomed by the local warlords and politicians, most notably Shamil Basayev, Zelimkhan Yandarbiev, Movladi Udugov and al-Khattab.

The third factor was the result of the joining of Salafist forces from both Chechnya and Dagestan and the increasing orientation away from the limited goal of the liberation of Chechnya to the more utopian ambition of the construction of an Islamic emirate in all of the North Caucasus. As such, Kebedov's collaboration and incorporation with the Chechen militants provided the context for an ambitious attempt to spread radical Islam throughout the region. In November 1998 there was the institutional unification of the Dagestani and Chechen radical Islamists through the formation of the Congress of the Peoples of Ichkeria and Dagestan, headed by Shamil Basayev (Souleimanov, 2005, p. 53). The following year in August 1999 there was the fateful invasion of Dagestan by about 2,000 insurgents led by Shamil Basyaev and Emir al-Khattab. The aim was inspired by Basayev's earlier open proclamation of the need for 'the formation of an independent Islamic state in the range of Chechnya and Dagestan' (Ware & Kisriev, 2010, p. 122). As such, the insurgency had now shifted decisively towards a more radical programme with a pan-Caucasian range coalescing around a radical Salafist ideology, which, however, also intensified and magnified intra-Caucasian divisions and cleavages (Moore, 2012, p. 1,789).

Putin's Strategy towards the North Caucasus and Islamic Radicalization

These developments in the North Caucasus coincided with the rise of Vladimir Putin from political obscurity to first prime minister in 1999 and then to president in 2000. Putin seized upon the opportunity of the increasingly serious and threatening situation emanating from the North Caucasus to cement his reputation and to ensure his enduring legitimacy and popularity. When he first came to power, he stressed that 'my mission, my historic mission—it sounds pompous but it is true—is to resolve the situation in the North Caucasus' (Gevorkan et al., 2000, p. 133). It is no overestimation to say that the North Caucasus in many ways defined and moulded Putin's presidency and that his democratic legitimacy was 'forged in war' (Rutland, 2000, p. 326). The underlying reason for this was that it was now evident, not just to those in the Kremlin but also to the wider Russian public, that the security situation in the North Caucasus was extremely serious and potentially threatened the very integrity of the Russian state. Chechnya had become a lawless territory, rife with criminality, violent conflict and hijackings, and, like Afghanistan, a breeding ground for Islamist jihadists and terrorists. The armed intervention into Dagestan by Chechen militants under Basayev's command demonstrated clearly the potential threat to the stability of the wider North Caucasus. For the more general Russian public, the sense of threat increased dramatically with the succession of bomb attacks on apartment blocks in Russian cities in September 1999, which caused over 300 deaths. This had a traumatic impact on Russians, not unlike that felt by the Americans after 9/11.[11]

Putin's strategies for dealing with the threat of Islamic radicalization and the associated threat of terrorism evolved over time, but the initial response was one of the demonstrative use of political power and military might. A second Chechen war was initiated in 1999 and, as against the perceived constant meddling of politicians in the Yeltsin period, Putin gave the military carte blanche to conduct the war in order to bring decisive victory. Compared with the occasionally tragicomic evolution of the first war, the second campaign was far more professional and effective.[12] The more assertive strategy was also evident in the position towards negotiations where a constant mantra was that there would be no negotiation with 'terrorists'. This set new rules for dealing with major terrorist incidents. In the response to the terrorist hostage crises in Budennovsk in 1995 and Kizlyar in 1996, the image of leading government figures negotiating with hostage-takers, agreeing to their demands and even facilitating their escape presented an image of a Russia abjectly humiliated. When Putin was confronted with similar challenges, most notably the hostage crises in the Moscow 'Dubrovka' theatre in 2002 and in Beslan in 2004, he brooked no negotiation and was willing to use deadly force (toxic gas in Moscow, flame-throwers in Beslan) to end the sieges, even at the cost of substantial loss of innocent life.

The political counterpart to this military campaign involved a much stronger assertion of the power of the federal centre and of the state more generally. The situation in the North Caucasus was presented as the extreme manifestation of the larger problems facing post-Soviet Russia and the particular legacy of the Yeltsin period—the threat of disintegration, the perceived penetration and subversion by foreign forces, the weakening of state structures as a result of criminality and terror, and Russia's basic inability to stand up for itself and its core national interests. The sense that this had, in part, been caused by the excessive federalization of power resulted in a number of measures to reassert control from the Kremlin. This included the establishment of super-regions or Federal Districts, with appointments made by the centre and which included the creation of the Southern Federal District and the appointment of the senior military figure, General Viktor Kazantsev (2000–2004), who had led the federal responses to the invasions of Dagestan in 1999. Republican laws and constitutions were enjoined to conform to federal laws and constitutions, which undermined some of the more creative legal and political adaptations to the ethnic and confessional particularities of the region, such as the multi-ethnic constitution of Dagestan. The link between insecurity in the North Caucasus and the legitimation of the recentralization of power was made most explicitly with the decision, after the hostage crisis in Beslan in 2004, to abolish direct election for subnational regional and republican leaders and reimpose a system of presidential appointment.

Military repression and the centralization of power did not, though, prove sufficient in resolving the situation in Chechnya. In practice, Putin gave the military free license up until the 2002 Moscow theatre siege, when it became clear that the Russian military would not be capable of overcoming the terrorist threat on its own and that the Chechen crisis could potentially spill over into an ever-broader terrorist campaign (Baev, 2005, p. 123). He realized that there was now a need to pursue a parallel political path, seeking to localize or de-internationalize the conflict through gaining a genuinely pro-Russian support base within Chechnya. This would involve, against the wishes of the military, devolution of both political and security responsibilities to the Chechens themselves, including those who could be tempted to switch sides from the rebels. To promote this, the Putin administration astutely chose Akhmad Kadyrov, the former Mufti of Chechnya, as the designated pro-Russian leader in June 2000 and who, as stated above, had earlier supported the resistance and even proclaimed a 'holy war' against Russia (Russell, 2007, p. 59). Kadyrov represented a significant coup not only because of the significance of his clan network but also because his co-option represented a significant schism in the Islamist opposition between the Sufi-influenced traditionalists and the increasingly intolerant salafist and radical extremists (Sokirianskaia, 2008, pp. 124–135). As Chechnya gained in stability, federal forces were gradually reduced, and local armed formations loyal to the Kadyrov clan were given increasing power, including taking control of a number of informal but lucrative economic resources.[13] With the assassination of Akhmad Kadyrov in 2004, power was increasingly devolved to his son, Ramzan, who was finally appointed president in 2007 (Baev, 2006, p. 2).

There are two other significant strands of Putin's strategy that were more generally directed to Russia's Muslim communities throughout Russia but which have also had a direct impact on Chechnya and the North Caucasus. The first was to end the laissez-faire policy of the Yeltsin period when foreign Muslim organizations had little difficulty in pursuing their work in Russia. Various foreign state-supported and private charities, such as al-Haramyan al-Sharifayn, al-Iqra'a and al-Igasa, were closed down.[14] Anti-terrorist legislation established, as in the US, a list of prohibited organizations, which included bodies such as the Muslim Brotherhood. More comprehensive anti-extremist legislation extended the field of surveillance and created a list of prohibited books. However, these more restrictive and exclusionary policies were counterbalanced by more active and interventionist support for the official 'loyal' Russian Muslim establishment. In contrast to the position of neutrality and neglect of the religious sphere during the Yeltsin period, the Putin administration provided direct financial support for Russia's Muslims, most notably through the Fund for Islamic Culture and Education, which has provided financial support for mosque building, the training of Imams, Muslim education and Islamic scholarship (Idrisov, 2007, pp. 6–8). Much of this support was directed through the established Muslim institutions, which tend to be loyal to Russia and traditionalist in doctrinal terms, and this significantly increased their financial strength and their social and political influence. This has given them a strengthened advantage in relation to the more radical salafist groups as well as all other Muslim groups that do not recognize the authority of the official established Muslim hierarchy.

The final strand of the more general strategy that Putin has adopted has been to develop a new 'national idea', replacing what was perceived to be the failure of liberal ideology in the 1990s, but which seeks to be inclusive of the indigenous Muslim communities and their interests. Naturally, for many Muslims, as with other minorities in Russia, there was concern that a quest for a new national conception could potentially lead to an assertion of an exclusive ethnic Russian nationalism. The Russian leadership has sought to counter any such dynamic by developing a national idea which, while being more conservative than liberal, is relatively moderate, promoting modernization, secularism, pragmatism and a civic nationalism rather than an ethnic or cultural heritage. There has been a conscious effort to excise the word *Russkii* (ethnic Russian) from official use in deference to Russian multinationality. For Putin, the 'Russian idea' is *Rossiiskaya* rather than *Russkaya* (March, 2012). The official doctrine is more statist rather than nationalist and this is evident in the conception of 'sovereign democracy', which was strongly supported in the late 2000s.[15] It is not a doctrine that privileges any one ethnic, national or religious group over another within Russia—what it does privilege is the authority and primacy of the state (March, 2012).

For Muslims in Russia, including those from the North Caucasus, the promotion of a Russian national idea, which maintains a certain uniqueness and distance from the West, has generally been welcomed, particularly if it helps to distance Russia from an exclusively European and Christian identity. The development of more assertive and ambitious Russian foreign policy towards the Middle East and the broader Muslim world has also helped to develop internal Muslim support. Under Putin, there has been a rapprochement with a wide array of Middle East countries, such as Turkey, Saudi Arabia and other Gulf states, which has re-established Russia's reputation in the region. The Russian government has also been willing to distance its Middle East policy from the West by, for example, dealing with Hamas and Hizbullah and by supporting the

Asad regime in Syria. Putin has even gone so far as to say that Russia is, in part, a 'Muslim country' (Makarenko, 2003). The decision in 2005 to accept Russia as an observer member of the Organization of Islamic Conference pleasantly surprised many Muslims in Russia, as it was believed that such a move was unlikely given the resistance of the Russian Orthodox Church. Through these various diplomatic moves, Putin succeeded to some extent in both defusing the hostility of the external Muslim world to Russian policies in the North Caucasus and increasing the sense of loyalty and inclusion of many Russian Muslims.

Understanding the Resurgence of the Islamist Insurgency

Yet, despite all these measures undertaken by Putin and the hubristic claims made during the parliamentary and presidential elections in 2007/8 that 'the war in Chechnya has ended ... we won', the insurgency has not been quelled (Markov, 2007). There had been a significant lull after 2004 after five years of a succession of waves of terrorist attacks, culminating in the large-scale terrorist attacks with the Nord Ost theatre siege in 2002 and the Beslan school siege in 2004 (Moore, 2012). But this was rudely interrupted in 2010 when two female suicide bombers from Dagestan blew themselves up in two Moscow metro stations, Park Kultury and Lubyanka, and killed 37 people (*The Economist*, 2010).

In the North Caucasus, the relative stability in Chechnya, which resulted in the official end of the 10-year 'counterterrorist operation' in the republic in April 2009, only appeared to disperse the conflict to other parts of the North Caucasus. From 2007 onwards, Ingushetiya became a serious site of violent conflict, with multiple attacks on law enforcement and government officials which targeted the widely reviled administration of President Murat Zyazikov, who was seen among most Ingush as corrupt and ineffective (Tlisova, 2008). Even his replacement in 2008 by Yunus-Bek Yevkurov, who has a much less tainted reputation, failed to stop the attacks, one of which led to his severe wounding and near assassination in June 2009. Nevertheless, the more consensual approach adopted by Yevkurov did eventually produce some dividends, with a significant reduction in terrorist attacks in 2011 and 2012 (International Crisis Group, 2012, p. 5). A similar escalation of armed conflict also occurred in Dagestan, where the 'Shariat Jamaat' engaged in widespread attacks on Dagestani officials, which included the assassination of many leading officials, including the Interior Minister, Adilgerei Magomedtagirov, in May 2009.[16] The geographical scale of the insurgency in Dagestan also expanded, including cities such as Derbent, which had previously not been affected. In 2011 and in 2012 there was also an escalation of the number of Muslim Imams and leaders killed in Dagestan, with over 10 leading Muslim clerics killed in 2012, including the most revered Sufi religious leader in the country, Said-Affandi Chirkei. Moreover, the claims of pacifications of Chechnya were rudely disrupted by an attack on the Chechen parliament in 2010, which resulted in three being killed (*Nezavisimaya gazeta*, 20 October 2010). A series of attacks in Kabardino-Balkaria, which included one on the Baksan hydroelectric plant in July 2010, brought to an end a period of relative stability in that republic.[17] Deadly bombings in Stavropol in May 2010, which resulted in seven killed, and in Vladikavkaz in September, which resulted in 19 deaths, were only the most visible and serious of a widespread and diffuse insurgency in the North Caucasus and southern region.

The Socio-economic and Political Sources

It has thus been increasingly implausible for the Kremlin to claim that the 'war' in the North Caucasus has been decisively 'won'. After his inauguration in 2008, Dmitry Medvedev confirmed, much like his predecessor Vladimir Putin in 2000, that the North Caucasus represents 'the country's most serious domestic political problem' and that this was caused by 'terrorism and an unprecedented level of corruption and clannism' (Medvedev, 2009). Medvedev's focus on the underlying political and economic causes of the crisis in the region represented an advance on the earlier predisposition to see the sources of conflict emanating primarily from external foreign sources and international terrorism, which require only a military resolution. It is this more socio-economic approach to the problems of the region that contributed to the appointment in January 2010 of a relatively young businessman and former governor of Krasnoyarsk region, Aleksandr Khloponin, to the newly created North Caucasus Federal District, which was carved out of the earlier Southern Federal District. His designated task, supported as much by Putin as by Medvedev, was to resolve the crisis in the North Caucasus through economic development and modernization.[18] In September 2010, he announced a socio-economic development plan for the region through to 2025, which would seek to produce 400,000 new jobs and which would include a development fund of 600 billion roubles (Sokolov, 2010). In 2012, this was expanded into a proposal for a 2.5 trillion rouble development plan for the region, of which 90% of the funds would come from extra-budgetary sources and about 235 billion from the federal budget (Alexandrovna, 2012).

The socio-economic and political lens through which the new envoy, Khloponin, interprets the roots of the insurgency in the North Caucasus can be seen in his response to the terrorist attack in Stavropol in May 2010 (Mukhin & Bondarenko, 2010). He argued that:

> The overall situation in the North Caucasus today is similar to the one we had in Russia in the 1990s ... This includes turf wars, corrupt government officials participating in those wars and clashes between criminal groups. We went through all of this in the 1990s. We see that sometimes ethnic conflicts and terrorism are used as a cover for turf wars'.[19]

This focus on the violence-inducing effects of systemic corruption in the clannish politics of the North Caucasus is not new. It had also been the principal approach taken by an earlier presidential envoy to the region, Dmitry Kozak, whose frank analysis in a confidential report in 2005 identified socio-economic collapse, the unpopularity and corruption of elites and their transgressions on democratic practice as incubators for extremism and terrorism (Khinshtein, 2005). In relation to Dagestan, he saw the widespread corruption and the clannish operations of the elites as leading inevitably to growing instability and as a breeding ground for extremism. This view that the 'root causes' of the conflict and regional instability are economic and political is also a view corroborated by recent Western social scientific studies, based on surveys conducted in the region, primarily in Dagestan. Holland & O'Loughlin (2010, p. 298) conclude that, based on their fieldwork, it is the salience of the more 'prosaic concerns, associated with employment, political corruption, and organised criminal elements' rather than 'Islamism' that are the main drivers of radicalization in the region.[20]

There is undoubtedly considerable validity in focusing on the underlying socio-economic and political sources of regional conflict and instability. There is a clear correlation between the levels of poverty and deprivation in the different North Caucasus republics and the strength of the Islamist insurgency. Dagestan, Ingushetiya and Chechnya remain some of the poorest parts of the Russian Federation and have the highest levels of unemployment. While in 2010 unemployment in Russia averaged 8.5%, in Ingushetiya it reached 50%, in Chechnya 34% and in Dagestan 28% (*Vedomosti*, 19 August 2009). Youth unemployment was even higher at levels of 50% in Kabardino-Balkaria, 84% in Ingueshetiya and 79% in Chechnya (*Vedomosti*, 15 September 2010). It is not surprising with such very high levels of unemployment that the youth in these republics feel alienated and disillusioned. The situation is exacerbated by the relatively high demographic growth rates in the region, with Dagestan alone needing to create 70,000 new jobs each year. The resurgence in violence from 2008 onwards also clearly has some link with what one Russian commentator has called the end of the 'fat 2000s' when the generally positive economic situation was disrupted by the start of the economic crisis in 2008 (Surkhov, 2009). This has only worsened the economic situation, not only in the North Caucasus but also in other parts of Russia where many North Caucasians seek employment.

The economic crisis has also exposed people from the North Caucasus to another source of alienation and discrimination, the rising anti-Caucasian and anti-immigrant sentiments of the majority ethnic Russian population. Despite the official attempts to promote a multi-national rather than explicitly nationalist Russian idea, such as the officially sanctioned concept of 'sovereign democracy' discussed above, there has nevertheless been a rise of more xenophobic and chauvinistic sentiments in Russian society. Analysts have noticed an increase of support for the slogan 'Russia for the Russians', and an increase in anti-Caucasus and anti-Muslim feelings, which have been encouraged by stereotypical images of the Caucasus and radicalized Islam in the media and popular culture (Verkhovsky, 2008). One expression of this was the large-scale ultra-nationalist riots in Moscow in December 2010, which were explicitly targeted against people from the North Caucasus and which Medvedev termed 'nationalist pogroms' (Gorst & Belton, 2010). The nationalist-led campaign to 'Stop Feeding the Caucasus' has become increasingly popular and has gained resonance even among liberal groups, such as those protesting against the flawed parliamentary elections in late 2011 and in 2012. For people from the North Caucasus, who are actually Russian citizens rather than migrants such as those from Central Asia or the South Caucasus, the particularly high levels of discrimination that they encounter only strengthen their sense of exclusion from Russian civil society.[21]

In the North Caucasus itself, the salience of clan and ethnopolitical networks of power and privilege, and the corruption associated with this, is also undoubtedly a factor behind youth and more general social alienation. This is rooted in the traditional structures of power that emphasize the salience of ethnic and subnational clan divisions and loyalties. In comparative terms, the North Caucasus political culture fits the general pattern of neo-patrimonialism found in many Middle Eastern and Muslim countries. However, these primordial roots of ethnic and clan division should not be exaggerated. The networks of privilege are also a more recent product of the chaotic post-Soviet redistribution of economic and political resources that greatly accentuated the degree of economic and political inequality in the region. Much of the energy of elites in the region in the post-Soviet period has been directed at gaining access to, or capturing the 'rent' of, the subsidies provided by the federal centre to the region. During the 2000s, these have become notably more generous and substantial, estimated to be in the region of 800 billion roubles during the course of the decade. Of the 280 billion rouble budget for the North Caucasus in 2010, 180 billion came in the form of federal subsidies (*Vedemosti*, 20 October 2010). Much of the relentless inter-ethnic and inter-clan struggle for power is directed towards gaining access to these considerable funds and this is a major factor fuelling the systemic and widespread corruption throughout the region. The fact that the majority of the population signally fails to benefit from these resources, most notably the disenfranchised and unemployed youth of the region, is clearly an important factor in the dynamic of radicalization.

The difficulties that the more enlightened presidential envoys, such as Kozak and Khloponin, have had in rooting out these corrupt patronage networks reflect the limited instruments and mechanisms for political change available to them. Much as the search for an illiberal and authoritarian national idea has helped to fuel rather than overcome inter-ethnic and inter-confessional tensions, so Putin's mix of the recentralization of power and the devolution of responsibilities to loyal but authoritarian leaders in the North Caucasus has as often undermined as strengthened anti-corruption and good governance measures. The model of the radical devolution of power to one clan group and local leader in Chechnya, the so-called process of 'Chechenization', is not one that has been easily transportable to other parts of the region. An example of this is in Ingushetiya, where Putin oversaw the replacement of Ruslan Aushev in 2002 with Murat Zyazikov, principally because Aushev was seen to be too independent from Moscow. Zyazikov, with his background in the FSB, was supposed to give a stronger and more effective role to the federal security services in the tense republic, but his rule proved to be deeply divisive and ineffective and he was viewed popularly as being deeply corrupt. This only exacerbated the insurgency in the republic and it was evident to Dmitry Kozak that a new leader and change in elites was required. However, this was never sanctioned by Putin while he was president, given his personal imprimatur to the original appointment. It was only with Medvedev that the decision was made in 2008 to replace Zyazikov with the less corrupt and more capable Yunus-Bek Yevkurov.

The simple replacement of one leader with another, however, even if more capable and effective, is not in itself a sufficient cure for the political and socio-economic problems of the region. One problem is that the very act of changing leaderships generates a renewed bout of inter-elite competition as existing patronage networks are disrupted and those affected resist their potential loss of economic and political power. This is often exacerbated by the fact that less corrupt and more capable leaders, who might have good links with Moscow, often lack a rootedness in the complex clan and ethnic patterns of local power. As mentioned earlier, Yevkurov only narrowly escaped an assassination attempt, and a sign of the difficulties he has had in transforming the political culture of the republic is that he was forced to sack his whole government in October 2009 (Bilevskaya & Samarina, 2010).

A similar problem can be seen in Dagestan, where Mukhu Aliev replaced the discredited long-time President Magomedali Magamedov in 2006 and where Aliyev was generally recognized to be a 'principled, competent, highly intellectual, and extremely hardworking technocrat' (Ware & Kisriev, 2010, p. 201). But his period of rule proved to be a disappointment as his many political virtues failed to include the capacity and sensitivity to deal with the complex inter-ethnic manoeuvring that is required for successful conflict resolution in Dagestan. In February 2010, Aliyev was replaced by the previous leader's son,

Magomedsalam Magomedov, who was himself replaced by Ramzan Abdullatipov in 2013 after signally failing to quell the crisis in Dagestan. Even when a more capable leader is appointed, such as was the case in Kabardino Balkaria with the appointment of Arsen Kanokov in 2005, the federal authorities are often reluctant to accord all the powers necessary for him to manage the situation. In an interview after his reappointment in 2010, he complained about the fact that most of the security and law enforcement chiefs are responsible to Moscow rather than to himself and use their connections to the centre to be able to remain in office even if they are incompetent and corrupt. From his perspective, the problem is that the Kremlin 'puts us in charge of our regions and expect us to show good results, but they have taken away the means of control' (*Kommersant*, 2010).

The essential underlying problem is that the Russian government's own mode of governance, which has become markedly more authoritarian and illiberal during the 2000s, operates on a personalized, neopatrimonial and factional basis. It does not provide the political capacity or processes that could radically transform the deeply embedded clan and ethnic networks of patronage and corruption in the North Caucasus region. As such, despite the best efforts of more enlightened and liberal federal envoys and local leaders, the general public in the North Caucasus remains deeply disenchanted with the seeming endemic and systemic corruption and the exclusive hold of economic and political power by an unrepresentative and uncaring elite. This deep political disillusionment certainly contributes significantly to the dynamics of radicalization.

The Religious and Theological Sources

All of these economic and political factors—economic degradation and poverty, unemployment, corruption, criminality and clannish and ethnic politics—are undoubtedly sources of radicalization in the region and help to explain many of the underlying conditions for the enduring Islamist insurgency in the region. However, there is a danger in focusing on these material factors of underplaying the more strictly religious and theological causes that have contributed to the dynamics and evolution of the insurgency. It is important to keep in mind that the insurgency is an *Islamist* insurgency, which has a religio-theological set of goals, however ambiguous and indeterminate these might be in practice. The insurgency can also be seen as a part of a global phenomenon of Islamist rebellion and violence in other parts of the world. As in countries such as Iraq and other parts of the Middle East, the North Caucasus insurgency is replicating the pattern of a more diffuse, network-centric and politically more ambitious and less nationalistically defined set of goals and ambitions.[22] Much of the attraction for the youth of the North Caucasus, and it is primarily the younger generation who are joining the insurgency, is to be part of this global 'umma' with its call for radical and violent action against injustice (Yarlykapov, 2010, pp. 142–143). Sociologists who have studied the causes of radicalization, such as Olivier Roy, highlight the attraction of radical Islam for those who feel deeply alienated from the particularist religious and cultural identities that they have inherited (Roy, 2004). In the North Caucasus, the younger generation feel both alienated from Russia, due to the discrimination that they encounter from broader Russian society, and to the Sufi-diffused traditional Muslim identity of the older Soviet generation that they consider to be ignorant and 'impure'.

Clearly, the problems of unemployment and the injustices of the economic and political structures play a role in engendering the shift to a violent Islamist orientation. However, a critically important additional dimension is the sense among many young Muslims that they are denied religious freedom and are victims of a forceful suppression of their legitimate commitment to a pious Muslim identity. This suppression of alternative Muslim identities has been supported by the policy shift of the Russian government to supporting 'moderate' and loyal 'traditional' Russian Muslim leaders in their struggle with 'Wahhabism'. The problem is that there is no clear hierarchy of authority and legitimacy in Islam, unlike in the Orthodox or Catholic churches, so the determination of what constitutes orthodox/heterodox or legitimate/illegitimate Islamic doctrine and practice is always deeply contested. In the North Caucasus, there have historically been multiple and competing forms of 'traditionalist' and 'moderate' Islam, with the most significant cleavage between Sufi and non-Sufi approaches. In fact, one of the consequences of the intra-Muslim struggle to be accorded official recognition by the Russian state, and the financial and other support that comes with this, has been a certain radicalization of the traditionalist Muslim establishment with markedly less tolerant relations to both secular society and to any manifestation of radical Islam.[23]

The case of Dagestan provides a good example of how the actions and activities of the traditionalist Muslim hierarchy have contributed significantly to the radicalization of a number of Muslim youth in the republic. The dominant religious figure in the traditional Muslim establishment was the Sufi Shaykh Said-Affandi Chirkei, who was assassinated in August 2012 and whose funeral attracted over 100,000 people. His religious allies control the official Muslim institution, the Spiritual Directorate of Muslims of Dagestan (DUMD), and his *murids* (followers) can be found in many parts of the Republican government and administration.[24] Said-Affandi cannot, though, be considered to have uncontested religious authority as it is estimated that only a third of the mosques in the republic are under the control of the DUMD and there are many other Muslim leaders and Sufi shaykhs who refuse to accept his authority. Said-Affandi's divisiveness was accentuated further by his significant influence and control over government policy and his generally intolerant attitude to challenges to his religious authority.

Until recently, this was expressed through describing such opponents as 'Wahhabis' and 'extremists'. This was made government policy in 1999 when the Dagestan government legally proscribed Wahhabism. But, as there was no clear legal definition of what actually constitutes 'Wahhabism', it has been the official religious establishment, effectively controlled by Said-Affandi, that has had a principal role in identifying the 'Wahhabis' and authorizing the security services and law enforcement bodies to take drastic measures to eliminate them. Evidence of the highly charged and conflictual context can be seen in the statement of the former head of the DUMD, Said-Muhammad Abubarakov, that those who kill a Wahhabi will themselves be rewarded by paradise (Knysh, 2007, p. 516). In the last year of his life, Said-Affandi did moderate his unconditional hostility to any compromise with the Salafist opposition, at least the moderate elements within it, and supported a Sufi-Salafi dialogue. However, his assassination in August 2012 by those opposed to the dialogue, whether on the part of official or radical Islam, has only turned the general policy back towards repression and a general rejection of pluralism and diversity in religious expression.

It is this atmosphere of officially sanctioned religious intolerance, supported by the repressive activities of the security forces, which has had a significant impact on the radicalization of Muslim youth in Dagestan. One of the most significant developments of the post-Soviet period among Russian Muslims has been the emergence of a new religious Muslim intelligentsia who have been trained in Islamic thought and doctrine in major centres in Russia or in the Muslim world. These young intellectuals tend towards more universal conceptions of Islam, influenced by such figures as Yusuf al-Qaradawi and Tariq Ramadan, and are critical of the more local culturally suffused Islamic traditions, which they perceive as being heterodox and incorporating non-Islamic elements.[25] However, these young Muslim religious elites might be radical but are not necessarily extremist; but, if they find that their right to express these views are illegitimately denied, and that they and their followers are actively repressed, this can lead to radicalization and a shift to a more violent and jihadist stance.

There are a number of examples in the North Caucasus of such young and dynamic individuals, who have genuinely sought to set out and define a distinctive Muslim identity in a non-violent manner, and who have ended up joining the Islamist insurgency. In Dagestan, these include Abuzagir Mantaev, a young intellectual who defended his doctoral dissertation on the topic of Wahhabism, and Yasin Rasulov, who was a graduate from Dagestan State University and a correspondent for the newspaper *Novoe Delo*. Both these figures sought in the aftermath of the 'Wahhabi' crises and conflicts in the late 1990s in Dagestan to reconstruct the more moderate and intellectual Salafist approach taken by Akhmad Akhtaev, which would be incorporated within, rather than seek to overthrow, the existing religious and political structures. However, it was the failure of the religious and political authorities to legitimate their activities, along with increasing levels of repression of them and their followers by the security and law enforcement services, which ultimately led them to join the underground 'Shariat Jamaat' and to engage in militant and violent activities (Makarov, 2004, pp. 159–160). A very similar process of radicalization can be seen in Kabardino-Balkaria, where the so-called 'New Muslims', under the leadership of Musa Mukojev and Anzor Astemirov who had studied in universities in Saudi Arabia and broadly subscribed to a moderate salafist position, nevertheless tried throughout the 1990s to promote dialogue to seek to dissuade young frustrated Muslims from turning to violence. However, the ever-increasingly anti-Wahhabi and anti-extremist repression from the late 1990s onwards forced Mukojev and Astemirov, and many of their followers, to go underground, and this led to their radicalization and the establishment of the Yarmuk jamaat in 2004, which openly called for jihad against the Kabardino-Balkaria government.[26]

Conclusion

Understanding the root causes of the continuing Islamist insurgency in the North Caucasus has many layers and cannot be reduced to any particular factor or element. There are, for instance, significant historical roots which include the deeply embedded mutual fears between Russians and the peoples of the North Caucasus resulting from their history of conflict and suppression. There is also the history of internal debates among North Caucasian Muslims about the role that Islam and *Shari'a* law should play in the region and where subservience to Russia has often been interpreted, as by Imam Shamil, to be due to a failure properly to observe the true dictates and demands of Islam.

There are also the particular experiences and developments in the post-Soviet period, most critically the ways in which the two brutal and bloody Chechen wars of the 1990s and 2000s contributed to the process of Islamic radicalization. Such radicalization was also aided by the influence of foreign Muslim fighters and ideologues as well as by indigenous North Caucasian religious leaders who came to challenge in increasingly more radical ways the existing Muslim practices and official Islamic establishments as corrupt, heterodox and co-opted by the secular Russian state. In the 2000s, the Russian military and political establishment under Vladimir Putin devised a multi-pronged strategy to seek to reduce and eliminate the growing threat from the region through a mix of military repression, devolution of power to loyal clans and leaders, and the co-option through financial and other support of the pro-Russian Islamic structures and institutions. This resulted in some significant successes, most notably the relative pacification of Chechnya.

These measures did not, however, ultimately quell the insurgency, which reignited with renewed force in the late 2000s. The nature of the insurgency also changed to be geographically more diffuse, to involve a larger set of networked jihadist groups, and to promote an ideological programme that was more Islamist and less nationalist. Some of the most critical factors behind the durability and transformation of the insurgency certainly include the poor socio-economic conditions in the region and the high levels of poverty and unemployment, particularly among the younger generation. They also include the systemic corruption, the inter-elite clannish competition for economic and political resources, and the high levels of criminality that this engenders. These are all powerful forces that breed resentment and alienation and where the call to a pure and pristine and uncorrupted Islam appears to be a powerful potential solution, including its justification of violent action to seek to put right the region's social and political injustices.

The strategic focus of Medvedev and Putin, through their appointment of Khloponin, on the economic development and modernization of the region is, in this regard, undoubtedly vital to bring stability and prosperity to the North Caucasus. As argued above, there are nevertheless real problems in the implementation of such a programme given the Kremlin's own modes of governance and its preference for authoritarianism and lack of transparency, which mirrors practices in the North Caucasus. However, there is another powerful source of radicalization that also needs to be addressed as energetically as these economic and political factors. This is the religious and religio-ideological dimension of the conflict, which involves a crucial debate over the political role of Islam. There is, currently, a highly intolerant intra-Muslim debate within the region that divides different generations, different social groups and even different families over the nature of Islamic orthodoxy and the legitimate forms of political power and authority in a Muslim-dominated society. Such religious intolerance is a powerful factor in radicalization, not only for those rejecting the existing political authority and resorting to violence but also for those defiantly defending traditional Islam. What is critically needed is a more pluralistic and tolerant religious environment where such an escalation of fears and hatreds can be overcome. But such a more open and tolerant religious setting is not something that can be easily imposed from Moscow. As such, it is this local intra-Caucasian dimension to the vibrancy and durability of the Islamist insurgency that significantly complicates the challenge facing Russian policymakers.

Notes

1. For Umarov's full declaration of a Caucasus Emirate, see Kavkaz-Tsentr (2007).
2. For example, Ivan the Terrible married a princess of Kabardia in order to cement relations with the region.

3. For an excellent recent history of the Caucasus, see King (2008). For the application of this history for understanding contemporary developments, see King & Menon (2010).
4. For a more extensive account of the nature of highland warfare, see Gordin (2000).
5. For the different sides of this debate, see Zelkina (2000) and Knysh (2002).
6. For an analysis of how these terms are ritually used in the North Caucasus jihadist media, see Kurbanov (2010).
7. For good accounts of the first Chechen war, see Dunlop (1998), Lieven (1998) and Gall & de Waal (1998).
8. For an excellent survey of the role of foreign Islamists in the Chechen conflict, see Moore & Tumelty (2008).
9. For an interesting account of the rhetoric of 'Wahhabism', see Knysh (2004). See also Dannreuther (2010).
10. See also Knysh (2007, pp. 515–517).
11. For accounts of the impact, see Trenin & Malashenko (2004, p. 37) and Russell (2005, p. 109).
12. For a Russian military perspective on the first war, see Troshev (2000).
13. For how taking over these markets involved clashes with federal military and interior forces, see Kots & Rodkin (2003).
14. See Silantev (2008, p. 141) and Malashenko (2007, p. 143).
15. See Orlov (2007).
16. This is but one of many attacks on senior officials from 2002 onwards. For details, see International Crisis Group (2008, pp. 8–10).
17. See Tlisova (2007) and Vatchagayev (2013).
18. For a more detailed analysis, see Markedonov (2010).
19. For a more detailed analysis of Kozak's strategy towards the region, see Slider (2008).
20. For similar evidence-based conclusions, see Gerber & Mendelson (2009).
21. For a more detailed analysis of the different aspects of Russian nationalism, and its societal implications, see March (2012).
22. On the general evolution of these networks, see Sageman (2008); and on how they apply to the North Caucasus, see Moore & Tumelty (2008) and Moore (2012).
23. On this phenomenon of 'neo-traditionalism', see Malashenko & *Yarlykapov (2009)*.
24. For more detailed analysis, see Matsuzato & Ibragimov (2010).
25. On the development of the young Muslim intelligentsia, see Makarov (2007).
26. See Yarlykapov (2006) and Sagramoso & Yemelianova (2010).

References

Alexandrovna, L. (2012) Money allocated to the North Caucasus to be less than expected, *ITAR-TASS*, 14 December.

Baev, P.K. (2005) Chechnya and the Russian military: a war too far? in: R. Sakwa (Ed.), *Chechnya: From Past to Future*, pp. 117–130 (London: Anthem Press).

Baev, P.K. (2006) Has Russia achieved a victory in its war against terror? *PONARS Policy Memo 415*, available online at: http://csis.org/files/media/csis/pubs/pm_0415.pdf

Bilevskaya, E. & Samarina, A. (2010) Modernization of the Caucasus, *Nezavisimaya gazeta*, 17 August.

Bobrovnikov, V. (2006) Traditionalist vs Islamist identities in a Dagestani collective farm, *Central Asian Survey*, 25(3), pp. 287–302.

Dannreuther, R. (2010) Russian discourses and approaches to Islam and Islamism, in: R. Dannreuther & L. March (Eds), *Russia and Islam: State, Society and Radicalism*, pp. 9–25 (London: Routledge).

Devji, F. (2005) *Landscapes of Jihad: Militancy, Morality, Modernity* (Cornell: Cornell University Press).

Dunlop, J. (1998) *Russia Confronts Chechnya: Roots of a Separatist Conflict* (Cambridge: Cambridge University Press).

Gall, C. & de Waal, T. (1998) *Chechnya: Calamity in the Caucasus* (New York: New York University Press).

Gammer, M. (2008) From the challenge of nationalism to the challenge of Islam: the case of Dagestan, in: M. Gammer (Ed.), *Ethno-nationalism, Islam and the State in the Caucasus: Post-Soviet Disorder*, pp. 178–198 (London: Routledge).

Gerber, T. & Mendelson, S. (2009) Security through sociology: the North Caucasus and the global counterinsurgency paradigm, *Studies in Conflict and Terrorism*, 32(9), pp. 831–851.

Gevorkan, N., Kolesnikov, A.V. & Timakova, N. (2000) *Ot pervogo litsa* (Moscow: Vagrius).

Gordin, I. (2000) *Kavkaz: Zemlia i krov* (Zvezda: St Petersburg).

Gorst, I. & Belton, C. (2010) Moscow police act to stem race riots, *Financial Times*, 15 December.

Hahn, G.M. (2013) Summary of CE terrorist activity, *Islam, Islamism and Politics in Eurasia* 64, available online at: http://csis.org/files/publication/130110_Hahn_IIPER_64.pdf

Holland, E.C. & O'Loughlin, J. (2010) Ethnic competition, radical Islam and challenges to stability in the Republic of Dagestan, *Communist and Post-Communist Studies*, 43(3), pp. 297–308.

Idrisov, Y.U. (2007) Musul'manskoye fondy i ikh zadachi v sovremennoi Rossii, *Islam v sovremennom mire*, 1(7), pp. 6–8.

International Crisis Group (2008) Russia's Dagestan: conflict causes, *Europe Report*, 192, pp. 1–25.

International Crisis Group (2012) The North Caucasus: the challenges of integration (II), Islam, the insurgency and counter-insurgency, *Europe Report*, 221, pp. 1–40.

Kavkaz-Tsentr (2007) Ofitsal'nyi reliz zaiavlenya Amira Dokki Umarova o provozglashenii Kavkazskogo Emirata, 21 November, available online at: http://www.kavkazcenter.com/russ/content/2007/11/21/54480.shtml

Kemper, M. (2002) Khalidiyya Networks in Dagestan and the question of jihad, *Die Welt des Islams*, 42(1), pp. 41–79.

Khinshtein, A. (2005) Sensatzionnyi doklad Dmitriya Kozaka, *Moskovskii komsomolets*, 15 June.

King, C. (2008) *The Ghost of Freedom: A History of the Caucasus* (Oxford: Oxford University Press).

King, C. & Menon, R. (2010) Prisoners of the Caucasus, *Foreign Affairs*, 89(4), pp. 20–34.

Knysh, A. (2002) Sufism as an explanatory paradigm: the issue of the motivations of Sufi resistance movements in Western and Russian scholarship, *Die Welt des Islams*, 42(2), pp. 139–173.

Knysh, A. (2004) A clear and present danger: 'Wahhabism' as a rhetorical foil, *Die Welt des Islams*, 44(1), pp. 3–26.

Knysh, A. (2007) Contextualising the Salafi–Sufi conflict (from the Northern Caucasus to the Hawdramat), *Middle East Studies*, 43(4), pp. 503–530.

Kommersant (2010) Interview with Arsen Kanokov, 1 October.

Kots, A. & Rodkin, A. (2003) The ambush, *Komsomolskaya Pravda*, 3 March.

Kurbanov, R. (2010) The information jihad and 'Shariat' Jamaat: objectives, methods and achievements, in: R. Dannreuther & L. March (Eds), *Russia and Islam: State, Society and Radicalism*, pp. 155–174 (London: Routledge).

Lieven, A. (1998) *Chechnya: Tombstone of Russian Power* (New Haven: Yale University Press).

Makarenko, V. (2003) Vladimir Putin recognizes Russia as a Muslim country, *Stolichnaya vechernaya gazeta*, 6 August.

Makarov, D. (2000) *Ofitsal'nyi i neofitsal'nyi Islam v Dagestane* (Moscow: Carnegie Foundation).

Makarov, D. (2004) Radikalizatsia Islama v Dagestane: Vozmozhnosti i predely dzhikhadizma, *Obshchestvennye nauki i sovremennost*, 6, pp. 159–160.

Makarov, D. (2007) Tendentsii intellektual'nogo rosta rossiiskogo musul'mankogo soobshchestva v sovremennyi period, *Islam v sovremennom mire*, 7, pp. 50–56.

Malashenko, A. (2007) *Islam dlya Rossiya* (Moscow: Carnegie Endowment for International Peace).

Malashenko, A. & Yarlykapov, A. (2009) Radicalisation of Russia's Muslim community, in: M. Emerson (Ed.), *Ethno-religious Conflict in Europe*, pp. 152–192 (Brussels: Centre for European Policy Studies).

March, L. (2012) Nationalism for export? The domestic and foreign policy implications of the new 'Russian idea', *Europe-Asia Studies*, 64(3), pp. 401–425.

Markedonov, S. (2010) Glavnyi po severnomu Kavkazu, *Neprikosnovenyi zapas*, 70, available online at: http://magazines.russ.ru/nz/2010/2/ma31-pr.html

Markov, S. (2007) Zadachu Ramzana Kadyrova, *Izvestiya*, 19 March.

Matsuzato, K. & Ibragimov, M.R. (2010) Tarikat, ethnichost' i politika v Dagestane, *Islamica.ru*, available online at: http://www.islamica.ru/?pageID=214

Medvedev, D. (2009) Presidential Address to the Federal Assembly of the Russian Federation, 12 November, available online at: http://eng.kremlin.ru/transcripts/297

Moore, C. (2006) Reading the hermeneutics of violence: the literary turn and Chechnya, *Global Society*, 20(2), pp. 179–198.

Moore, C. (2012) Suicide bombing: Chechnya, the North Caucasus and martyrdom, *Europe-Asia Studies*, 64(9), pp. 1,788–1,815.

Moore, C. & Tumelty, P. (2008) Foreign fighters and the case of Chechnya: a critical assessment, *Studies in Conflict and Terrorism*, 31, pp. 412–433.

Moore, C. & Tumelty, P. (2009) Assessing unholy alliances in Chechnya: from communism and nationalism to Islamism and Salafism, *Journal of Communist Studies and Transition Politics*, 25(1), pp. 73–94.

Mukhin, V. & Bondarenko, M. (2010) Terrorist cluster, *Nezavisimaya gazeta*, 28 May.

Orlov, D. (Eds) (2007) *Suverennnaya democratiya: ot idei k doktrine* (Moscow: Evropa).

Roy, O. (2004) *Globalised Islam: The Search for a New Ummah* (London: Hurst).

Russell, J. (2005) Terrorists, bandits, spooks and thieves: Russian demonisation of the Chechens before and since 9/11, *Third World Quarterly*, 26(1), 101–116.

Russell, J. (2007) *Chechnya—Russia's 'War on Terror'* (London: Routledge).

Rutland, P. (2000) Putin's path to power, *Post-Soviet Affairs*, 16(4), pp. 313–354.

Sageman, M. (2008) *Leaderless Jihad: Terror Networks in the Twenty-first Century* (Philadelphia: University of Pennsylvania Press).

Sagramoso, D. & Yemelianova, G. (2010) 'Islam and ethno-nationalism in the north-western Caucasus, in: G. Yemelianova (Ed.), *Radical Islam in the Former Soviet Union*, pp. 120–130 (London: Routledge).

Silantev, R. (2008) *Islam v sovremennoi Rossii; entsiklopedia* (Moscow: Algoritm).

Slider, D. (2008) Putin's 'Southern Strategy': Dmitriy Kozak and the dilemmas of recentralization, *Post-Soviet Affairs*, 24(2), pp. 177–197.

Sokirianskaia, E. (2008) Ideology and conflict: Chechen political nationalism prior to, and during, ten years of war, in: M. Gammer (Ed.), *Ethno-nationalism, Islam and the State in the Caucasus: Post-Soviet Disorder*, pp. 102–138 (London: Routledge).

Sokolov, D. (2010) North Caucasus: buying reforms, *Vedemosti*, 15 September.

Souleimanov, E. (2005) Chechnya, Wahhabism and the invasion of Dagestan, *Middle East Review of International Affairs*, 9(4), pp. 48–71.

Surkhov, I. (2009) Test in the south, *Vremya Novostei*, 19 August.

The Economist (2010) Terror in Moscow, 29 March.

Tlisova, F. (2007) Kabardino-Balkaria faces long-term guerilla war, *Jamestown Foundation Eurasian Daily Monitor*, 2(195), available online at: http://www.jamestown.org/single/?no_cache=1&tx_ttnews%5Bswords%5D=8fd5893941d69d0be3f378576261ae3e&tx_ttnews%5Bany_of_the_words%5D=Tlisova&tx_ttnews%5Bpointer%5D=2&tx_ttnews%5Btt_news%5D=30996&tx_ttnews%5BbackPid%5D=7&cHash=f5cc90245e76803dced5a0f7303e88e8#.UgCjxRbvxmA

Tlisova, F. (2008) Events in Ingusheitiya spin out of Moscow's hands, *Jamestown Foundation Eurasian Daily Monitor*, 9(40), available online at: http://www.jamestown.org/single/?no_cache=1&tx_ttnews%5Bswords%5D=8fd5893941d69d0be3f378576261ae3e&tx_ttnews%5Bany_of_the_words%5D=Tlisova&tx_ttnews%5Bpointer%5D=1&tx_ttnews%5Btt_news%5D=5239&tx_ttnews%5BbackPid%5D=7&cHash=bb5353df9c5b43b236cc3226cd43e6fc#.UgCigBbvxmA

Trenin, D.V. & Malashenko, A.V. (2004) *Russia's Restless Frontier: The Chechnya Factor in Post-Soviet Russia* (Washington, DC: Carnegie Endowment for International Peace).

Troshev, G. (2000) *Moya voina: Chechenskiii dnevnik okopnogo generala* (Moscow: Vagrius).

Vatchagayev, M. (2013) The Yarmuk Jamaat and the Sochi Olympics, *Jamestown Foundation Eurasian Daily Monitor*, 10(69), available online at: http://www.jamestown.org/programs/edm/single/?tx_ttnews%5Btt_news%5D=40727&cHash=76af407275ef183793aa323585d822b6#.UgCg_BbvxmA

Verkhovsky, A. (2008) The Putin's government's response to increased xenophobia, *Kennan Institute Meeting Report*, XXV(9), available online at: http://www.wilsoncenter.org/event/the-putin-governments-responses-to-increased-xenophobia

Ware, R.B. & Kisriev, E. (2010) *Dagestan: Russian Hegemony and Islamic Resistance in the North Caucasus* (Armonk, NY: Sharpe).

Yarlykapov, A. (2006) Islamskie obshschiny Severnogo Kavkaza: Ideologiya i praktika, *Aziya i Afrika sevogdnya*, 1, pp. 45–49.

Yarlykapov, A. (2010) The radicalisation of North Caucasian Muslims, in: R. Dannreuther & L. March (Eds), Russia and Islam: State, Society and Radicalism, pp. 137–154 (London: Routledge).

Zelkina, A. (2000) *In Quest for God and Freedom: The Sufi Response to the Russian Advance in the North Caucasus* (London: Hurst).

Ethnopolitics, 2014
Vol. 13, No. 4, 396–417, http://dx.doi.org/10.1080/17449057.2014.906150

Citizenship, Federalism and Powersharing: Nigeria's Federal Character and the Challenges of Institutional Design

BRANDON KENDHAMMER

Ohio University, USA

ABSTRACT   If, as a number of recent proponents have argued, 'pluri-national' federalism holds great promise as a means of democratization and conflict resolution in deeply divided societies, why has it so rarely been tried in sub-Saharan Africa, home to arguably the world's most ethnically diverse nations? Using Nigeria—Africa's largest and oldest federal system—as a case study, it is argued that the legacy of late colonial, indirect rule institutions on citizenship and the politics of belonging pose a serious challenge for designing successful consociational powersharing arrangements. In particular, Nigeria's dependence on a primordial notion of ethnic citizenship undermines the ability of its federal institutions to mediate and cross-cut ethnic conflicts, a problem most clearly reflected in the functioning of the nation's most important official powersharing institution, the Federal Character Commission (FCC). Although the quota systems for governmental employment operated by the FCC are officially tied to Nigeria's 36 states, in both administrative law and practice they enforce a highly discriminatory 'indigeneity' system that privileges ethnic origins over federal citizenship.

Introduction

Early in 2008, Aliyu Magatakarda Wamakko, the newly elected governor of Sokoto State in north-western Nigeria, announced a seemingly minor adjustment to the formula for calculating public school fees, creating a single flat rate for all Sokoto residents. Among Nigerians, school fees (and the challenges of paying them) are a frequent topic of discussion, but these sorts of announcement rarely attract much press attention. This time, however, the proposal garnered national media coverage, picked up by newspaper and radio reporters across the country as a centrepiece of the Wamakko administration's first term (*Daily Champion*, 2008).

Why did such a seemingly innocuous policy change attract so much attention? The revolutionary aspect of Wamakko's proposal had nothing to do with the size of the fees

---

Correspondence Address: Brandon Kendhammer, Department of Political Science and African Studies Program, Ohio University, Athens, OH 45701, USA. Email: kendhamm@ohio.edu

© 2014 The Editor of Ethnopolitics

themselves, but with its elimination of the extra charge applied to the state's 'non-indi-gene' families. In Sokoto, as in all of Nigeria's 36 states, Nigerian nationals whose ethnic ancestry is not local to their official state of residence face systematic discrimination that denies them full local and state-level citizenship and the political rights that come with it. In many jurisdictions across Nigeria, it is effectively impossible for ethnic 'strangers to gain 'indigene' status in their state of residence, even if they have lived there since birth. Despite the efforts of Wamakko and a few others, the legacy of primordialism embedded in Nigerian citizenship policy has rendered nearly all of the country's extensive consocia-tional powersharing arrangements little more than window-dressing for millions of the country's citizens living outside their ancestral (and legally defined) 'homelands'.

Moreover, conflicts over the qualifications for local citizenship are among the leading cause of communal violence in Nigeria (Human Rights Watch, 2006; Milligan, 2013). In Plateau State, a long-standing history of ethnic and religious conflict between Christian members of the Birom community and their Muslim Hausa and Fulani neighbours is rooted in colonial and postcolonial policies that classify resident Muslims as 'settlers' and 'non-indigenes', despite the fact that they lack specific, recognizable links to another homeland. Battles over the 'ownership' of ethnically mixed communities in Plateau have caused sporadic communal riots for decades, but since the return to democ-racy this tension has been magnified by 'do or die' electoral competitions. In 2008, accu-sations that the Birom governor of Plateau, Jonah Jang, had illicitly engineered the victory of his preferred candidate in the divided Jos North electoral district helped to inspire a series of religious riots that displaced at least 10,000 citizens and killed 400 more (Ostien, 2009).

Nigeria is a nation divided by citizenship—by the legal categories its federal and state governments use to define membership in subnational political communities. Like most African nations, it operates a system of ethnically based 'dual citizenship' (Osaghae, 1990, 1998; Ejobowah, 2013) in which membership in the national political community is mediated by membership in a state-recognized 'indigenous' ethnic or racial group. The prevalence of the 'dual citizenship' problem in African politics can be readily traced back to the governing practices of 'late colonialism', particularly the connection between colonial citizenship and legal status with membership in a specific 'customary' ethnic community (Mamdani, 1996, 2001, 2012; Fanthorpe, 2001; Geschiere, 2009). Today, policies that preserve the role of ethnic identity in defining national citizenship have been adopted by contemporary political entrepreneurs to deny their opponents the right to vote, run for office, and seek government employment outside their 'native' com-munities (Ceuppens & Geschiere, 2005). Discriminatory citizenship is at the heart of many of the continent's recent civil wars and internal conflicts, and its effects have proved to be devilishly difficult to undo during the process of post-conflict reconciliation and insti-tutional design (Dorman *et al.*, 2007). Even where citizenship conflicts have not led directly to rebellion and war, they have undermined the consolidation of democracy by entrenching clientelist and neopatrimonial patterns of authority and reinforcing the role of ethnic community membership in determining access to state services and benefits.

This article explores the connection between 'citizenship troubles' in Nigeria and other African states and another puzzling problem on the continent—the widespread failure or underperformance of consociational and ethnofederal models of powersharing and demo-cratic state-building. Despite growing enthusiasm within many academic and policymak-ing camps for consociational powersharing and 'pluri-national' federalism as means of managing ethnic diversity and promoting democratization (Lijphart, 2002; O'Leary, 2005; McGarry & O'Leary, 2009; Anderson, 2013), such models have rarely translated into success on African soils (Spears, 2002; Lemarchand, 2007). I argue that whereas successful ethnic powersharing institutions provide a 'roof of rights' spanning equally over the heads of all citizens, including those who define themselves culturally and politically primarily as members of subnational communities (Stepan *et al.*, 2011, p. 21), most African states use membership in 'customary' ethnic communities to circumscribe or limit national citizenship. Post-conflict and democratic institutional design projects in Africa often underestimate how firmly exclusionary citizenship policies and practices are entrenched in law and in practice, with the result that institutions intended to ensure broad ethnic representation in politics often become inadvertent tools of exclusion that undermine the success of powersharing principles.

As the possessor of both Africa's oldest and largest federal system and a complex history of ethnic violence and institutional innovation, Nigeria has long served as a test case for proponents of both consociational powersharing (Lijphart, 1977, p. 164; Njoku, 1999) and 'centripetalism' (designed to 'pull parties towards moderate, compromising policies') (Sisk, 1995, p. 19; Horowitz, 1985; Anderson, 2013, pp. 134–163). Beginning in earnest following its destructive 1967–1970 civil war, Nigeria has experimented with crafting institutions designed both to limit sectarian conflict *and* institutionally recognize and protect the country's ethnic and religious diversity. As Rotimi Suberu has argued, these efforts have largely succeeded in preventing the reoccurrence of the sort of large-scale ethnic outbidding that drove the country to civil war, 'channelling ethnic conflict along constructive, or negotiable, rather than destructive, or non-negotiable, lines' (Suberu, 2001, p. 9). Critics note, however, that a stunningly large number of these post-war engineering efforts have 'boomeranged' back on their crafters, worsening the ethnic tensions and political violence they were intended to prevent (Bach, 1989; Osaghae, 1998; Kendhammer, 2010); and as scholars of neopatrimonial politics and its Nigerian variants (Joseph, 1987; Adebanwi & Obadare, 2013) have long argued, they have also done little to dampen the country's long-standing and highly destructive 'struggle for control of the enormous socio-economic powers and resources of the state' (Diamond & Suberu, 2002, p. 422), and much to reinforce it. In this failure, I argue, the inability of three distinct generations of Nigerian framers to recognize and repair the damage done by the 'dual citizenship' problem has been central.

One of the most important sites of conflict between consociational ideals and citizenship realities in Nigeria is the 'federal character' project, a loosely related set of principles and institutions introduced in the 1978 constitution as a means of guaranteeing ethnic proportionality in governmental and military services. Over the past 35 years, the scope and influence of the 'federal character' has expanded dramatically, becoming a massive, formal ethnic powersharing structure administered by the Federal Character Commission (FCC), a federal ministry created in 1996 to manage the increasingly complex ethnic quota systems introduced across the federal and state civil services. While the FCC has attracted relatively little attention from scholars (cf. Mustapha, 2009), its responsibilities have (inadvertently, it would seem) made it the source of nearly all administrative law on subnational citizenship. Relying on an analysis of FCC-related legislature and practice, as well as on a series of interviews with mid-level FCC programme staff conducted in June 2013, I argue that by enforcing a fundamentally primordial perspective on what it means to be an 'indigene' in today's Nigeria, the FCC perpetuates the connection between federal, consociational powersharing and 'dual citizenship'. Although the FCC and the federal character 'principle' have both had limited success in creating a more ethnically representative balance in Nigerian public life, their efforts have also entrenched ethnic-based state and local citizenship as a major site of political mobilization and conflict.

Citizenship and 'Pluri-national Federalism' in Postcolonial Africa

Despite the ferocity with which critics (Snyder, 2000; Rothchild & Roeder, 2005) and defenders (McGarry & O'Leary, 2009) debate the merits of ethnically based powersharing and 'pluri-national federalism' as solutions for cooling tensions in post-conflict societies, most of their evidence is drawn from a relatively geographically constrained set of 'Western' cases (cf. Kymlicka, 2006; Anderson, 2013) that fails to conceptualize fully the challenges of institutional design in postcolonial societies. More promising, however, is the recent work of Stepan, Linz and Yadav, who begin their discussion of federal solutions to ethnic conflict by acknowledging that for most postcolonial societies, the classic model of state-directed nation-building is no longer a viable path for transforming plural societies into nation states. Faced with an inability to simply overwrite their cultural and linguistic diversity—and growing international support for preserving and providing autonomy for minority cultures (Nimni, 2007; Kymlicka, 2007)—plural states such as India have chosen to recognize that citizens possess multiple, strong cultural identities beyond their nationality, even as they attempt to build both pride and trust in the state project (Stepan *et al.*, 2011, p. 7). Organizationally, this is accomplished by a system of 'nested' policies, including asymmetric federal institutions providing legal and cultural autonomy to ethnic and religious communities, and the promotion of 'centric-regional' electoral institutions that facilitate national elite bargaining and coalition-building. Stepan, Linz and Yadav's work is significant because they take the challenge of applying their model to the Global South seriously. By focusing on India, a nation with a long history of ethnic and religious violence, democratic setbacks and poverty that has nonetheless succeeded in creating a strong sense of national pride and identity, they aim to demonstrate that so long as institutions are reasonably inclusive and popular commitment to democracy remains robust, traditional nation-building is not the only path to peace and stability.

Ostensibly, the 'state-nation' model, with its reliance on federal and consociational policies for balancing national unity and ethnic autonomy, would seem to hold particular promise in sub-Saharan Africa, home to the most ethnically diverse set of countries on earth (Easterly & Levine, 1997). Yet Africa has long been seen as a 'virtual graveyard of federal experiments', with none of the initial cohort of independence-era federal systems surviving into the present in their original forms (Suberu, 2009). Despite a significant wave of institutional reforms across the continent in the 1990s, apart from three cases—post-apartheid South Africa, which adopted a regionalist system that devolves relatively little power to its constituent units (Klug, 2000), Ethiopia's post-civil war (1994–present) ethnic federalism (Keller & Smith, 2005), and Nigeria's own federal experiment—federal, consociational arrangements have remained a dead letter on the continent.

Why have these alternative, federal/consociational models of 'state-nation' building failed to work as well in sub-Saharan Africa as elsewhere? One explanation is that the pressures of political and economic modernization in postcolonial Africa have driven states towards centralized political control. Combined with the weak, low-capacity states most African nations inherited at independence, movements for ethnic and regional autonomy are often interpreted not as opportunities to engineer peace, but as threats to national security and integrality (Suberu, 2009, p. 70). This legacy of central control, as well as many African states' dependence on revenue from resource extraction, means that subnational units rarely possess their own independent fiscal bases. Local ethnic and regional elites rarely care as much about achieving autonomy from the centre as they do about gaining access to nationally held resources, a process that undermines the quality of regional governance (Gervasconi, 2010). Not surprisingly, both of Africa's most prominent federal systems (Ethiopia and Nigeria) are widely regarded as little more than unitary states possessing the exterior trappings of federalism (Keller & Smith, 2005, pp. 272–277).

Another explanation, broadly emphasized by critics of ethnofederalism, is that it is simply too difficult to both provide ethnic communities with significant territorial and cultural autonomy *and* foster national identity through integrative institutions. When power dynamics between ethnic communities become unbalanced, these arrangements invariably embolden secessionist movements without offering any particular advantages in governance and stability (Hale, 2004). In sub-Saharan Africa, however, secessionist movements have never been as common as the continent's artificial borders would suggest. Buoyed by the powersharing agreements they negotiate at the behest of Western powers, regional elites often find that access to weak but sovereign and internationally recognized state authority is more valuable than independence (Englebert & Hummel, 2005).

A third possibility is that African legal regimes, particularly those around citizenship, disrupt efforts to build 'statenation' communities. Sadly, academic proponents of ethnofederalism have been largely silent on the question of how to negotiate the legal relationship between national citizenship and subnational group membership. In the vast majority of federal systems, particularly those in Europe (Switzerland excepting) and North America, citizenship at the national level is 'controlling' in the sense that membership in the national polity entitles one to membership in a subnational community, and nearly all guarantee that citizens can acquire new subnational citizenship based on residency. In 'holding-together' federalisms (Stepan, 1999)—formerly unitary states that choose to provide autonomy to subnational units as part of a broader strategy for managing pluralism—the story is roughly the same. Even when, as in India, consociational strategies are used to create quotas or other mechanisms for ensuring 'balanced' representation for historically marginalized groups, national citizenship is generally legally determinative, with constitutional and case law affirming a 'single, national concept of citizenship' (Jackson, 2001, p. 137). As a result, Indian citizens have the possibility of leading what Stepan *et al.* (2011, pp. 20–21) call 'polity-wide' lives—participating fully in civil and political affairs wherever they choose to make their homes, or wherever their careers take them.

Why have Nigeria and other multi-ethnic African states consistently given ethnic identities pride of place in national citizenship policies? Here, the answer lies in the nature of the 'late' colonial state in Africa, and its emphasis on establishing an ethnographic understanding of 'traditional' or 'native' societies in order to effect their integration into colonial empires. As Karuna Mantena (2010) and Mahmood Mamdani (2012) argue, these efforts have their origin in the failures of 'direct rule' strategies of colonial governance pioneered by the British in India and elsewhere in the mid-nineteenth century. Driven by the experience of the Indian 'Sepoy Mutiny' of 1857, in which 130,000 Indian soldiers engaged in open revolt against colonial rule, British colonial administrators such as Sir Henry Maine argued for a fundamental reconceptualization of the role of colonial government, away from the universalist impulse that saw colonial subjects as a single, undifferentiated mass to be subjected to a 'single legal order' (Mamdani, 1999, p. 867) and towards the legal recognition of native 'differences' as a means of more effectively governing 'traditional societies' (Mantena, 2010, p. 2).

Beginning in the mid-nineteenth century, European agents experimented with governing through local adjuncts, co-opting their 'traditional' legitimacy for their own ends in a strategy that came to be known as 'indirect rule' (Perham, 1934). Indirect rule depended on the ability of the colonial state to recognize, classify and codify 'traditional' authority, culture and practice in the form of 'customary law'. The administrative genius of indirect rule was to define ethnicity ('nativeness') not as a 'cultural, but [as] a legal distinction', with each group possessing its '*own* law' under which it could be (cheaply and efficiently) governed (Mamdani, 2001, p. 655). Colonial rule in sub-Saharan Africa hinged on the distinction between 'natives'—those who possessed a 'customary law' and could be governed accordingly—and 'non-natives', who occupied an entirely 'different legal universe' (Mamdani, 2001, p. 654; Mamdani, 2012). The local rulers of ethnic communities—the 'native authorities'—were recognized as the sole possessors of customary power, and alternative loci (women's and religious groups, in particular) were often shut out entirely. In Nigeria, 'sole native authorities' were granted significant power over access to land and economic opportunity, a barrier that proved particularly important for resident non-members of the local 'tribe', who (whatever their history in the area might have been) were classified as 'strangers' or 'settlers', unable ever to become 'natives' by assimilation or tenure.

Although most African nationalist movements adopted the language of nation-building and were formally non-ethnic in their official discourse, practice was something else (Smith, 2007, p. 572). 'Mainstream' nationalism reproduced colonial narratives of custom and authenticity, promising not simply to provide 'natives' with the civil rights they had been denied under colonial rule, but to privilege their 'indigenous' status in law and state policy (Mamdani, 2001, p. 658). Providing these benefits meant codifying the arbitrary colonial boundaries, often restricting citizenship to members of ethnic groups 'native' or 'indigenous' to the territory at the time of colonization or (as in Ethiopia, and, until 1993, Botswana) by allowing only the father's lineage to pass on citizenship rights to children (Manby, 2009, pp. 34–35). To be a citizen in the African postcolony means being an 'indigene', possessing an ethnic identity recognized by colonial fiat more than a century ago.

As Peter Ekeh (1975) has described, another result of maintaining the colonial distinction between 'natives' and 'non-natives' after independence was that most Africans found themselves members not of a single national community, but rather, two separate 'publics', one defined by the relatively thin bonds of national citizenship, and the other by cultural (and, equally importantly, legal) association with a 'native' community. Members of ethnically defined 'primordial publics' share the benefits that come with belonging to a network of dense social connections, as well as a moral obligation for this community's well-being. Membership in the 'civic public', on the other hand—primarily, the realm of the state and other areas of society governed by 'legal-rational rules' (Osaghae, 2003, p. 7)—provides access to formal rights but little else. This distinction encouraged national and subnational political elites to mobilize around 'primordial publics' and their memberships by offering 'special rights to those who "really" belonged where they lived' (Geschiere, 2009, p. 40). With the decline of single-party regimes and the growing economic challenges of the 1980s, the power to define citizenship became an important tool for insecure autocrats and democrats alike to exclude their political opponents from national political life. In Zaire, Mobutu's manipulation of the date speci- fied in Congolese law for determining whether or not an ethnic group was indigenous (and thus eligible for citizenship) allowed him to buy the loyalty of key members of the Banya- mulenge, a community in the eastern region with linguistic and cultural links to Rwanda. However, when the group fell out of favour, their citizenship could be (and was) easily revoked, contributing to their eventual participation in the conflicts that became the First and Second Congo Wars (Manby, 2009, p. 9; Stearns, 2010, pp. 57–65). In the Ivory Coast, Henri Bedié and Laurent Gbagbo's reliance on the doctrine of 'Ivoirite'— a policy that distinguished between 'autochthonous' ('of the soil') and foreign ethnic com- munities for the purpose of excluding their political opponents from the full rights of citi- zenship—helped to inaugurate a series of civil wars that ravaged that country in the late 1990s and 2000s, as well.

How does Africa's 'dual citizenship' heritage affect the ability of ethnofederal systems to foster a successful 'state-nation'? As Stepan *et al.* describe it, the advantage of feder- alist, consociational systems in deeply divided societies is that they offer the possibility of recognition and autonomy for potentially secessionist minorities *and* the prospect of developing a sense of national pride around joint participation in and ownership of national institutions. Their institutional proposals for achieving this balance, what they call the 'nested policy grammar of state-nations', is premised on many of the same choices African nations already make, including official recognition for 'collective rights' (including state support for multiple languages and religions), as well as electoral institutions that force ethnic constituencies into broad coalitions at the federal level. But as important as these accommodations are, Stepan *et al.* also recognize the importance of building some measure of national community, particularly through access to 'polity- wide' careers, and personal opportunities limit the need to rely on ethnic and 'primordial public' networks (Stepan *et al.*, 2011, pp. 17–22). Exclusionary citizenship rules built upon local autochthony or indigeneity render even members of the largest ethnic commu- nities (or even worse, the nation's most cosmopolitan citizens) as incomplete participants in nearly all communities they might choose to reside in outside their legally defined homelands. While mobile citizens might be able to find homes in metropolitan areas or national capitals (Kinshasa, Abidjan, or Abuja), African 'dual citizenship' regimes ensure that they remain practically and politically tied to their home communities when it comes to access to the state and its resources.

Indirect Rule and Unequal Citizenship in Nigeria

As most Nigerians understand it, their 'federal heritage' began in 1914, with the amalga- mation (or 'coming-together') of Northern and Southern Nigeria. In this reading, contem- porary Nigeria is a 'primordial' federal state, defined by the collapse of well-defined, sovereign political structures into a single nation state forged out of little more than British administrative convenience and economic interest (Umesjesi, 2012, p. 52). Amal- gamation is widely regarded as a 'mistake' or 'fraud' that has shackled fundamentally incompatible societies together, and only the slow process of devolution of the federal scope, first to three (Northern, Western and Eastern) 'regions' and eventually to the contemporary 36 states, has restored a measure of that natural order.

In practice, the story is a bit more complicated. Post-amalgamation Nigeria did not spring into life fully formed as a federation of well-defined 'nations . . . "culture areas," or . . . "linguistic areas"' (Afigbo, 1991, p. 15). Rather, the incentives of colonial administrative and economic institutions fostered the intensification of ethnic mobilization, creating new patterns of group belonging that, as generations passed, provided them with an air of 'naturalness' that they did not initially possess. For example, the ethnic community that is now understood as modern 'Yorubaland', encompassing the former Western Region, is largely the product of British administrative decisions that empowered political elites associated with 'ancestral city' identities and minimized an equally 'real' religious divide between Muslims and Christians (Laitin, 1986, pp. 109–135). Similarly, in Northern Nigeria, where colonial administrators were dependent on the existing political elites—the emirs and the *masu sarauta*, or title-holding class—efforts were made to isolate these communities and their cultural and religious values from the influx of 'native foreigners' (Nigerian colonial subjects from the south) who arrived to serve in administrative posts. By separating newcomers into officially established *sabon gari* ('new town') communities on the periphery of established cities such as Kano and Zaria, they were placed outside the jurisdiction of the local 'native administrators', who retained legal and administrative control over all 'local natives'. A 1934 Order in Council in Northern Nigeria defined natives as colonial subjects in possession of a 'general mode of life' the same as that of the 'general native community' in a particular area (Keay & Richardson, 1966, pp. 165–166). In other words, being a native—and falling under the jurisdiction of a Native Authority and its law—meant 'looking' like a native to the British.

These definitions were more complicated in cities without clear ethnic or religious 'ownership'. In Jos, one of Nigeria's most ethnically heterogeneous communities, colonial uncertainty about who precisely to devolve 'native authority' to in a city without a discrete precolonial history laid the groundwork for generations of future conflict. Initially, the British assigned this status to a small but growing 'Hausa Settlement' that had cropped up in the area around the mining industry, adopting the classic *Sabon Gari* model for other, mostly Christian communities comprised of both southern immigrants and local 'indigenous' peoples. In 1921, colonial policy flipped, eliminating the position of Hausa 'District Head' and transferring new powers to members of the local Birom community. The resulting tensions, simmering over some 20 years, eventually produced Nigeria's first full-scale ethnic riot in 1945 (Plotnicov, 1971).

With the emergence of nationalist movements in Southern Nigeria in the late 1940s, negotiations with the British began to flesh out an explicitly federal future. Both the 1946 and 1951 colonial constitutions provided for a federal system centred around three large regions (North, East and West), each of which possessed considerable ethnic heterogeneity. The question, however, was what the relationship would be between these three regions and their ethnic majorities (Hausa and Fulani in the North, Yoruba in the West, and Igbo in the East), none of which enjoyed a national plurality. One vision, advanced by future Eastern Region Premier and Nigerian president Nnamdi Azikwe (1963–1966), proposed that federalism function as an administrative convenience, not a means of recognizing ethnic diversity. States would be smaller than the current regions and multi-ethnic in their make-up, with a strong federal government over the top. From the West, Obafemi

Awolowo, future leader of the Action Group party and a Yoruba nationalist who once famously declared that Nigeria was not a nation state but rather a 'mere geographical expression' (Awolowo, 1947, p. 47), argued that the diversity of Nigeria's ethnic communities—including, importantly, their very different levels of economic achievement— could only be accommodated in a near-confederal system built around homogenous ethnic 'nations' (Awa, 1964, pp. 25–27). Like Awolowo, the Northern elite, including Sir Ahmadu Bello, leader of the Northern Peoples' Congress (NPC), preferred a loose confederal arrangement, but one that by contrast also preserved the large regional system, which ensured the North's numerical dominance in any federal bodies.

The system that carried Nigeria into its First Republic (1960–1966) was a compromise, ostensibly rejecting the ethnofederal proposals of Awolowo and others in favour of preserving the tripartite regional structure and a limited federal government. At the time, this arrangement was interpreted as a victory for Northern interests, backed in turn by British support for their long-time colonial collaborators. In the long run, however, the strong regional arrangement also proved to be enormously beneficial to ethnic majorities in all three regions. As the pioneering scholar of Nigerian federalism Eme Awa noted at the time, both Azikwe and Awolowo ultimately abandoned their quest for smaller federal units during the 1953–1954 London Constitutional Convention, in no small part because they arrived at the conclusion that the political structures in each of the three regions— single-member districts, for the most part, with a strong regional premier at the top— would ensure the continued electoral dominance of Igbo and Yoruba interests as well as smaller, more homogenous states. The result of the regionalist bargain was that federalism in Nigeria was reduced to little more than a 'philosophy of opportunity'—a means of ensuring that each of the three dominant ethnic communities would be able to 'progress' according to their own trajectories, with minimal competition from the others (Awa, 1964, pp. 46–49). In the Yoruba-dominated Western Region, this meant the opportunity to capitalize on the region's advantages in education and industry without being held back by the much larger but far less developed North. For Northern leaders such as Bello, it meant the Northern elite could prevent the incursion of better-trained southerners into their region's civil service and business sectors, preserving opportunities for locals and ensuring NPC control over the region's resources.

Interestingly, the autonomous regional system did not include a clear insistence on 'dual citizenship'. At the Ibadan General Conference in 1950, Northern delegates succeeded at inserting a clause into the draft constitution permitting only 'native' Northerners with at least three years' consecutive residency to stand for election. Aimed squarely at the Igbo immigrant population in the North, the proposal was received harshly by representatives of the Eastern Region, who pushed back against the 'evil of denial of citizenship status and equal franchise to African "aliens" born or resident in villages and towns outside their clan, tribe, or region', and neither the Eastern or Western Regions adopted similar limits (Awa, 1964, pp. 33–34). The absence of official discrimination did not, however, mean that non-natives and minorities were accorded full political rights or access to state resources. In particular, Bello's NPC succeeded in maintaining a virtually unreconstructed version of the 'Native Authority' system as the administrative and legal apparatus of the Northern Region, relying heavily on this system as a means of controlling and excluding minorities and other political opponents from political power. And across the country, the recommendations of a 1958 Minorities Commission, which had argued for granting minority communities within each region special protections and access to development resources, went largely unimplemented.

As Larry Diamond notes in his comprehensive review of First Republic politics, the 'small number of regions ... allowed few opportunities for the capture of sub-central power, and so made each particular opportunity enormous in its potential reward' (Diamond, 1988, p. 73). Following the 1961 regional election, which saw the NPC (relying heavily on a slate of candidates drawing from the precolonial ruling classes and officers of the 'native administration') nearly entirely eliminate its domestic opposition, power in the federal centre tilted decidedly northwards (Mackintosh, 1966, pp. 535–544). Over the next four years, political competition became increasingly violent, as the NPC and its regional counterparts (Azikwe's NCNC (National Council of Nigeria and the Cameroons) in the East and Samuel Akintola's NNDP (Nigerian National Democratic Party) in the West, which had unseated Awolowo's Action Group in alliance with the NPC) fought desperately to hold the reins of state power and the economic resources that accompanied it. Veiled ethnic threats soon gave way to riots, escalating further following the 1966 coup led by a group of Igbo military officers. Pogroms against Ibgos in Kano, Jos and elsewhere pushed the nation the rest of the way off the cliff, leading to the East's secession in May 1967 and the deadly two-and-a-half-year civil war.

Nigeria's 'Federal Character': Consociational Solution or Powersharing Run Amok?

Looking back as they began the process of crafting the country's next set of democratic institutions in the late 1970s, most Nigerian statesmen had little difficulty identifying the origin of the problem. As then-military ruler General Olusegun Obasanjo put it on the eve of the country's second democratic transition in 1979, the previous era's failures had been caused by leaders who had, in their pursuit of power, 'concentrated on the part and ignored the whole', allowing 'regionalism, tribalism, sectionalism and ethnicity' to erode the political process from the inside out. Speaking two years later as Nigeria's first nationally elected president, Shehu Shagari argued that the First Republic's system of autonomous regions had created a national culture of 'ignorance and unfamiliarity, and therefore fear and mistrust' (Kirk-Greene, 1983, pp. 457–458). Under this logic, a weak confederal state would hardly work. Yet there was little interest in a unitary state, either—particularly one that did not recognize Nigeria's diversity as the basis for the allocation of national resources, including the nation's growing coffers of oil revenues.

The new order was based on an odd, even contradictory combination of policies and institutions that sought both to downplay ethnic conflict through coalition-building and the activation of cross-cutting cleavages, and to formalize consociational commitments to ethnic communities. Geographically, Nigeria's post-war federalism is primarily 'ethnoterritorial', seeking to balance the protection and recognition of minorities by dividing the largest ethnic communities among multiple states. The process began in 1967 when, in a last-ditch effort to maintain the nation's unity, new military head of state Yakubu Gowan formally abolished the regional system in favour of 12 states. In 1976, that number was increased to 19. By splitting the northern Hausa and Fulani majority across 12 states, the Yoruba across five, and the Igbo into two, control of any individual state would be far less consequential and far more dependent on the mobilization of local minority groups, who now formed significant voting blocs (and, in several states, absolute majorities) in their own right. Beginning in the Second Republic (1979–1983) and continuing ever since, state politics have served as the primary space for mobilizing political ethnicity.

A parallel set of reforms introduced in the 1978 constitution were intended to create a set of strong incentives for cross-ethnic, federal-level coalition-building. Here, the key was the adoption of a presidential system, in the hope that it would produce a unifying national leader with a national constituency. Reinforcing this goal was a slate of regulations requiring that a truly national leader fill the presidency. Political parties organized around exclusivist ethnic imagery or restricted to a particular region were banned, and all national parties were required to operate offices in all federal states. All successful presidential candidates were required to win at least 25% of the vote in at least two-thirds of the states, again ensuring that demographic shifts could not swing control to any particular ethnic bloc (Horowitz, 1979, pp. 197–198). Despite the collapse of the Second Republic in 1983, 16 subsequent years of military rule, and several major efforts to revisit these arrangements culminating in the new 1999 constitution, these requirements have largely remained in place (Bogaards, 2010).

As significant as these innovations were (the fate of the 1979 presidential elections came down to the Supreme Court's interpretation of the 'two-thirds' rule), the ethnofederal, consociational components of the 1978 constitution have had a far greater long-term impact on contemporary politics. The most important innovation was a collection of interlocking constitutional and informal policies that have collectively come to be known in Nigerian political parlance as the 'federal character'. The term 'federal character' was first introduced by military ruler General Murtala Mohammed during a speech before the initial meeting of the Constitutional Drafting Committee (CDC) in 1976. In his usage, which was carried forward by the CDC into the final document (in Section 277), he referred to '... the distinctive desire of the peoples of Nigeria to promote national unity, foster national loyalty and give every citizen of Nigeria a sense of belonging in the nation' (Kirk-Greene, 1983, pp. 460–462). In practice, the command to 'recognize Nigeria's "federal character"' translated into a constitutional commitment, formulated primarily in ethnic and regionalist terms, to ensure an 'equitable' balancing of power and resources between federal units. In Section 14(4), the federal government was charged with ensuring that no major areas of administration (ambassadorial and ministerial positions, the military officer corps) were dominated by a 'predominance of persons from a few States or from a few ethnic or other sectional groups', while Section 203(2)b required that the executive committees of all political parties should represent no 'less than two-thirds of all the States comprising the Federation'. In effect, the goal of the federal character principle was to facilitate a visible 'balance' in public life, ensuring that no community could claim that they had been unfairly excluded by those in power.

In its initial formulation, the federal character 'principle' was hardly a principle at all. Its components were scattered across a handful of constitutional clauses and sections, lacking a unified operational definition. In the CDC debates, efforts to promote national unity (by, among other things, providing 'full residence rights for all citizens in all parts of the country') (*Report of the Constitutional Drafting Committee*, 1976, pp. viii–ix) clashed with equally forceful commitments to addressing long-standing fears, held by minority and majority groups alike, of 'domination', 'marginalization' and 'alienation', often through the adoption of implicit quotas or proportionate balancing schemes. But while these initial federal character commitments were judiciously circumscribed to application in a limited number of fields, it soon became clear that the legal apparatus necessary to enforce them would inevitably have much larger consequences. In particular, ensuring the 'fair' distribution of government positions along state lines required a fixed legal definition of state citizenship, something that the First Republic framers had preferred to leave vague in the name of national integration. What they turned to was the colonial doctrine of 'nativeness' in its nearly pristine form. Section 135(3) specified that to meet the distributional requirements of the federal character principle, appointments needed to be filled by 'indigenes', those who belonged (via parentage or grandparentage) to an ethnic community 'indigenous' to that state. And in the absence of a formal definition of indigeneity—a definition did not appear anywhere in the 1978 constitution—it was defined largely (if often unofficially) by a community's legal status under colonial rule. Under the Second Republic, 'Nigerian citizens [had] no right to indigeneity outside the state ascribed to them on the sole basis of their genetic antecedents', no matter how deep their ties to the community might become (Bach, 1997, p. 337). In an effort to promote national unity, the 1978 framers had inadvertently backed into a definition of citizenship that ensured Nigerians remained legally categorized and divided by their ethnic heritage.

How did the (re)introduction of 'indigeneity' as a legal concept affect the trajectory of Nigerian federalism? After the launch of the 1978 constitution, the number of states more than doubled (to 36 by 1996), with the majority of these claims being framed explicitly in ethnic terms (Kraxberger, 2005). Paradoxically, most successful demands came not from minority groups seeking autonomy, but from regional majority groups seeking further subdivisions. Under the 1978 constitution, states received 50% of the national revenue as budgetary support (since 1999, 36%, with 20% going directly to local governments), which encouraged majority ethnic communities to demand that they be subdivided further into more states, each of which would receive its own allocation (Osaghae, 1991, p. 249). In effect, the largest ethnic communities had cracked the code of state creation, recognizing that by demanding more states they could capture a greater overall share of federal resources, undermining the spirit of the entire exercise in the process (Akinyele, 1996, p. 88). As long as the federal character principle remains in place, nearly every community in Nigeria possesses a language that justifies the creation of new state and local government areas (LGAs), even if there is no demonstrable administrative need or long-standing history of 'marginalization' to repair.

Over time, the idea of the federal character has evolved into perhaps the single most important concept in Nigerian public life, a logical framework into which nearly every demand on state resources is fitted and through which every grievance is expressed. It is invoked to debate the ethnic and religious make-up of the roster of the national football team, to analyse the admissions rolls published by all federal universities, and to compare the spatial allocation of market stalls. Moreover, popular understandings of fairness and representativeness in politics have been deeply influenced by the procedural 'headcounting' carried out by most federal character policies, even when the issues at hand are not directly related to ethnicity. In particular, organized religious interests have eagerly adopted federal character language and claim-making, particularly for expanding governmental funding for religious affairs. In perhaps the most notable example, in the mid-1980s Christian organizations lobbied for and received funding for 'Christian pilgrimages' to Rome and Jerusalem in exchange for withdrawing their objections to state support for the annual *hajj*.

The pressure of meeting federal character goals also contributed to the rapid growth of the Nigerian state, expanding opportunities for rent-seeking and other forms of 'prebendalist' corruption (Joseph, 1987). The Shagari presidency, which overlapped with the height of an oil boom that more than doubled petroleum revenues from $9.8 billion in 1978 to $25 billion in 1980 (Lewis, 2007, p. 155), earned a reputation for profligacy and cronyism, tripling administrative costs as a share of federal expenditures during its four-year run. Much of this increase was driven by the need to create a series of expensive new federal ministries (40 cabinet positions in total) and top-level positions in order to meet federal character requirements. Following the collapse of the Second Republic at the end of 1983, the use of federal character justifications to control access to patronage opportunities expanded even more dramatically. As Peter Lewis (1996) has argued, the combination of precipitous economic decline (again, tied to fluctuations in international oil markets) and uncertain political legitimacy forced the Babangida (1985–1993) and Abacha (1993–1998) military regimes to adopt increasingly roundabout strategies for maintaining the support of key constituencies. Beginning with Babangida's ill-fated decision to announce Nigeria's accession to membership in the Organization of Islamic Cooperation (OIC) in 1986, his regime began an informal (but very public) policy of carefully managing the religious and ethnic distribution of cabinet-level positions, not only publically to defuse potential claims of marginalization, but also as a cost-saving measure that allowed the regime to pay off supporters indirectly through expanded access to informal, ethnically based patronage networks. In response, ethnic and religious communities across the country began printing elaborate 'scorecards' in pamphlets and the popular press, detailing the exact ethnic and religious affiliations of nearly all administrative offices and decrying even seemingly minor imbalances as concerted efforts at 'marginalizing' their communities. Current ministerial arrangements (there are 19) require the appointment of multiple 'Ministers of State' (effectively, deputy ministers with cabinet-grade statuses) to attain the 36 total, all of whom receive among the highest compensation packages of any government officials in the world (Pindiga & Nuruddeen, 2013).

Consociationalism and Neopatrimonialism in Federalism: The Nigerian Federal Character Commission

Arguably the most powerful engine for transforming exclusive claims of indigeneity into access to federal resources in Nigeria today is the FCC. The FCC's creation in 1996 marked the culmination of a shift, begun under Babangida, to expand and proceduralize the federal character principle, expanding it beyond its original constitutional mandate into nearly all realms of Nigerian public service. The idea for a formal bureaucratic structure to enforce federal character provisions originated with the 1989 draft constitution, which proposed for the first time to institute formal quota systems for a wide range of institutions, including the boards of parastatal corporations and federal universities. However, it was not until after the failed 1993 democratic transition that an institution for managing formal quotas was actually constructed, this time by the Abacha regime as part of its own transition programme. Today, the FCC's authority is based on the mandate laid out in Part I of the Third Schedule of the 1999 constitution (reinforced in a 2004 legislative act), which provides it with supervisory jurisdiction over the hiring processes of 'all bureaucratic, economic, media, and political posts at all levels of government', with the goal of ensuring the 'fair and equitable distribution of socio-economic amenities and infrastructural facilities throughout the federation' (FCC, 2011a, p. 11). It is also charged (although often hamstrung by inadequate funding and the weakness of the national legal system) with broad powers to sanction and prosecute government bodies and officials that fail to 'imbibe' the spirit of the federal character in their hiring practices.

Beginning with the initial 1996 authorizing law, the FCC's primary task was the enforcement of a public service quota system, fixing the expected representation of indigenes from each state in each institution it supervised at between 2.5% and 3% of total employees. Quotas are also assessed at the 'zonal' level (another Abacha-era invention), six geographic clusters of states (North-West, North-East, North-Central, South-West, South-East and South-South). The system is also supposed to take state and zonal population size and access to education and training into account, increasing the allotments for both the largest states and those with the most qualified candidates. The current formula entitles the Muslim-majority North-West and North-East zones to 15% and 18% of all federal appointments, respectively, while the Yoruba-dominated South-West (including Lagos, with an estimated population of 21 million) are allotted a full 22%. Within states, similar formulas exist to divide appointments between the country's 744 LGAs. There are also safeguards in place intended to prevent quota allotments from serving as 'lever[s] to elevate the incompetent' (FCC, 1996, cited in Mustapha, 2009). The FCC handbook specifies that unqualified candidates cannot be shortlisted for positions based solely on the need to fill zonal quotas, although hiring units are warned to consider personnel who fulfil minimum qualifications *and* originate from under-represented states over better-trained applicants who do not (FCC, 2011b, p. 24).

Officially, these quotas do not revolve around ethnic or religious identities, but to geographic units. However, just as in the original federal character 'principle' formulation, state and LGA citizenship remain determined by indigeneity. For their part, most FCC staff I spoke with were explicit about the ethnic nature of idigeneity in Nigeria. To them, ethnic identity was the content that filled in the indigeneship 'box', providing the common experiences and understandings that made it real. Rather than shying away from the ethnic connotations of the federal character, they embraced the possibility of using the FCC's formal rules and procedures to temper the fears of 'marginalization' that they acknowledged run deeply in the national popular culture. By offering a legal framework for delineating precisely who could lay claim to state benefits (including, implicitly, access to patronage through the appointment of co-ethnics to civil service and parastatal posts), they imagined taking the wind out of the sails of ethnic chauvinists, even if doing so required acknowledging the basic justice of distributing these resources along ethnic lines in the first place.

But if the FCC understands indigeneship in primordialist, ethnic terms, what role does it play in resolving or adjudicating the inevitable conflicts around who qualifies? Just as in the 1978 constitution, the 1999 version does not offer an explicit definition of indigeneity, nor does it provide any official mechanism for resolving disputes around indigeneship status. Indeed, the closest Nigerian law comes to a definition of subnational idigeneity is in the 2004 'Federal Character Commission (Establishment, Etc) Act', which states that:

(1) An indigene of a local government means a person

(a) either of whose parents or any of whose grandparents was or is an indigene of the local government concerned; or

(b)   who is accepted as an indigene by the local government;
        Provided that no person shall claim to more than one local government. (FCC, 2011b,
        p. 16)

The individual qualifications for indigeneship (birth) here are clear, but they are far less so
for groups or communities. The language of Section 1(b) parallels the colonial policy
referenced earlier—effectively, an indigene is someone who 'looks' like an indigene to
the rest of the community—but does not offer any formal guidance for how such a determination might be codified. By virtue of both this statute and its role in administering the
quota system, the FCC would seem to possess the de facto power to determine indigene
status for most federal and state purposes. However, despite this potential authority,
FCC officials suggested to me that they rarely exercise it, and the agency has never established any formal internal mechanism for addressing conflicts over indigeneship status or
maintained any official lists of ethnic groups that quality for indigeneship status in particular jurisdictions. So who actually defines the ethnic terrain of indigeneship? Since the mid-
2000s, the FCC has come to rely on the LGAs to do this work for them, particularly
through the issuance of 'indigeneship certificates' to qualified citizens. Given the lack
of federal oversight, the criteria for assigning indigeneship within LGAs—particularly
around Clause 1(b)—vary tremendously, swayed by the dynamics of local ethnic (and,
where they overlap, religious) conflicts and the results of (often violently contested)
LGA elections. In effect, as Philip Ostien (2009, p. 7) put it, 'whoever controls the
local government controls the issuance of indigene certificates'. Some LGAs (particularly
in metropolitan Lagos) award indigene status to citizens meeting a simple residency
requirement, others refuse to issue them to members of particular ethnic groups entirely
in what appears to be an ad hoc manner (Nigeria Research Network, 2014). In general,
the FCC has chosen to recognize these certificates as they are issued, meaning that the
act of certifying indigeneity has been effectively devolved into the hands of those (local
elected officials) who have the greatest potential interest in manipulating it.

    Not surprisingly given the direct link between political control of LGAs, indigeneity
definitions and access to the primarily oil-derived resources of the Nigerian federal
state, many Nigerians still think of the federal character quota system primarily in neopatrimonial terms—as a tool for advancing the interests of co-ethnics and protecting indigeneity 'rights'; in no small part because the state remains the primary source of wealth
and class advancement in Nigeria and, for many job-seekers, access to co-ethnics with
control over hiring provides the most certain path to state employment. In some instances,
federal character considerations seem to have led ethnic minority communities systematically to pursue admittance and advancement in certain bureaucratic organizations, taking
advantage of unrecognized quota-based opportunities to secure communal access to state
resources (Owen, 2013, pp. 166–168).

    Far from allowing ethnic communities and organizations to relax, secure in the knowl-
edge that the FCC is promoting unity through 'equity, fairness, and justice' (FCC, 2011a,
p. 12), federal character logic compels ethnic actors constantly to cry 'marginalization',
lest any opportunity to secure a foothold in a key agency or office be lost. To cite one
recent example, in October 2013, Yushau Shuaib, a public relations officer for the National
Emergency Management Agency (NEMA), was fired following the publication of an
article in which he accused the federal minister of finance, Ngozi Okonjo-Iwaela, of
'playing an ethnic game' in pursuing the appointment of her 'Igbo kinsmen' over

Northerners (read: Muslims) to key positions in the financial regulatory section (Shuaib, 2013; *Punch*, 2013). But as Okojo-Iwaela herself recounted in an interview at the height of the controversy, the hiring process she oversaw adhered to strict federal character controls, including the appointment of a nominations committee with representatives from each zone and the use of outside consulting firms to craft shortlists. That such a process had not produced a perfectly proportional ethno-regional balance in any given agency was, from her perspective, a secondary concern. In his spirited defence of the minister, then-Central Bank chairman Sanusi Lamido Sanusi (a northern Muslim) argued that by identifying the federal character principle with ethnic headcounting, many Nigerians had lost sight of its original purpose—to build national unity through the assurance that the 'diversity of Nigeria' would be reflected in its corridors of power. Instead, he observed, this distorted logic forces 'loyal' co-ethnics to defend even the most corrupt and inefficient appointees from the consequences of their actions:

> Diversity is not just ethnicity-driven, but you still have Muslims, Christians; north-erners, southerners, women, men; and that is what is called federal character. Apart from all these ridiculous things of accusing someone of who you appoint and did not appoint, the entire concept about inclusion and diversity have [*sic*] been so abused that anyone who loses a position, for instance, you sack the management of an insti-tution for fraud and someone says it is ethnic cleansing. You all know what we went through in the banking industry when people stole people's money and we removed them, it was seen as a northern agenda. So is it southern agenda to steal N192 billion of depositors' fund? So, we need to outgrow this. (Gabriel, 2013)

In principle, as most FCC staff members suggested to me, the rules and procedures relied on by Okojo-Iwaela are the best defence against these claims, followed closely by trans-parency with respect to quota fulfilment. As one senior FCC official told me, he regarded his office's most challenging job not to be the management of the quota system itself (although technical and recordkeeping challenges reared their heads constantly), but rather the effort to counter metaphorical, overly broad uses of the federal character language and to replace them with a focus on the rules and procedures the FCC oversees. But can reliance on rules and procedures really meet the challenge the FCC has set for itself to 'promote one indissoluble Nigeria' (FCC, 2012)? The evidence is mixed, trending negative. On their own terms, it has proved nearly impossible for the FCC to ensure the achievement of quota targets in federal ministries and parastatals, and over the past decade the FCC's own documentation suggests that there has been relatively little move-ment in the percentages of state indigenes represented in the civil service. In its 2011 annual report, the FCC found, not surprisingly, that the Muslim-majority northern states remain significantly under-represented on the federal payroll (a fact that is almost certainly connected to their under-representation in federal universities and, more broadly, to their greater poverty and poorer educational systems), as do several smaller states in the south. In all, only seven states have staff contingents that fall within the official quota range (FCC, 2011a, pp. 184–190) and, by their own account, the FCC's broader mission to ensure the even distribution of 'socio-economic amenities' remains largely untouched.

In the FCC's favour, the venal pressures of the Nigerian political process, which ensure that a significant proportion of the national wealth is distributed illicitly, put the goal of promoting substantive equality outside the reach of any individual agency. Similarly,

Nigeria's rapidly growing income and wealth inequality speaks to larger, systematic failures of distributive justice. Yet within both the halls of the FCC and Nigerian society at large, attachment to the federal character principle, at least in this distributive sense, remains quite strong. Much like the national fuel subsidy, a manifestly inefficient policy that is nonetheless popularly beloved because of its tangibility as evidence that the Nigerian state is doing *something* for ordinary citizens, the federal character principle and the FCC's quota system serves to soothe the deeply ingrained suspicions many Nigerians hold that, without constant vigilance, they too might find themselves marginalized. However, as the guardians of legal indigeneship, the FCC runs the risk of driving the very divisiveness they were meant to contain.

Nigeria's Unfinished State-nation

Although it is not often discussed in these terms, Nigeria's federal system is perhaps best understood as a post-conflict powersharing arrangement, one that has endured (despite 16 years of military rule) in roughly the same form for over 35 years. Given the continental standards to which it might be compared, this represents something of a success story. Both of Nigeria's post-war constitutions demonstrate a commitment to the notion that a broad and inclusive ruling coalition, one that grants access to power and state resources and recognition to as many communities as possible, is the safest path to popular political legitimacy and stability a divided nation can travel. Yet despite the entrenchment of federal, consociational powersharing principles—most importantly, the 'federal character'—in Nigerian political life, sectarian claim-making remains a frequent and intense source of conflict and violence, particularly in the very ethnically and religiously divided communities that should have seen the greatest benefit from these new arrangements.

In this article, I have argued that although ethnic powersharing institutions such as the Nigerian FCC offer transparent processes for sharing and distributing access to state employment and resources, they can also play the unintentional role of reinforcing fundamental inequalities of citizenship. These inequalities originated in the indirect rule strategies of late nineteenth and early twentieth century colonial rule, but in the postcolonial era they have achieved the status of constitutional law and, even more strikingly, 'common sense' in many Nigerian communities. Indigeneity, indigeneship certificates and 'native/settler' conflicts need not be central components of consociational powersharing systems, but in the face of an entrenched legacy of 'dual citizenship' they become difficult outcomes to avoid. In Nigeria, this problem is magnified by a federal system that, despite its efforts to devolve power away from ethnic majorities and towards local, pluralist communities, reinforces the primacy of subnational, ethnic belonging over national citizenship. Perhaps not surprisingly, Nigerians demonstrate some of the lowest commitments to national pride and identity of any citizens on the continent (Robinson, 2009).

In this sense, the real influence of the FCC on national political life comes not from its earnest efforts to achieve national unity through the 'fair' distribution of state employment, but from its endorsement of a primordialist vision of subnational citizenship that encourages Nigerians to view ethnic group membership as the primary vehicle for access to state resources. Ethnic powersharing principles such as the federal character were meant to reduce the stakes of political competition, channelling demands for state resources within institutions designed to manage and contain them. But as Mamadou

Gazibo (2013, pp. 84–85) has argued, democracies facing down a legacy of neopatrimonial rule often struggle with the 'coexistence of contradictory norms'—both formal rules and procedures and informal networks and pathways—by which elites and citizens alike pursue access to power and wealth. In the case of the FCC, quota systems based (ultimately, if not directly) on ethnic group membership serve not to provide a sense of belonging and security to potentially 'marginalized' communities, but to link the formal institutions of the federal state with the informal ethnic patronage networks that most Nigerians still trust to provide them with their best chance at upward mobility (Daloz, 2005); and in a federal structure where centralized oil revenues remain the primary funding source for state and local governments, restrictive citizenship rules reinforce the notion that asserting indigeneity claims is a winning strategy for capturing state resources.

Although there is not space here for a more detailed comparison, it is interesting to contrast the Nigerian experience with consociational powersharing and federalism with that of India, where, according to Stepan *et al.* (2011), the 'state-nation' building project has paid significant democratic dividends. Like Nigeria, India's federal powersharing system is not entirely consociational, but it does formally recognize a range of sectarian identities for accommodation. From Stepan *et al.*'s perspective, one of the great successes of Indian federalism was its tolerance towards its citizens' possession of multiple identities, built on the core assumption that it was not necessary to build the political community around dominant Hindu/Hindi religious and linguistic models. As a result, cultural nationalist movements such as those among the Tamils in the south found it possible both to retain their particularity *and* to participate in national political life (Stepan *et al.*, 2011, pp. 129–134).

Unspoken in this story, however, is the role of citizenship policy in fostering the successful balancing of national and subnational identities. Indeed, Stepan *et al.* seem to assume that language and culture are the largest barriers to 'polity-wide careers', to be overcome (although, particularly in regional politics, not necessarily easily) by retaining English as the medium of governance over Hindi (Stepan *et al.*, 2011, p. 128). But although late colonial India witnessed a distinct move towards using ethnic and religious identities as justifications for legal pluralism (particularly in terms of property rights) (Newbigin, 2013), this never carried over into the establishment of 'dual citizenship' for members of different ethnic or religious communities. At independence, the question of how to define national citizenship was a thorny one, embedded in broader debates about the role of religion, language and territoriality in defining Indian nationality, and heavily contested between supporters of Nehru's 'secular nationalism' and the Hindu nationalist community (Adeney & Lall, 2005). However, there seems to have been no serious thought given to creating legal categories of 'indigeneship' that assigned special rights to residents of particular communities based on their 'nativeness', even for territories governed by 'native authorities' under indirect rule-style arrangements during the colonial era.

Perhaps in no small part due to the fact that Indian citizenship is and has always been a national affair, problems of neopatrimonialism and the centrality of the state as a source of resource accumulation have not proved as difficult and divisive in India as across much of Africa, either. Tellingly, Stepan *et al.* (2011) ignore this problem altogether in their discussion of India, despite the fact that, as Kanchan Chandra has observed, the state still 'controls the bulk of resources in Indian society', and that federal politics in India clearly revolve around securing access to these resources through ethnic, religious and linguistic claim-making (Chandra, 2005, pp. 239–240). In this sense, the absence of a 'dual citizenship' heritage seems to free up the operation of federal institutions to focus on the goals of good governance rather than on the procedures of distributing resources. As Kenneth Wheare (1943, p. 43) once famously warned, 'federalism is not an end in itself'. When it becomes—as it so often has in Nigeria—simply a means of accessing wealth, it serves to entrench, rather than mediate, the differences between federal units and their citizens,

The federal character 'principle' and the FCC's quota system remain quite popular in Nigeria, but there is also a growing awareness that the 'dual citizenship' model, particularly as embedded in institutions such as the FCC, drives patronage politics and undermines the universal application of human rights (Nwachukwu, 2005; Ejobowah, 2013). These concerns have even received federal acknowledgement, in the form of a 2011 constitutional amendment (Section 42[1]) that prohibits both the assignment of 'disabilities or restrictions' and 'priviledge[s] or advantage[s]' on the basis of ethnicity, place of origin and religion. However, laws that 'impose restrictions with respect to the appointment of any person to any office under the State' are excluded, meaning that, for the foreseeable future, indigeneity will continue to be a deciding factor in the allocation of many important state resources. Can the FCC's balancing act succeed in contributing to the development of a 'state-nation' in Nigeria, one that rallies Nigerians around a common sense of trust and pride in the nation while retaining respect for difference? As long as ethnic powersharing serves to divide Nigerians more than it brings them together, I remain unconvinced.

References

Adebanwi, W. & Obadare, E. (Eds) (2013) *Democracy and Prebendalism in Nigeria: Critical Interpretations* (New York: Palgrave-Macmillan).

Adeney, K. & Lall, M. (2005) Institutional attempts to build a 'national' identity in India: internal and external dimensions, *India Review*, 4(3–4), pp. 258–286.

Afigbo, A.E. (1991) Background to Nigerian federalism: federal features in the colonial state, *Publius*, 21(4), pp. 13–29.

Akinyele, R.T. (1996) States creation in Nigeria: the Willink report in retrospect, *African Studies Review*, 39(2), pp. 71–94.

Anderson, L. (2013) *Federal Solutions to Ethnic Problems: Accommodating Diversity* (New York: Routledge).

Awa, E. (1964) *Federal Government in Nigeria* (Berkeley: University of California Press).

Awolowo, O. (1947) *Path to Nigerian Freedom* (London: Faber and Faber).

Bach, D. (1989) Managing a plural society: the boomerang effects of Nigerian federalism, *Journal of Commonwealth & Comparative Politics*, 27(2), pp. 218–245.

Bach, D. (1997) Indigeneity, ethnicity, and federalism, in: L.J. Diamond, A.H.M Kirk-Greene & O. Oyediran (Eds), *Transition Without End: Nigerian Politics and Civil Society Under Babangida* (Boulder, CO: Lynne Rienner).

Bogaards, M. (2010) Ethnic party bans and institutional engineering in Nigeria, *Democratization*, 17(4), pp. 730–749.

Ceuppens, B. & Geschiere, P. (2005) Autochthony: local or global? New modes in the struggle over citizenship and belonging in Africa and Europe, *Annual Review of Anthropology*, 34, pp. 385–407.

Chandra, K. (2005) Ethnic parties and democratic stability, *Perspectives on Politics*, 3(2), pp. 235–252.

Daily Champion (Lagos) (2008) Editorial: fresh air from Sokoto, 3 January.

Daloz, J.P. (2005) Nigeria: trust your patron and not the institutions, *Comparative Sociology*, 4(1–2), pp. 129–146.

Diamond, L. (1988) *Class, Ethnicity, and Democracy in Nigeria: The Failure of the First Republic* (Syracuse, NY: Syracuse University Press).

Diamond, L. & Suberu, R. (2002) Institutional design, ethnic conflict management, and democracy in Nigeria, in: A. Reynolds (Ed.), *The Architecture of Democracy: Constitutional Design, Conflict Management, and Democracy* (Oxford: Oxford University Press).

Dorman, S., Hammett, D. & Nugent, P. (2007) *Making Nations, Creating Strangers: States and Citizenship in Africa* (Leiden: Brill).

Easterly, W. & Levine, R. (1997) Africa's growth tragedy: policies and ethnic divisions, *Quarterly Journal of Economics*, 62(4), pp. 1,203–1,250.

Ejobowah, J.B. (2013) Ethnic conflict and cooperation: assessing citizenship in Nigerian Federalism, *Publius*, 43(4), pp. 728–747.

Ekeh, P. (1975) Colonialism and the two publics in Africa: a theoretical statement, *Comparative Studies in Society and History*, 17(1), pp. 91–112.

Englebert, P. & Hummel, R. (2005) Let's stick together: understanding Africa's secessionist deficit, *African Affairs*, 104, pp. 399–427.

Fanthorpe, R. (2001) Neither citizen nor subject? 'Lumpen' agency and the legacy of native administration in Sierra Leone, *African Affairs*, 100, pp. 363–386.

Federal Character Commission (2011a) *Federal Character Commission 2011 Annual Report* (Abuja: Government Printer).

Federal Character Commission (2011b) *The Presidency: Federal Character Commission Handbook, 2011 Revised Edition* (Abuja: Xavier Communications).

Federal Character Commission (2012) Federal Character Commission—Mandates, Achievements, Constraints and Areas Assistance is Required: A Brief Presented to Public Accounts Committee of House of Representatives on Status Inquiry of MDAs, 2007–2011, unpublished report in possession of author.

Gabriel, O. (2013) Nigerians push federal character to the extreme, *Vanguard* (Lagos), 29 April.

Gazibo, M. (2013) Can neopatrimonialism dissolve into democracy?, in: D. Bach & M. Gazibo (Eds), *Neopatrimonialism in Africa and Beyond* (London: Routledge).

Gervasconi, C. (2010) A rentier theory of subnational regimes: fiscal federalism, democracy and authoritarianism in the Argentine provinces, *World Politics*, 62(2), pp. 302–340.

Geschiere, P. (2009) *The Perils of Belonging: Autochthony, Citizenship, and Exclusion in Africa and Europe* (Chicago: University of Chicago Press).

Hale, H. (2004) Divided we stand: institutional sources of ethnofederal state survival and collapse, *World Politics*, 56(2), pp. 165–193.

Horowitz, D. (1979) About-face in Africa: the return to civilian rule Nigeria, *Yale Review*, 68(2), pp. 192–206.

Horowitz, D. (1985) *Ethnic Groups in Conflict* (Berkeley: University of California Press).

Human Rights Watch (2006) *'They Do Not Own This Place': Government Discrimination Against 'Non-indigenes' in Nigeria* (New York: Human Rights Watch).

Jackson, V. (2001) Citizenship and federalism, in: T.A. Aleinikoff & D.B. Klusmeyer (Eds), *Citizenship Today: Global Perspectives and Practices* (Washington, DC: Brookings Institution Press).

Joseph, R. (1987) *Democracy and Prebendal Politics in Nigeria: The Rise and Fall of the Second Republic* (New York: Cambridge University Press).

Keay, E.A. and Richardson, S.S. (1966) *The Native and Customary Courts of Nigeria* (London: Sweet & Maxwell).

Keller, E. & Smith, L. (2005) Obstacles to implementing territorial decentralization: the first decade of Ethiopian federalism, in: P. Roeder & D. Rothchild (Eds), *Sustainable Peace: Democracy and Power-dividing Institutions after Civil Wars* (Ithaca, NY: Cornell University Press).

Kendhammer, B. (2010) Talking ethnic but hearing multi-ethnic: the Peoples' Democratic Party (PDP) in Nigeria and durable multi-ethnic parties in the midst of violence, *Commonwealth & Comparative Politics*, 48(1), pp. 48–71.

Kirk-Greene, A. (1983) Ethnic engineering and the 'federal character' of Nigeria: boon of contentment or bone of contention?, *Ethnic and Racial Studies*, 6(4), pp. 457–476.

Klug, H. (2000) How the centre holds: managing claims for regional and ethnic autonomy in a democratic South Africa, in: Y. Ghai (Ed.), *Autonomy and Ethnicity* (New York: Cambridge University Press).

Kraxberger, B. (2005) Strangers, indigenes and settlers: contested geographies of citizenship in Nigeria, *Space and Polity*, 9(1), pp. 9–27.

Kymlicka, W. (2006) Emerging western models of multination federalism: are they relevant for Africa?, in: D. Turton (Ed.), *Ethnic Federalism: The Ethiopian Experience in Comparative Perspective* (Athens, OH: Ohio University Press).

Kymlicka, W. (2007) National cultural autonomy and international minority rights norms, *Ethnopolitics*, 6(3), pp. 379–393.

Laitin, D. (1986) *Culture and Hegemony: Politics and Religious Change Among the Yoruba* (Chicago: University of Chicago Press).

Lemarchand, R. (2007) Consociationalism and power sharing in Africa: Rwanda, Burundi, and the Democratic Republic of the Congo, *African Affairs*, 106, pp. 1–20.

Lewis, P. (1996) From prebendalism to predation: the political economy of decline in Nigeria, *Journal of Modern African Studies*, 34(1), pp. 79–103.

Lewis, P. (2007) *Growing Apart: Oil, Politics, and Economic Change in Indonesia and Nigeria* (Ann Arbor, MI: University of Michigan Press).

Lijphart, A. (1977) *Democracy in Plural Societies: A Comparative Exploration* (New Haven: Yale University Press).

Lijphart, A. (2002) The wave of democratic power-sharing, in: A. Reynolds (Ed.), *The Architecture of Democracy: Constitutional Design, Conflict Management, and Democracy* (Oxford: Oxford University Press).

Mackintosh, J. (1966) *Nigerian Government and Politics: Prelude to the Revolution* (Evanston: Northwestern University Press).

Mamdani, M. (1996) *Citizen and Subject: Contemporary Africa and the Legacy of Late Colonialism* (Princeton, NJ: Princeton University Press).

Mamdani, M. (1999) Historicizing power and responses to power: indirect rule and its reform, *Social Research*, 66(3), pp. 859–883.

Mamdani, M. (2001) Beyond settler and native as political identities: overcoming the political legacy of colonialism, *Comparative Studies in Society and History*, 43(4), pp. 651–664.

Mamdani, M. (2012) *Define and Rule: Native as Political Identity* (Cambridge: Harvard University Press).

Manby, B. (2009) *Struggles for Citizenship in Africa* (London: Zed).

Mantena, K. (2010) *Alibis of Empire: Henry Maine and the Ends of Liberal Imperialism* (Princeton, NJ: Princeton University Press).

McGarry, J. & O'Leary, B. (2009) Must pluri-national federations fail?, *Ethnopolitics*, 8(1), pp. 5–26.

Milligan, M. (2013) Fighting for the right to exist: institutions, identity, and conflict in Jos, Nigeria, *Comparative Politics*, 45(3), pp. 313–334.

Mustapha, A.R. (2009) Institutionalizing ethnic representation: how effective is affirmative action in Nigeria?, *Journal of International Development*, 21, pp. 561–576.

Newbigin, E. (2013) *The Hindu Family and the Emergence of Modern India Law, Citizenship and Community* (New York: Cambridge).

Nigeria Research Network (2014) Indigeneity, Belonging, & Religious Freedom in Nigeria, *NRN Policy Brief No. 5*.

Nimni, E. (2007) National–cultural autonomy as an alternative to minority territorial nationalism, *Ethnopolitics*, 6(3), pp. 345–364.

Njoku, R.C. (1999) Consociationalism: its relevance for Nigeria, *Nationalism and Ethnic Politics*, 5(2), pp. 1–35.

Nwachukwu, I. (2005) Challenges of local citizenship for human rights in Nigeria, *African Journal of International and Comparative Law*, 13, pp. 235–261.

O'Leary, B. (2005) Debating consociational politics: normative and explanatory arguments, in: S. Noel (Ed.), *From Power-sharing to Democracy: Post-conflict Institutions in Ethnically Divided Societies*, pp. 3–43 (Vancouver: University of British Columbia Press).

Osaghae, E. (1990) The problems of citizenship in Nigeria, *Africa*, 45(4), pp. 593–611.

Osaghae, E. (1991) Ethnic minorities and federalism in Nigeria, *African Affairs*, 90, pp. 237–258.

Osaghae, E. (1998) Managing multiple minority problems in a divided society: the Nigerian experience, *Journal of Modern African Studies*, 36(1), pp. 1–24.

Osaghae, E. (2003) Colonialism and civil society in Africa: the perspective of Ekeh's two publics, presented at the *Symposium on Canonical Works and Continuing Innovation in African Arts and Humanities*, Accra, Ghana. Sharia Debates in Africa Project, University of Bayreuth.

Ostien, P. (2009) Jonah Jang and the Jasawa: ethno-religious conflict in Jos, Nigeria, *Muslim–Christian Relations in Africa*.

Owen, O. (2013) Positions of security and the security of position: bureaucratic prebendalism inside the state, in: W. Adebanwi & E. Obadare (Eds), *Democracy and Prebendalism in Nigeria: Critical Interpretations* (New York: Palgrave-Macmillan).

Perham, M. (1934) A re-statement of indirect rule, *Africa*, 7(3), pp. 321–334.

Pindiga, H. & Nuruddeen M.A. (2013) Investigation: Nigeria pays ministers higher than US, UK, SA, *Daily Trust* (Abuja), 25 July.

Plotnicov, L. (1971) An early Nigerian civil disturbance: the 1945 Hausa-Ibo riot in Jos, *Journal of Modern African Studies*, 9(2), pp. 297–305.

Punch (Lagos) (2013) FG sacks ex-NEMA spokesman over article on Okonjo-Iweala, 9 October.

Report of the Constitutional Drafting Committee (1976), Vol. 1 (Lagos: Federal Ministry of Information).

Robinson, A.L. (2009) National versus Ethnic Identity in Africa: State, Group, and Individual Level Correlates of National Identification, *Afrobarometer Working Paper No. 112*.

Rothchild, D. & Roeder, P. (2005) *Sustainable Peace: Power and Democracy After Civil Wars* (Ithaca, NY: Cornell University Press).

Shuaib, Y. (2013) Still on Okonjo-Iweala over controversial appointments, *Sahara Reporters*, accessed 13 November, available online at: http://saharareporters.com/article/still-okonjo-iweala-over-controversial-appointments-yushau-shuaib

Sisk, T. (1995) *Democratization in South Africa: The Elusive Social Contract* (Princeton: Princeton University Press).

Smith, L. (2007) Voting for an ethnic identity: procedural and institutional responses to ethnic conflict in Ethiopia, *Journal of Modern African Studies*, 45(4), pp. 565–594.

Snyder, J. (2000) *From Voting to Violence* (New York: W.W. Norton).

Spears, I. (2002) Africa: the limits of powersharing, *Journal of Democracy*, 13(3), pp. 123–136.

Stearns, J. (2010) *Dancing in the Glory of Monsters* (New York: Public Affairs).

Stepan, A. (1999) Federalism and democracy: beyond the U.S. model, *Journal of Democracy*, 10(4), pp. 19–34.

Stepan, A., Linz, J. & Yadev, Y. (2011) *Crafting State-nations: India and Other Multinational Democracies* (Baltimore: Johns Hopkins University Press).

Suberu, R. (2001) *Federalism and Ethnic Conflict in Nigeria* (Washington, DC: US Institute of Peace Press).

Suberu, R. (2009) Federalism in Africa: the Nigerian experience in comparative perspective, *Ethnopolitics*, 8(1), pp. 67–86.

Umesjesi, I. (2012) The nation state, resource conflict, and the challenges of 'former sovereignties' in Nigeria, *African Studies Quarterly*, 13(3), pp. 47–66.

Wheare, K. (1943) What federal government is, in: P. Ransome (Ed.), *Studies in Federal Planning*, pp. 17–38 (London: Palgrave MacMillan).

Ethnopolitics, 2014
Vol. 13, No. 4, 418–427, http://dx.doi.org/10.1080/17449057.2014.921485

DEBATE

Non-territorial Autonomy in Canada: Reply to Chouinard

RÉMI LÉGER

Simon Fraser University, Canada

There is an impressive amount of scholarship on the broad topic of multiculturalism and minority rights in Canada. A significant number of researchers have explored central issues related to our federal system, nationalism and nation-building, Aboriginal self-determination and religious or cultural accommodations. Key works—such as Charles Taylor's 'The politics of recognition' (1994), James Tully's *Strange Multiplicity* (1995) and Will Kymlicka's *Multicultural Citizenship* (1995)—have gone on to shape research agendas and global debates on citizenship and democracy in diverse societies. An influential counter scholarship has also emerged. It refutes the dominant interpretations of the state's successes in dealing with minority rights-claims and accommodations—see, for example, Gerald Kernerman's *Multicultural Nationalism* (2006) or Rita Dhamoon's *Identity/Difference Politics* (2009).

Stéphanie Chouinard's article—'The rise of non-territorial autonomy in Canada: towards a doctrine of institutional completeness in the domain of minority language rights' (2014)—engages with this scholarship on two fronts. She first explores the case of Canada's francophone minority communities (FMCs)—the close to one million French-speakers living in provinces and territories outside Québec. As an increasing number of researchers have noted over the past few years, these minorities have been rendered invisible in the scholarship on multiculturalism and minority rights in Canada (Thériault *et al.*, 2008, p. 22; Cardinal & Hidalgo, 2012, p. 55; Poirier, 2012, pp. 67–68). Second, Chouinard also introduces the seldom-used notion of non-territorial autonomy (NTA) to examine the claims of FMCs as well as state responses to their claims. She aims to show that NTA has emerged in Canada through the equivalent notion of institutional completeness.

I divide my comments on Chouinard's article into two main parts and a conclusion. I begin by discussing her original thesis—the contention that FMCs have claimed NTA

Correspondence Address: Rémi Léger, Department of Political Science, Simon Fraser University, 8888 University Drive, Burnaby, British Columbia, Canada V5A 1S6. Email: rleger@sfu.ca

© 2014 The Editor of Ethnopolitics

and that the state, pushed along by the courts, has responded with NTA. I then explore the scholarship on NTA in order to show how Chouinard reproduces some of its definitional problems, and how these problems weaken the promising notion of institutional completeness. Finally, I conclude with a very general defence of institutional completeness both as an analytical lens and as a normative benchmark.

An Original Thesis

I first want to situate Chouinard's article within recent scholarship on NTA as well as on multiculturalism and minority rights in Canada. Her twofold submission that FMCs have claimed NTA and that the federal government has responded with NTA is an original thesis. In Canada, there is a rich scholarship on *territorial* autonomy as it relates to francophones in Québec (Gagnon & Iacovino, 2007), the Inuit in Nunavut (Loukacheva, 2007) or even in Nunavik and Nunatsiavut (Rodon & Grey, 2009), and finally Aboriginal peoples across the country (Otis & Papillon, 2013). As for NTA, it is scarcely mentioned in relevant academic debates or policy research. Political scientists, normative philosophers and legal experts have dissected the ins and outs of territorial autonomy in Canada, and have, in essence, snubbed NTA.

As for the emerging scholarship on the applications and normative justifications of NTA, Canada is generally not cited. Common examples or case studies include Belgium (Jacobs & Swyngedouw, 2003), Estonia (Alenius, 2007), Hungary (Dobos, 2007), Russia (Osipov, 2010) and increasingly the Roma in Central and Eastern Europe (Klimova-Alexander, 2007; Lajcakova, 2010). In a recent article, Bertus de Villiers (2012), aiming to highlight the latest advances on NTA, examines the cases of Estonia, Slovenia, Kosovo and Finland. There is no mention of Canada. Indeed, de Villiers (2012, p. 171) lists Belgium and Russia as the only federations to have formal arrangements of NTA. More broadly, NTA is often seen as a promising tool for new democracies or democratizing countries, not for Canada or other such established liberal democracies. For many, the important reflections on and developments in NTA are taking place in Central and Eastern Europe. As per André Liebich (2008, p. 279), this area has 'some of the most imaginative solutions to the co-existence of different peoples, such as Austro-Marxist schemes of cultural or non-territorial autonomy'.

Another strand of research on NTA concerns ethnic conflicts and human rights. In this scholarship, NTA is a tool of conflict prevention or resolution. It is a set of normative principles and institutional mechanisms that are aimed at existing political situations. These detailed prescriptions are inspired from contemporary or historical case studies as well as from theoretical proposals. Sherrill Stroschein (2008), Christopher Decker (2007) and Andreas Follesdal's (2011) respective works on Kosovo, Romania and Nepal are powerful examples of this research. Stroschein's work, for example, makes a case for 'dispersed state control' whereby state functions—such as educational or health affairs—are allocated to subunits that need not be territorial. As a result, individuals within the same subunit might be dispersed throughout Kosovo and not concentrated in a neat geographical area. The subunits have an ethnocultural rather than territorial basis. As with the scholarship on existing or historical forms of NTA, Canada is also not featured in this second strand of research concerned with conflicts and human rights.

With that said, there are nevertheless a handful of exploratory works on the promise and possibilities of NTA in Canada. These are exploratory in the sense that they are theoretical reflections on what could be or what ought to be as opposed to works that explore existing constitutional design or institutional mechanisms.[1] David Elkins was the first to give serious consideration to the possibilities of NTA in Canada in a reflection on territory and territorial politics in the contemporary era (Elkins, 1995; see also Elkins, 1992). Starting from the premise that 'the social distribution of population' in Canada does not coincide with our 'territorial division of protagonists', Elkins (1995, pp. 147–155) promotes the creation of two non-territorial provinces, one for francophones living outside Québec, and another for Aboriginals across the country. Non-territorial provinces would enable these groups to exercise powers of control over matters deemed crucial to their flourishing, including education and health services.

Tim Nieguth (1999, 2009) has also written about NTA in Canada. His two articles take as their starting point the works of Austro-Marxists Karl Renner and Otto Bauer—I discuss these two authors in the second part of this reply. After examining the institutional content and the normative justification of their scheme, Nieguth suggests that NTA is worth considering as part of a broader package of rights and accommodations, which could include settling land claims with Aboriginal peoples and enshrining Québec's national character in the constitution. In specific relation to FMCs, not much is said. In two brief passages, the author mentions that 'certain powers' could be devolved to public corporations representing FMCs, and that the scheme 'could be a particularly useful tool' for FMCs and other historic minorities (Nieguth, 2009, pp. 12–13).

Finally, Johanne Poirier (2008, 2012) has recently reflected on the possibilities and difficulties associated with granting autonomy to FMCs. As with Elkins and Nieguth, Poirier's writings are theoretical reflections on institutional mechanisms and normative principles. Of particular interest to her are what could be or what ought to be. Her two articles discuss a range of institutional options, including territorial solutions such as a new province or new territories, and non-territorial solutions such as cultural autonomy or personal federalism (Poirier, 2008, pp. 535–550). For her, any institutional accommodation of FMCs, whether territorial or non-territorial, must account for their rights-claims and their broader aspirations (Poirier, 2012, p. 85).

To return to Chouinard, the synopsis provided here would seem to confirm that her thesis distinguishes itself from the existing relevant scholarship because hers is not an exercise in theoretical proposals or normative prescriptions. Her thesis is original because she submits that NTA already exists in the Canadian context. She affirms that 'NTA [was] claimed by the FMCs', and that, in response to these claims, Canadian courts have defined a 'right to NTA through various judgments' relating to minority language educational rights and official language rights (Chouinard, 2014, pp. 142, 146). In summary, Chouinard flips the existing scholarship on NTA on its head.

What is Non-territorial Autonomy?

Chouinard asserts that NTA in Canada has emerged through the equivalent notion of institutional completeness. She writes: 'from 2000 to today, a clearer definition of a right to non-territorial autonomy has developed, through the concept of institutional completeness' (Chouinard, 2014, p. 146). In this second part, I explore definitional problems that continue to cloud the scholarship on NTA, and I explain how Chouinard falls prey to some of them in the process of equating institutional completeness to NTA. In my view, institutional completeness is a poorer analytical lens and normative benchmark when equated to NTA.

The past 20 years have witnessed the re-emergence of NTA in political and academic debates on multiculturalism and minority rights as well as on ethnic conflicts. NTA has elicited growing interest from academics as well as from a number of social actors and policymakers in Central and Eastern Europe. Political scientists, for example, have identified and evaluated existing political mechanisms that are consistent with theories and principles of NTA. Examples include Estonia's 1993 Law on Cultural Autonomy for National Minorities, Hungary's 1993 Law on the Rights of National and Ethnic minorities, Russia's 1996 Law on National-Cultural Autonomy and Slovenia's 1994 Law on Self-managing Ethnic Communities (see Coakley, 1994; Smith, 2013). For their part, normative theorists have explored the main conceptual features of NTA, as well as reflected on how these features relate to liberal principles of justice and equality (Bauböck, 2004; Nootens, 2006; Kymlicka, 2007). Taken together, these efforts have shed light on the trajectory of NTA, and have made NTA an increasingly credible institutional option for the protection and promotion of ethnocultural groups.

The scholarship on NTA remains, however, fraught with definitional problems. Alexander Osipov (2013, p. 3), a leading scholar of NTA, wrote: 'there is no uniform definition and no commonly accepted understanding of what NTA may actually mean'. In no particular order of importance, NTA can reference the scheme elaborated for the Austro-Hungarian Empire at the turn of the twentieth century, the laws implemented in Estonia and Latvia in the 1920s, the scheme envisioned by the Congress of European Nationalities during the interwar period, the Russian experiences ensuing from its Law on National-Cultural Autonomy, and recent institutional mechanisms created over the past 20 years in Central and Eastern Europe. Of course these various iterations of NTA can share certain features, but they also differ in terms of content and objectives. For example, as David Smith (2010, p. 85) observed in relation to the Minorities Congress, 'debates were clearly inspired by the theories of Renner and Bauer', but at the same time they 'also drew directly upon the practical work and experiences of a range of minority political activists'.

Chouinard runs into and reproduces some of these definitional problems. In her article, NTA is presented as a specific, clearly defined scheme for the protection and promotion of ethnocultural groups. Indeed, she equates NTA with the works of Karl Renner and Otto Bauer during the final days of the Austro-Hungarian Empire. These two social democratic theorists aimed to 'enable the working class of the various national groups of the Empire to reconcile the quest for their respective nationalist goals with a common socialist action against capitalism' (McRae, 1975, p. 37). For Renner and Bauer, there was no logical connection between nationality and territory. Membership in a nation was to be a personal declaration, regardless of where an individual resided within the state. A German living on predominantly Czech territory could declare him/herself a German national. Nations could thus include concentrated and/or dispersed populations. Their scheme revolved around a complex federal structure with overlaid territorial and non-territorial administrative units. Non-territorial national councils were to have powers to legislate on cultural matters, and the territorial provinces would have regulated non-cultural matters. More directly, it involved four core features: (1) individuals were to declare their national identity on a register upon reaching voting age; (2) each nation would have been considered a public law corporation endowed with collective rights; (3) nations were to elect national councils on the basis of their membership register; and (4) these councils would have had the power to legislate in educational and cultural affairs and to tax their co-nationals to finance their institutions and services.

Chouinard's analysis of court decisions does not confirm the emergence of a right to NTA à la Renner and Bauer. This specific scheme of NTA has no legal or political basis in Canada, regardless of the relation there may be between institutional completeness and NTA. Francophone minority communities are not established as public law corporations and Canadians do not declare their national identity upon reaching voting age. Moreover, if FMCs have developed complex networks of community organizations and institutions in every province and territory, these do not amount to national councils (see Johnson, 2010). For Renner and Bauer, these councils were to be elected and would have had powers to govern their own cultural affairs—akin to the separation of powers in a federation. A national council could have elaborated a cultural policy or an education policy, and it would have had the power to tax co-nationals. Francophone minority communities are not entrusted with such legislative or taxation powers. The bulk of their responsibilities are delegated not devolved, and thus jurisdiction remains with the state. In addition, their networks are largely funded through agreements signed with federal departments, and their organizations and institutions are involved in the delivery of services and activities designed to support the development of the French language and cultures (Forgues, 2007; Cardinal et al., 2008).

It is much more plausible that Chouinard had another, more general understanding of NTA in mind. This other understanding of NTA denotes constitutional or institutional arrangements that do not entail exclusive control over a territory. Its aim is to enable ethnocultural groups to manage their own affairs such as culture or education. As Edmund Aunger wrote (1996, p. 192): '[it] means minority rule, not in all domains, but in the area of the minority's exclusive concern'. Non-territorial autonomy thus entails minority control over a particular matter not over a particular territory. Take as an example English- and French-language school boards in Canada. Generally speaking, these school boards share a territory over which neither has exclusive control. The two school boards recruit students from the same catchment area. Ephraim Nimni, a leading scholar of NTA, recently called upon this more general understanding. He wrote that NTA is 'not a specific model', but rather a 'generic term that refers to diverse practices and theories of minority community empowerment and self-determination that does not entail exclusive control over territory' (Nimni, 2013, p. 1). Nimni discussed a number of examples of NTA, including the scheme elaborated by Renner and Bauer, but also the Ottoman millet system and Bolivia's new constitution.

This general understanding is a much more plausible candidate for Chouinard's analysis of the evolution of NTA in Canada. For example, her article identifies three areas of overlap between NTA and institutional completeness: (1) the recourse to a personal rather than a geographic principle; (2) the emphasis on contentious matters or functions; and (3) the importance of minority control and its legitimacy. These overlaps are much more in line with the generic rather than the specific understanding of NTA. The scheme elaborated by Renner and Bauer is specific and clearly defined. It imposes more rigorous normative and institutional standards than these three overlaps. Moreover, Chouinard's discussion of the emergence of NTA in Canada boils down to how the network of institutions and activities that follows from institutional completeness need not have exclusive control over a territory. These institutions are about FMCs having jurisdiction over cultural, educational or health matters. Her discussion of the *Lalonde* case, for example, reveals that the goal of the legal challenge was the safeguard of the only French-language hospital in the National Capital Region, and not making that hospital the exclusive health services provider in the geographic area. In other words, plaintiffs were not vying for exclusive control of the territory. Their aim was to administer their hospital because it is a matter of minority concern.

In my view, however, institutional completeness loses much of its analytical and normative purchase when equated with this general understanding of NTA. Institutional completeness goes from being a promising notion with some constitutional and perhaps even legislative basis in Canada to a general principle about how minority control does not entail exclusive control over a territory. If the first understanding of NTA means too much to have any basis in Canadian legislation or court decisions, this second understanding means too little to shed analytical light on case studies as well as to offer normative guidance to social actors or policymakers. In essence, institutional completeness becomes a poorer analytical lens and normative benchmark. Beyond the important idea that the power to legislate can be separated from the exclusive control of a territory, it does not provide any guidance to hard questions around group institutions and representation, constitutional design or powers that the minority ought to control. Its lack of content and specifications leaves us ill-equipped to examine existing arrangements or to prescribe new ones. It merely enables one to determine whether or not a given constitutional or institutional arrangement entails exclusive control over a territory.

Recent works also hint at similar reservations in regard to the analytical and normative purchase of this general understanding of NTA. In her influential work on Kosovo, Stroschein turns to the scholarship on NTA, and draws from it 'a *functional premise of control*—meaning that substate units need not be territorial' (Stroschein, 2008, p. 656, emphasis in original). However, aiming to provide additional normative guidelines, she does not resort to the label of NTA in describing and defending her scheme. Her work instead uses the term 'functional governance'. This scheme enables her to shed important light on the new Kosovar constitution and its implications for the Balkans region. Osipov has also expressed serious doubts (and frustrations) on the analytical and normative purchase of NTA; not only can scholars 'do without resorting to such a notion as NTA', but also they 'could even more clearly express themselves and defend their arguments with alternative terminology and research tools which are already in place' (Osipov, 2013, p. 9). Perhaps inspired from Stroschein, he opines that functional autonomy represents a 'more appropriate' scheme for analysing existing arrangements relating to the protection and promotion of ethnocultural groups (*ibid.*, p. 10). Even Nimni, a leading proponent of NTA for a number of years, has shifted the focus of his research. His recent works discuss examples of NTA as a way to document and defend a paradigm shift in the governance of diverse societies (Nimni, 2009, 2013). Nimni no longer seems to conceive of NTA as an analytical tool that can shed light or a normative benchmark that can prescribe guidelines regarding case studies. For him, NTA is a symbol of a broader intellectual and political movement that aims to reconsider the 'state-centric view of the world'—the view that nations correspond to states, and that states are bestowed with territorial sovereignty (Nimni, 2013, p. 2).

Overall, I hope to have shown in this second part that equating institutional completeness to NTA has analytical and normative costs because NTA either means too much (NTA à la Renner and Bauer) or too little (NTA as a family of theories and practices).

Conclusion

In conclusion, I want to offer a very general defence of institutional completeness both as an analytical lens and as a normative benchmark. I have argued that the move to view institutional completeness through NTA weakens rather than strengthens it. That move would seem to transform institutional completeness into a poorer analytical lens and normative benchmark. This is especially disappointing because the past few years have witnessed the emergence of new and exciting scholarship on institutional completeness. As Chouinard notes, Raymond Breton coined the term in a study of the integration of immigrants in Montréal, Canada, in the 1960s. Breton's research showed that ethnocultural groups that have their own institutions—such as churches, socio-economic organizations and newspapers—were having more success in attracting and retaining their members. In his words: 'the presence of formal organizations in the ethnic community sets out forces that have the effect of keeping the social relations of the immigrants within its boundaries' (Breton, 1964, p. 196). In the 1980s and 1990s, the notion of institutional completeness was used in research on FMCs, including by Breton himself (see Breton, 1984, 1985; Bernard, 1988; Denis, 1993).

More importantly, recent research has brought institutional completeness in new and exciting directions. Sociolinguist Rodrigue Landry has elaborated and promoted a scheme of cultural autonomy for FMCs that relies in an important way on institutional completeness (Landry et al., 2007, 2010). In his research, institutional completeness, as part of the broader scheme of cultural autonomy, becomes a normative benchmark that states ought to respect if their goal is to ensure the promotion and protection of ethnocultural groups. In a recent article, Linda Cardinal and Eloisa Gonzalez Hidalgo (2012) elevated institutional completeness to the level of moral and political principle—that is, a principle that ought to guide our political actions. If national minorities have a right to self-determination and ethnic groups a right to non-discrimination (see Kymlicka, 1995), these two scholars argue that FMCs ought to have a right to institutional completeness. These works are examples of how institutional completeness can become a sound normative benchmark for the treatment of FMCs and perhaps even other analogous ethnocultural groups.

Another strand of research further enhances institutional completeness as an analytical lens. In a recent book chapter, political scientist Edmund Aunger set out to measure whether or not the existence of minority institutions has an impact on the continued use of the minority language. The initial step of the research consisted of identifying French-language institutions in 1,861 municipalities with francophone residents (in Canadian provinces and territories excluding Québec). Then, relying on official language data from Statistics Canada, Aunger was able to show that there is a positive relation between institutional completeness and linguistic vitality. 'When the number of institution increases,' he wrote, 'the use of the French language also increases, and that in a linear fashion' (Aunger, 2010, p. 73, personal translation). It is my sense that this more robust definition of institutional completeness could enable one to shed important light on the impact of government policies and programmes that aim to promote the flourishing of minority languages.

In summary, I strongly believe that institutional completeness holds great analytical and normative promise. Indeed, I would urge scholars working on the promotion and protection of ethnocultural groups in Central and Eastern Europe and even elsewhere in the world to borrow from Breton as well as from the more recent scholarship on institutional completeness. As for the relation between institutional completeness and NTA, in my view it is scholars of NTA that would benefit from a turn to institutional completeness and not the other way around.

Note

1. The exception to the rule is the following undeveloped statement from Kymlicka (2007, p. 387): 'In Canada, for example, strong TA for the French-majority province of Quebec co-exists with significant non-territorial linguistic and cultural rights to Francophones who live outside Québec (and with non-territorial rights for "internal minorities" within Quebec)'. Notice that it speaks to non-territorial *rights* not NTA per se.

References

Alenius, K. (2007) The birth of cultural autonomy in Estonia: how, why, and for whom?, *Journal of Baltic Studies*, 38(4), pp. 445–462.

Aunger, E. (1996) Dispersed minorities and segmental autonomy: French-language school boards in Canada, *Nationalism and Ethnic Politics*, 2(2), pp. 191–215.

Aunger, E. (2010) Profil des institutions francophones, in: *Territoires Francophones: Études Géogrpahiques sur la Vitalité des Communautés Francophones du Canada* (Québec: Septentrion).

Bauböck, R. (2004) Territorial or cultural autonomy for national minorities, in: *The Politics of Belonging: Nationalism, Liberalism, and Pluralism*, pp. 221–257 (Lanham: Lexington Books).

Bernard, R. (1988) *De Québécois à Ontarois: La Communauté Franco-ontarienne* (Hearst: Le Nordir).

Breton, R. (1964) Insitutional completeness of ethnic communities and the personal relations of immigrants, *American Journal of Sociology*, 70(2), pp. 193–205.

Breton, R. (1984) Les institutions et les réseaux d'organisations des communautés ethnoculturelles, in: *État de la Recherché sur les Communautés Francophones hors Québec: Actes du Premier Colloque National des Chercheurs* (Ottawa: Fédération des francophones hors Québec).

Breton, R. (1985) L'intégration des francophones hors Québec dans des communautés de langue française, *Revue de l'Université d'Ottawa*, 55(2), pp. 77–90.

Cardinal, L. & Hidalgo, E.G. (2012) L'autonomie des minorités francophones hors Québec au regard du débat sur les minorités nationales et les minorités ethniques, *Minorités Linguistiques et Sociétés*, 1, pp. 51–65.

Cardinal, L., Lang, S. & Sauvé, A. (2008) Les minorités francophones hors Québec et la gouvernance des langues officielles: portrait et enjeux, *Francophonies d'Amérique*, 26, pp. 209–233.

Chouinard, S. (2014) The rise of non-territorial autonomy in Canada: towards a doctrine of institutional completeness in the domain of minority language rights, *Ethnopolitics*, 13(2), pp. 141–158.

Coakley, J. (1994) Approaches to the resolution of ethnic conflict: the strategy of non-territorial autonomy, *International Political Science Review*, 15(3), pp. 297–314.

de Villiers, B. (2012) Protecting minorities on a non-territorial basis—recent international developments, *Beijing Law Review*, 3, pp. 170–183.

Decker, C. (2007) The use of cultural autonomy to prevent conflict and meet the Copenhagen criteria: the case of Romania, *Ethnopolitics*, 6(3), pp. 437–450.

Denis, W. (1993) La complétude institutionnelle et la vitalité des communautés fransaskoises en 1992, *Cahiers franco-canadiens de l'Ouest*, 5(2), pp. 253–284.

Dhamoon, R. (2009) *Identity/Difference Politics: How Difference is Produced and Why it Matters* (Vancouver: UBC Press).

Dobos, B. (2007) The development and functioning of cultural autonomy in Hungary, *Ethnopolitics*, 6(3), pp. 451–469.

Elkins, D. (1992) Where should the majority rule? Reflections on non-territorial provinces and other constitutional proposals, *Points of View* (Centre for Constitutional Studies, University of Alberta), 1, pp. 1–21.

Elkins, D. (1995) *Beyond Sovereignty: Territory and Political Economy in the Twenty-first Century* (Toronto: University of Toronto Press).

Follesdal, A. (2011) Federalism, ethnicity and human rights in Nepal. Or: Althusius meets Acharya, *International Journal on Minority and Group Rights*, 18, pp. 335–342.

Forgues, E. (2007) *Du Conflit au Compromis Linguistique: L'État et le Développement des Communautés Francophones en Situation Minoritaire* (Moncton: Canadian Institute for Research on Linguistic Minorities).

Gagnon, A.-G. & Iacovino, R. (2007) *Federalism, Citizenship, and Quebec: Debating Multinationalism* (Toronto: University of Toronto Press).

Jacobs, D. & Swyngedouw, M. (2003) Territorial and non-territorial federalism in Belgium: reform of the Brussels Capital Region, 2001, *Regional & Federal Studies*, 13(2), pp. 127–139.

Johnson, M. (2010) Community governance of the francophone minority: a cultural heritage, *Encyclopaedia of French Cultural Heritage in North America*. http://www.ameriquefrancaise.org/en/article-560/Community_Governance_of_the_Francophone_Minority:_a_Cultural_Heritage.html

Kernerman, G. (2006) *Multicultural Nationalism: Civilizing Difference, Constituting Community* (Vancouver: UBC Press).

Klimova-Alexander, I. (2007) Transnational Romani and indigenous non-territorial self-determination claims, *Ethnopolitics*, 6(3), pp. 395–416.

Kymlicka, W. (1995) *Multicultural Citizenship: A Liberal Theory of Minority Rights* (New York: Oxford University Press).

Kymlicka, W. (2007) National cultural autonomy and international minority rights norms, *Ethnopolitics*, 6(3), pp. 379–393.

Lajcakova, J. (2010) Advancing empowerment of the Roma in Slovakia through non-territorial national autonomy, *Ethnopolitics*, 9(2), pp. 171–196.

Landry, R., Allard, R. & Deveau, K. (2007) Bilingual schooling of the Canadian francophone minority: a cultural autonomy model, *International Journal of the Sociology of Language*, 185, pp. 133–162.

Landry, R., Allard, R. & Deveau, K. (2010) *Schooling and Cultural Autonomy: A Canada-wide Study in Francophone Minority Schools* (Ottawa and Moncton: Canadian Heritage and Canadian Institute for Research on Linguistic Minorities).

Liebich, A. (2008) How different is the 'new Europe'? Perspectives on states and minorities, *CEU Political Science Journal*, 3, pp. 262–292.

Loukacheva, N. (2007) *The Arctic Promise: Legal and Political Autonomy of Greenland and Nunavut* (Toronto: University of Toronto Press).

McRae, K. (1975) The principle of territoriality and the principle of personality in multilingual states, *International Journal of the Sociology of Language*, 4, pp. 33–54.

Nieguth, T. (1999) Accommodating ethnic minorities: the Austro-Marxist personality principle and Canada's multicultural condition, *Canadian Review of Studies in Nationalism*, 26, pp. 91–105.

Nieguth, T. (2009) An Austrian solution for Canada? Problems and possibilities of national cultural autonomy, *Canadian Journal of Political Science*, 42(1), pp. 1–16.

Nimni, E. (2009) Nationalism, ethnicity and self-determination: a paradigm shift?, *Studies in Ethnicity and Nationalism*, 9(2), pp. 319–332.

Nimni, E. (2013) The conceptual challenge of non-territorial autonomy, in: *The Challenge of Non-territorial Autonomy: Theory and Practice*, pp. 1–24 (Bern: Peter Lang).

Nootens, G. (2006) Liberal nationalism and the sovereign territorial ideal, *Nations and Nationalism*, 12(1), pp. 35–50.

Osipov, A. (2013) Changing the Angle: Does the Notion of Non-territorial Autonomy Stand on Solid Ground?, *ECMI Issue Brief*, 29, 14 pp.

Osipov, A. (2010) National cultural autonomy in Russia: a case of symbolic law, *Review of Central and East European Law*, 35, pp. 27–57.

Otis, G. & Papillon, M. (Eds) (2013) *Fédéralisme et Gouvernance Autochtone* [Federalism and Indigenous Governance] (Sainte-Foy: Presses de l'Université Laval).

Poirier, J. (2008) Au-delà des droits linguistiques et du fédéralisme classique: favoriser l'autonomie institution-nelle des francophones minoritaires du Canada, in: *L'Espace Francophone en Milieu Minoritaire au Canada: Nouveaux Enjeux, Nouvelles Mobilisations*, pp. 513–562 (Québec: Fides).

Poirier, J. (2012) Autonomie politique et minorités francophones au Canada: réflexions sur un angle mort de la typologie classique de Will Kymlicka, *Minorités Linguistiques et Sociétés*, 1, pp. 66–89.

Rodon, T. & Grey, M. (2009) The long winding road towards self-government: the Nunavik and Nunatsiavut experience, in: *Northern Exposure: Peoples, Powers and Prospects in Canada's North*, pp. 317–343 (Montréal: Institute for Research on Public Policy).

Smith, D. (2010) Non-territorial cultural autonomy in contemporary Europe: reflections on the revival of an idea, in: *After the Nation? Critical Reflections on Nationalism and Postnationalism*, pp. 84–102 (Basingstoke: Palgrave Macmillian).

Smith, D. (2013) Non-territorial autonomy and political community in contemporary Central and Eastern Europe, *Journal on Ethnopolitics and Minority Issues in Europe*, 12(1), pp. 27–55.

Stroschein, S. (2008) Making or breaking Kosovo: applications of dispersed state control, *Perspectives on Politics*, 6(4), pp. 655–674.

Taylor, C. (1994) The politics of recognition, in: *Multiculturalism: Examining the Politics of Recognition*, pp. 25–73 (Princeton: Princeton University Press).

Thériault, J.Y., Gilbert, A. & Cardinal, L. (2008) *L'Espace Francophone en Milieu Minoritaire au Canada: Nouveaux Enjeux, Nouvelles Mobilisations* (Québec: Fides).

Tully, J. (1995) *Strange Multiplicity: Constitutionalism in an Age of Diversity* (Cambridge: Cambridge University Press).

Ethnopolitics, 2014
Vol. 13, No. 4, 428–430, http://dx.doi.org/10.1080/17449057.2014.921484

DEBATE

Rethinking Non-territorial Autonomy through Institutional Completeness: A Response to Léger

STÉPHANIE CHOUINARD

University of Ottawa, Canada

I welcome the opportunity to respond to Rémi Léger's rigorous commentary on my article, 'The rise of non-territorial autonomy in Canada: towards a doctrine of institutional completeness in the domain of minority language rights'. The crux of Léger's reply touched on the first part of the paper, where a normative link is drawn between the broad concept of non-territorial autonomy (NTA) and the more specialized, less explored notion of institutional completeness (IC). Léger's argument is presented in two parts. He begins by situating my research within the existing scholarship on NTA and minority rights. He makes a thorough review of the existing literature on NTA and its uses in contemporary settings, to demonstrate how my research fits in this body of work. He writes: 'Her twofold submission [is] that [francophone minority communities] have claimed NTA and that the federal government has responded with NTA'. In the first instance, I would like to clarify that the argument presented in the article was based on the *courts*—not the government—and how they had responded to the claims of the francophone minority communities with a gradual evolution in the jurisprudence regarding language rights in Canada. This evolution, over 30 years, culminated with an enunciation of a right to IC in certain domains. The article only claims to analyse the judicial discourse, and makes no mention of state reaction to the enunciation of such rights.

Non-territorial Autonomy and Institutional Completeness: Related, but not Equivalent

In the second part of his response, Léger postulates that my demonstration uses IC as an 'equivalent' to the notion of NTA. The article, by highlighting a certain familiarity in the

Correspondence Address: Stéphanie Chouinard, School of Political Studies, Social Sciences Pavillion, University of Ottawa 120, Ontario, Canada K1N 6N5. Email: schou015@uottawa.ca

© 2014 The Editor of Ethnopolitics

conceptual relationship between NTA and IC, attempts to demonstrate a more nuanced theoretical argument. More precisely, I highlight (p. 145) three ways NTA and IC appear to be normatively related: (1) they both rely on the *personal* (rather than territorial) principle; (2) they target the same *domains of contention* between the majority and minority related to the sustainability of the minority group (such as education and social services); and (3) they take into consideration the *democratic principle* and the *representation* of minority institutions. Because of these normative ties, which are explored in further detail in the article, IC could be considered a proper fit to be welcomed under the broader conceptual umbrella that is NTA. This does not mean that a distortion or a watering-down of the concept of IC is necessary. In fact, IC could and should rather be used as a normative tool to *revitalize* the debates on NTA, and it is with this intent that both concepts are used in the article. Furthermore, by showing how IC had appeared to have some traction in recent Canadian jurisprudence regarding minority language rights, notably in the recognition of certain institutions belonging to the francophone minority, the article aims to explore how the case of Canada can shed some light on new possibilities for NTA as a normative tool.

The Analytical Usefulness of Non-territorial Autonomy in Question

Léger then proceeds to argue that IC is a more useful normative and analytical benchmark than that of NTA to promote and protect certain types of minority. He appears to discredit the usefulness of NTA in the understanding and articulation of minority rights. He cites Alexander Osipov (2013, p. 3), according to whom 'there is no uniform definition and no commonly accepted understanding of what NTA may actually mean'. Osipov's approach has many strengths and offers a valuable basis to show how the normative connections between NTA and IC may be useful both in rethinking NTA and by calling on scholars of NTA to consider IC in their research. In this manner, I agree with Léger when he suggests that 'scholars of NTA ... would benefit from a turn to institutional completeness'.

It is also important to note that, in the general domain of minority rights, the lack of uniformity and official definition emphasized by Osipov and Léger in the broader literature on NTA is more a commonality than an exception. It is still a matter of contention today to distinguish who is or belongs to a minority and who is not or does not. According to the United Nations (2010, p. 2), 'the existence of a minority is a question of fact and ... any definition must include both objective factors (such as the existence of a shared ethnicity, language or religion) and subjective factors (including that individuals must identify themselves as members of a minority)'. This definitional problem leads to another lack of common understanding that is related to the types of right to be granted to different types of minorities. Kymlicka's (1996) typology, which earned its stripes in the last two decades among liberal scholars, recognizes different sets of rights for national and ethnic minorities, but leaves the question of minorities that are not 'just' ethnic yet fall short of full-fledged national minority status, such as language minorities, in a theoretical gap. Cardinal and González Hidalgo's groundwork suggests that IC could become the liberal benchmark of recognition for language minorities 'in the same way [as] the principle of self-determination towards national minorities and that of non-discrimination towards ethnic minorities' (Cardinal & González Hidalgo, 2012, p. 52). The article aims to demonstrate how the Canadian jurisprudence on language minority rights may already prove them right in the apparition of the notion of IC since the last decade, and how these advances may be considered in a comparative context. In this context, a greater dialogue between scholars of IC and NTA may be valuable.

To conclude, it is clear that Léger and I share the view that IC holds an undeniable potency as an analytical benchmark, or reference point, for the recognition of the rights of certain types of minority that have been left out of the liberal framework, such as language minorities. I agree that IC is a solid enough tool to stand on its own and does not 'need' to be read under the umbrella concept of NTA. However, the normative ties between the two concepts are significant and highlighting them may help, on the one hand, to bolster the recognition of IC within the literature on minority rights, and on the other hand, to reinforce the discussions on the usefulness of NTA as an analytical tool. Finally, I wish to thank Rémi Léger for the questions he addressed in his reply to the original article, and for allowing me to clarify the theoretical framework used in my analysis of the recent Canadian jurisprudence on minority language rights.

References

Cardinal, L. & González Hidalgo, E. (2012) L'autonomie des minorités francophones hors Québec au regard du débat sur les minorités nationales et les minorités ethniques, *Minorités Linguistiques et Société* [Linguistic Minorities and Society], 1, pp. 51–65.

Kymlicka, W. (1996) *Multicultural Citizenship. A Liberal Theory of Minority Rights* (Oxford: Oxford University Press).

Osipov, A. (2013) Changing the angle: does the notion of non-territorial autonomy stand on solid ground? *ECMI Issue Brief*, 29.

United Nations (2010) *Minority Rights : International Standards and Guidance for Implementation* (New York and Geneva: United Nations).